INTERTEXTUAL WAR

Frontispiece of Swift's *Battle of the Books* (1710).
Photo courtesy of the Division of Rare and Manuscript Collections, Cornell
University Library.

INTERTEXTUAL WAR

Edmund Burke and
the French Revolution
in the Writings of
Mary Wollstonecraft,
Thomas Paine, and James Mackintosh

Steven Blakemore

Madison • Teaneck
Fairleigh Dickinson University Press
London: Associated University Presses

Associated University Presses
440 Forsgate Drive
Cranbury, NJ 08512

Associated University Presses
16 Barter Street
London WC1A 2AH, England

Associated University Presses
P.O. Box 338, Port Credit
Mississauga, Ontario
Canada L5G 4L8

The paper used in this publication meets the requirements of the American National Standard for Permanence of Paper for Printed Library Materials Z39.48–1984.

Library of Congress Cataloging-in-Publication Data

Blakemore, Steven.
    Intertextual war : Edmund Burke and the French Revolution in the writings of Mary Wollstonecraft, Thomas Paine, and James Mackintosh / Steven Blakemore.
        p. cm.
    Includes bibliographical references and index.
    ISBN 0–8386–3751–5 (alk. paper)
    1. Burke, Edmund, 1729–1797. Reflections on the Revolution in France. 2. France--History--Revolution, 1789–1799--Literature and the revolution. 3. France--History--Revolution, 1789–1799--Historiography. 4. Wollstonecraft, Mary, 1759–1797--Views on French Revolution. 5. Paine, Thomas, 1737–1809--Views on French Revolution. 6. Mackintosh, James, Sir, 1765–1932--Views on French Revolution. I. Title.
    DC150.B9B54   1997
    944.04--dc21
                                                                        96–52533
                                                                        CIP

PRINTED IN THE UNITED STATES OF AMERICA

In Memoriam
Anna Rae Nagle (10 July 1935–20 June 1995)
Mario Cajina Vega (11 February 1929–10 November 1995)

Contents

Acknowledgments

I am very grateful to the following friends and colleagues who responded to portions of this book: Frances Ferguson, Daniel E. Ritchie, and Fred Hembree. I owe a special debt of gratitude to John E. Faulkner for generously reading versions of the manuscript and replying to numerous inquiries.

Abbreviations

Works cited throughout this study are identified by the following short titles in the text and notes:

Collected Letters   Wardle, Ralph M., ed. *Collected Letters of Mary Wollstonecraft*. Ithaca: Cornell University Press, 1977.

Correspondence   *The Correspondence of Edmund Burke*. Edited by Thomas W. Copeland et al. 10 vols. Chicago: The University of Chicago Press, 1958–78.

CW   *The Complete Writings of Thomas Paine*. Edited by Philip S. Foner. 2 vols. New York: The Citadel Press, 1945, in which is to be found *Rights of Man*.

Enquiry   Burke, Edmund. *A Philosophical Enquiry into the Origin of our Ideas of the Sublime and Beautiful*. 1757. Edited by J. T. Boulton. New York: Columbia University Press, 1958.

Reflections   Burke, Edmund. *Reflections on the Revolution in France*. 1790. Edited by Conor Cruise O'Brien. Harmondsworth: Penguin Classics, 1986.

Vindiciae   Mackintosh, James. *Vindiciae Gallicae*. 1791. Reprint. 1st ed. Spelsbury, Oxford: Woodstock Books, 1989.

Vindiciae in *Works*   Mackintosh, James. *Vindiciae Gallicae*. 1791. 3rd ed. In *Works*.

Works   Mackintosh, James. *The Miscellaneous Works of the Right Honourable Sir James Mackintosh*.

Edited by Robert J. Mackintosh. 3 vols. in one. New York: D. Appleton, 1870.

WMW   *The Works of Mary Wollstonecraft*, edited by Janet Todd and Marilyn Butler. New York: New York University Press, 1989, in which are to be found *Analytical Review* (1788–97), 7:13–502; *The Female Reader; or Miscellaneous pieces in Prose and Verse; Selected from the Best Writers, and disposed under proper heads; for the Improvement of Young Women* (1789), 4:53–350; *A Vindication of the Rights of Men, in a Letter to the Right Honourable Edmund Burke; Occasioned by his Reflections on the Revolution in France* (1790), 5:1–78; and *A Vindication of the Rights of Woman: With Strictures on Political and Moral Subjects* (1792), 5:79–266.

INTERTEXTUAL WAR

Introduction

On 1 November 1790, Edmund Burke's *Reflections on the Revolution in France* precipitated a debate over the French Revolution that has continued for two centuries. In Britain, the debate erupted into a great ideological war over the significance of the past, for the Revolution was, in many ways, a referendum on history. Both opponents and supporters represented the Revolution as an apocalyptic event that would either destroy or transform the world; thus the revolutionary controversy impinged not only on the meaning of the Revolution but on the canonical meaning of England and Europe. Burke's *Reflections*, consequently, inspired or provoked hundreds of replies, igniting a voluminous intertextual war that continues today—for, unlike other revolutions, the French Revolution still evokes passionate loyalties and furious denunciations. We still read the "terms" of the controversy into the language of contemporary thought.

In the late eighteenth century, one of the principal reasons for the controversy over the *Reflections* was Edmund Burke himself. Burke, an Irishman of modest background and means, had, by exuberant talent and effort, raised himself to public prominence: author of a well-received political satire and an aesthetic treatise, he had, in the 1760s, aligned himself with the political opposition, the Rockingham Whigs, promoting a variety of progressive causes—among them, opposition to royal patronage and court influence, support of the Americans in their remonstrations against exorbitant British interference, and defense of the oppressed people of Ireland and India. Given Burke's progressive reputation, supporters of the French Revolution in both Britain and America assumed that he would also support the liberating revolution in France. They were consequently stunned when Burke publicly announced in the House of Commons (9 February 1790) that he would oppose the Revolution in a forthcoming publication. Writing in 1798, William Godwin recalled that "Burke had been warmly loved by the most liberal and enlightened friends of freedom, and they were proportionally inflamed and disgusted by the fury of his assault, upon what they deemed to be its sacred cause."[1] It was not just anyone who opposed the Revolution: it was a celebrated and admired member of the House of Commons with a record of support for progressive causes—a man who could not easily be dismissed as "reactionary." Subsequently, Burke's character and reputation were deconstructed by his respondents, but, in February 1790, their immediate task was to organize a series of replies to Burke's forthcoming *Reflections*.

Throughout the spring and summer, his opponents were meeting and planning to contest him on every point and from every direction. This accounts for the flurry of replies appearing shortly after 1 November. Among the most memorable, Mary Wollstonecraft's *A Vindication of the Rights of Men,* appeared on 29 November, and the first volume of Helen Maria Williams's *Letters from France* appeared at the end of the year. On 23 November, Richard Price responded in the fourth edition of *A Discourse on the Love of our Country* to Burke's personal criticisms in the *Reflections*. In January 1791, Joseph Priestly published his *Letters to the Right Honourable Edmund Burke*. In March, the first part of Thomas Paine's *Rights of Man* was published, followed in April and May by James Mackintosh's *Vindiciae Gallicae* and Thomas Christie's *Letters on the Revolution of France*.

Not everyone who replied to Burke was part of the organized opposition, but London society was small, and in the interval between February and November 1790, most of Burke's respondents undoubtedly knew the people who would be replying and the topics and themes they would be discussing. While the specific details of the *Reflections* were not yet available, Burke's opponents could surmise that he would cover certain subjects, including the French Constitution and controversial events such as the October Days of 1789. In addition, he would most likely deal with the Revolution's "causes." In the meantime, Burke's character and reputation could begin to be revised. When the *Reflections* appeared, his respondents quickly addressed the specifics of Burke's antirevolutionary critique, for even more than Burke himself, the book's radiant power generated an ongoing literature of response so that, in Britain and America, to participate in the revolutionary controversy meant, at some level, to engage in the controversy over the *Reflections*. With its publication, admirers of the Revolution were suddenly confronted with a correlative antirevolutionary force. Thus, while there was considerable overlap by Burke's respondents with regard to specific details after its publication (Burke's apostrophe to Marie Antoinette was a godsend), there was also a recognizable intellectual division of labor.

Paine, for instance, had been living in France and had rushed back to London (April 1790), where he began meeting with Burke's adversaries and awaiting Burke's *Reflections*. During this time, he met Thomas Christie, who was planning to deal with the Revolution's "origin" and "causes" but who had decided, instead, to concentrate on the French Constitution, once he learned that Paine was also interested in these topics.[2]

While it is unclear whether or not Mary Wollstonecraft and Helen Maria Williams were part of the organized opposition, both of their works also had a specific emphasis, suggesting an ideological division of labor: Wollstonecraft focuses on Burke's character and reputation while Williams emphasizes her personal response to the Revolution—having just returned from a visit to revolutionary France (July–September 1790), she uses her personal authority to contradict allusively Burke's misrepresentations. Even James Mackintosh, who was relatively unknown before the publication of *Vindiciae Gallicae*, refers to other anonymous respondents who would, in future publications, be dealing with France's Constitution and economy—the former an allusion to Thomas Christie (*Vindiciae*, 146, 232). Having read the principal replies to Burke (Wollstonecraft, Williams, and Paine), Mackintosh decided to ground his attack on Burke's reading of history and its relevance to the Revolution.

The classic, celebrated responses to Burke were hence formulated in a period (1790–91) that constituted the Revolution's prelapsarian moment—a time when the Revolution seemed, to many, impendingly triumphant and the world's regeneration axiomatically inevitable. The Terror (1793–94) changed all this, creating a crisis in representation, compelling writers such as Wollstonecraft and Williams to rewrite the Revolution and revise their representations of Burke. My focus here, however, is on the period that produced the classic critiques of Burke's *Reflections*. While he was not always the focal point, Burke represented not merely one side but rather a constant reference point for the Anglo-American debate on the Revolution. My specific focus, given the plethora of replies, is on the three primary works that continue to be cited against Burke: Mary Wollstonecraft's *A Vindication of the Rights of Men*, Thomas Paine's *Rights of Man*, and James Mackintosh's *Vindiciae Gallicae*. These writers established the dominant anti-Burke paradigms that continue to reverberate in Anglo-American criticism and the Revolution's historiography. They formulated the terms that created the counterrevolutionary "Other," just as Burke created the revolutionary as other. To understand the significance of what they contend is being revealed is to begin to see what is being obscured—occult and striking resemblances between themselves and the enemy they denounce. The strategies, language, and contexts they employ to inscribe superior difference may also be fruitfully refigured in other great intertextual events founded on difference, most conspicuously the Reformation and the Enlightenment.

In the voluminous intertextual war of the 1790s, Paine is an obvious choice: from the beginning he was linked antithetically to Burke, and it is still common to find dialectic editions of both the *Reflections* and *Rights of Man* in libraries and bookstores. Better known for *A Vindication of the Rights of Women* (1792), Wollstonecraft, in her first *Vindication*, was recognized as one of the best respondents by her contemporaries. Today the renewed interest in Wollstonecraft has generated a renewed consideration of her oeuvre, and I concentrate on the ways in which her first *Vindication* was read by her contemporaries contra Burke. Mackintosh, in *Vindiciae Gallicae*, wrote what is still considered the best intellectual response, contesting Burke on his own learned ground. While I discuss other writers as well, I selected these three because of their ideological relation to both Burke and the French Revolution.

Their personal relationships with Burke are sometimes pertinent and can be briefly summarized. In Wollstonecraft's case, there was no relationship: she never met Burke and was responding to both his attack on the Revolution and on Richard Price, a prominent dissenting minister and a personal friend.

Paine, in contrast, had first met Burke in England, in 1787. They got along well and seemed to have initially considered each other political allies—having both supported the American "cause," albeit for different reasons. In 1788, Paine renewed his acquaintance with Burke, spending a week at Burke's home in Beaconsfield. During this time, Burke introduced Paine to influential members of the Whig opposition and helped him promote a plan for a bridge Paine hoped to build. While both Burke and Paine seemed to like each other, and while both seemed initially to consider themselves political allies, they both ultimately misjudged each other.

Paine, for instance, subsequently wrote Burke from Paris (17 January 1790), sending a glowing account of the Revolution's progress, at approximately the same time Burke was reading Richard Price's *A Discourse on the Love of our Country* with both alarm and disgust. Burke of course did not find Paine's account reassuring, especially his comment that "the Revolution in France is certainly a forerunner to other Revolutions in Europe."[3] Assuming Burke was an ideological ally who would enthusiastically embrace the Revolution, Paine was unhappily surprised when he learned that Burke (9 February) had announced his forthcoming opposition to the Revolution. Paine consequently interpreted

Burke's announcement as a personal affront, apparently believing that Burke was rejecting his own personal authority and that of Thomas Jefferson, whom he had also cited in his January letter. After he read the *Reflections*, he also seems to have believed that Burke's book contained an allusive attack on his political positions and hence himself.

James Mackintosh did not meet Burke until 1796, subsequently beginning a slow but emphatic conversion to Burke's side. Because most readers are not likely to be as familiar with his life and writings, I have included a brief biographical essay establishing the contexts of his intertextual war with Burke.

Context, a word containing the conspicuous *text*, begins with the prefixal *con*, meaning "with or together," conjuring up a supportive text it joins or reinforces. The word can also be counterread as a text that is in conflict with or in opposition to—con or contra the antagonistic text it confronts or resists. In this sense, Burke's *Reflections* was and is, for the Revolution's admirers, the great "counter-context" of the revolutionary debate.

Because Wollstonecraft, Paine, and Mackintosh were reading other texts in opposition to Burke, there was a great intertextual war reverberating in their respective writings. Every debate or controversy over a major political event is, to some degree, intertextual, but the French Revolution was profoundly so because it called into question the traditional world as well as the histories and texts that had articulated and sustained that world. The new battle of texts thematically resembled the previous battle of books, and issues of tradition and authority versus progress and modernity were refought by eighteenth-century partisans of the ancients and moderns. Because the controversy entailed a war over the past, both sides read a variety of bellicose texts into their representations of the Revolution. Anglo-American writers additionally contextualized the war by reading previous revolutions "in" or "out" of the French Revolution in order to establish antithetical distinctions or reassuring resemblances.

Antirevolutionaries, for instance, linked the 1789 Revolution with the English Civil War, with regicidal republicans and Levellers, while its supporters either denied the resemblance or used it as an instructive example for benighted reactionaries at home. In France, the English Civil War and the Cromwellian Protectorate were also principal paradigms by which the French Revolution was either compared or contrasted. In England, the significance of the Glorious Revolution was also central to the revolutionary debate. In the *Reflections*, Burke had vehemently denied any resemblance between the Glorious and French Revolutions— a resemblance initially seen by those British writers who also saw the

French Revolution as the restoration of a constitutional monarchy and ancient liberties and, later, as the deposition of a king and the election of a national convention. In *Vindiciae Gallicae* (1791), James Mackintosh emphasized the resemblances and then subverted them, contrasting the Glorious Revolution with the French Revolution that was consummating what the English Revolution had botched. Mackintosh's attack on the Glorious Revolution was simultaneously an attack on the British constitution and English institutions. Indeed, the French Revolution revivified the ideological battles of the seventeenth century, allowing British dissidents to promote the old radical agenda (extended suffrage, parliamentary reform, and religious freedom) in the seemingly new language of natural rights and the French Revolution. The American Revolution was yet another "text" used to read the paradigms of the past into the ongoing French Revolution. A historical paradigm is, as Hayden White notes, "the model of what a set of historical events will look like once they have been explained."[4]

This raises the problem of "translation" that J. G. A. Pocock has discussed: how do you translate a radical, alien event, how do you translate a French Revolution into English discourse, without distortion? British dissidents, Pocock notes, had to translate the Revolution through accessible Anglo-American discourses.[5] There were, of course, a variety of French discourses, but they were usually domestically contextualized to make them recognizable to Anglo-American eyes. Thus the war over the Revolution was simultaneously a war over former ideological issues, in which the past was read into the present and vice versa. In this respect, the writers of the 1790s were engaged in a great intertextual war, in which prior texts were either evoked or expunged, sometimes both— written "out" in the paradoxical sense of exposure and erasure.

The war over the Revolution's meaning was, simultaneously, a war over the traditional canon. Burke opposed the Revolution with a series of classical and biblical texts, while his respondents countered with rebellious readings of the English constitution and "Tory" dictionaries, the traditional meaning of the Glorious Revolution, and the texts of Burke himself. His opponents tried to reconstitute both radical tradition and a new revolutionary canon—the triumphant texts and histories they cited contra Burke. In their appeal to authorities, both sides repeatedly (author)ized their own canonical, authoritative readings. The textual, canonical war—a war for the hearts and minds of Europe—corresponded to the nascent military war that was coalescing and that would soon conflagrate Europe. Since Burke and his respondents envisioned the Revolution as a defining moment in human history—a revolution that would either destroy or regenerate mankind—they textually attempted to annihilate each other. Writers on both sides employed military metaphors to represent what eventually became a total textual war. Both sides engaged in campaigns of propaganda and disinformation, waging internecine psychowars in journals and newspapers, pamphlets, letters, and books—in all the available genres of eighteenth-century discourse. They attacked the character and language of antagonistic authors, invading enemy texts and occupying or obliterating the semantic territory with their own dominant readings. This involved assaulting the opposing author's readings of the texts and histories by which he or she attacked or defended the Revolution.

To enter this great intertextual war, we need to recover the contexts that impinge on both the writing of the Revolution and the revision of Burke. For every text, there were a series of subtexts: for Wollstonecraft, it was the language of madness and gender; for Paine, it was the language of drama and radical tradition; for Mackintosh, it was the dissident histories of the Glorious Revolution and the explanatory texts of the French Revolution. Recoveries of these contexts crystallize the languages and hence the ways in which Burke's respondents read and were being read in the eighteenth century. In my study, I begin to reconstruct the intertextual war that impinged on the ways Burke and his opponents read and were read, while rereading pertinent contemporary contexts into its significance. My aim is that elusive "fusion of horizons"—the timeless historical dialogue that continues across the centuries. Concentrating on Burke's respondents, I show how the terms of their critique—Burkean contradiction and misrepresentation—inevitably constitute their own reflexive representations, providing another context with which they can be read.

The issue of correct representation, whether as a true historical account, the mirrored relation between the voter and the representative, the reflective connection between money and the value it represents, and a variety of other associations based on "true" and "natural" correspondences was a primary issue of writers involved in the war over the Revolution's "real" significance. The corollary was the unnatural distortion of these correspondences. Hence, the central theme of the Revolution was the reformulation of the ancient distinction between illusion and reality. This fundamental concern of Western metaphysics preoccupied all those engaged in the intertextual war—it was, in essence, an old story rewritten anew in the contemporary contexts of the Revolution. Intertextual adversaries accused each other of illusion and error while reaffirming their own representations in terms of reality and truth. Each accused the other of misrepresentation and contrasted the confusion of cause with effect, the etiology of error, with the

Revolution's authentic origins. Contradiction and truth, madness and sanity were major tropes in the intertextual war. In the *Reflections*, Burke reinscribed these tropes and themes, and his opponents responded by rewriting Burke's primal script in terms of counterrevolutionary insanity and error. The intertextuality of these exchanges, specifically the absorption and transformation of the *Reflections* in rival texts, is implicit throughout. The problem of the Revolution reintroduced the problem of representation into a new social, political context, resulting in a myriad of conflicting yet complicit configurations. The demonization of oppositional texts meant that difference could be condemned as an alien "other," but since they shared a series of mutual assumptions, warring writers essentially repeated disguised versions of the same story. Engaged in strong, critical commentaries of antagonistic texts, both sides reread and rewrote the other in their own image. Wollstonecraft and Paine, for instance, reconceived Burke in terms of their own textual image(s), and yet they both inadvertently inscribed various covert resemblances and identifications with their counterrevolutionary enemy. They project onto Burke suppressed errors and "weaknesses," while presenting psychological readings of Burke's "real" self.

Since I deal with how Burke was read by his adversaries and the texts and contexts that underwrite their representations, I am not primarily concerned with their or Burke's misrepresentations. I do address some of these, especially when charges of misrepresentation ironically implode, but I am essentially concerned with how Burke was being read and reconceived by his opposition. Thus I do not address whether every reading by this opposition was accurate or fair. Readers will be able to decide for themselves. Similarly, since I concentrate on one intertextual moment (the period between 1790 and 1792), I do not consider subsequent responses, clarifications, or revisions—such as Wollstonecraft's *Historical and Moral View of the French Revolution* (1794)—all these have an immense life of their own, constituting what became a crisis in representation for writers during the Terror (1793–94), the subject of another book. The one exception is James Mackintosh, whose subsequent revisions fit succinctly within the chronology of the final four chapters and anticipate thematically the revisions of Wollstonecraft, Paine, and others during the crisis the Terror produced. Because I include a biographical chapter on Mackintosh and discuss his subsequent revisions of Burke and the Revolution, while dealing with those of Wollstonecraft and Paine in another book, Mackintosh's section is necessarily longer.

In this book, I examine how difference was rewritten within the same repetitive tradition (mutual assumptions about illusion and reality) and how historical paradigms (the English Civil War, the Glorious Revolution) were refigured in texts whose resemblances belied their disparity. Specifically, with regard to Wollstonecraft, I discuss how she subverts Burke's character and his *Reflections* by feminizing both with a variety of "mad," misogynous languages. This pejorative feminization conjures up and confronts another Burkean text, *A Philosophical Enquiry into the Origin of our Ideas of the Sublime and Beautiful*, first published in 1757. While critics have touched on her pejorative references to the *Enquiry*, I show that the references and allusions are much more extensive and that Wollstonecraft's reading of the *Enquiry* is central to her reading of both Burke and the French Revolution. In addition, I show how she repeatedly resembles Edmund Burke by engaging in the very Burkean misrepresentations she contends she has exposed and "reprobated." Similarly, Wollstonecraft describes Burke in personal language that she used to describe herself in private letters to her family and friends. Since these letters were not available to the eighteenth-century reader, we have an additional context with which to reread Wollstonecraft's first *Vindication*: thematically and linguistically, the distinction between Burke and herself turns into a redounding resemblance.

Paine's *Rights of Man* provides a similar and a different kind of context and resemblance. Paine accuses Burke of receiving a secret pension and then, in subsequent publications, suggests how Burke's botched concealment of the pension compromises and explains his opposition to the French Revolution. Paine, however, engages in his own concealments, resembling Burke as he criticizes him, projecting onto Burke the very charge of which he himself had been accused: a compromising fund drawn secretly in 1782. Some of the details of Burke's pension have been told before, but what has not been examined are the links between Paine and other writers in the campaign to discredit Burke and Paine's own misrepresentations of Burke's Civil List Act of 1782, by which Paine engages in the same distortions he accuses Burke of performing, ironically underscoring an identification of himself with the Burkean "other." Because Paine also pursues themes pertinent to his attacks on Burke in works other than *Rights of Man*, I also deal with these writings, although my central focus is on the former. In chapter 5, I examine yet another resemblance between Paine and Burke. In the *Reflections*, Burke had criticized the revolutionaries in France and England for reproducing parodic history, absurd theater, and ideological insanity, and his respondents reascribed his critique in their correspondent indictment of Burke and the counterrevolution. Both Burke and his respondents insisted that they were writing history, while the "other" was writing fiction. This distinction, however, turned into another resemblance: their correspondent emphasis on true history was the poetic fiction of their respective plots. Paine, in *Rights of Man*, insists on this distinction, opposing his "sober history" to Burke's counterrevolutionary "tragedy." He establishes a criterion, Burke's suppression of "causes," to highlight Burke's drama, but in doing so, he writes "out" his own revolutionary drama. Like Wollstonecraft, the very criteria he uses to condemn Burke subvert his authoritative text.

Numerous commentators have, for two centuries, quoted Paine's comments approvingly, reaffirming his distinction and focusing, as Paine does, on the two paragraphs in the *Reflections* dealing with the events of 6 October—the invasion of Marie Antoinette's bedroom and the forced removal of the royal family to Paris. Since Paine's account has been privileged by many, if not most, critics, I reexamine Paine's distinction and discuss how his representations mutually replicate what he contends are Burke's misrepresentations. The, by now, traditional emphasis on the distinctions between Burke and his adversaries ineluctably obscures significant similarities that the preoccupation with difference distorts. My focus consequently is on the ways in which Paine and other canonical writers of the eighteenth century provide the reflexive "terms" for reading their own texts as well as those they oppose. One reason, I suggest, is because both revolutionaries and antirevolutionaries write in and "out" of the same system of representation, even though they both distinguish between true representation and oppositional misrepresentation. Paine is pertinent in this regard, since he claimed to be *writing* a revolution radically different from any previous revolution or representation. In this context, I explore his textual war against the Burkean canon and underscore what I believe is his enduring contribution to the revolutionary debate: the creation of the writer as *ur*-revolutionary.

After the publication of *Vindiciae Gallicae*, James Mackintosh spent much of the rest of his life contextually repudiating its positions. The book itself, however, is a radical critique that contests Burke on a variety of historical and thematic battlegrounds. In my exposition, I recover the submerged contexts that underwrite his reading of Burke and the French Revolution. Mackintosh's analyses of the Glorious Revolution, corporate property, and economic and electoral representation illustrate something fundamental to all of Burke's respondents: by emphasizing Burkean "fiction" and the contradictions by which Burke misrepresents the Revolution, they insist on a higher and truer representation, repeatedly rewriting the "new" revolutionary debate in the traditional terms of illusion and reality—the terms that Burke himself reinscribes in his critique of the Revolution. Thus, while I focus on the contradictions and misrepresentations in classic "radical" texts of the late eighteenth century, I am not suggesting that similar contradictions do not exist in Burke and other antirevolutionary writers. My implicit thesis is that they proliferate in the antagonistic texts of the 1790s because both sides were ultimately writing within the same system of representation. Indeed, Burke's criticisms of the Revolution contain similar resemblances to the discourse he condemns. This does not suggest that there is some kind of moral equivalence between Burke and his adversaries, but that there are a variety of covert resemblances belying the strident, oppositional readings of late eighteenth-century discourse. I recognize, however, that the emphasis on resemblances and similarities may irritate or even antagonize both the admirers of Burke (of whom I count myself one) and the admirers of his eighteenth-century respondents.

There are, of course, real and outstanding differences between Burke and his respondents, many of which I address, but by dealing with thematic, paradoxical similarities and resemblances, I am interested in redressing a scholarly imbalance. By concentrating on resemblances and similarities rather than the conventional distinctions and differences, my focus is restricted to a specific perspective rather than the whole panorama. It is not the entire picture but rather a significant, neglected, and often obscured view that needs to be incorporated into our discussion of the great intertextual wars of the 1790s. My concentration on those similarities and resemblances also admittedly obscures occult and striking differences between Burke and his respondents—a caveat that needs to be remembered in the endeavor to address an imbalance that I believe results frequently in a one-sided story. Just as Burke established the dominant paradigms that were and continue to be cited against the Revolution, Wollstonecraft, Paine, and Mackintosh formulated the principal paradigms that are reemployed against an opposition that is, ipso facto, counterrevolutionary. Critics and historians who study this discourse of difference easily get caught up in the same ironic repetitions and resemblances. In a fundamental sense, we continue to repeat the antithetical terms that Burke and his contemporary critics provided us and, in this context, Anglo-American discourse continues to validate the conventional oppositions of late eighteenth-century discourse.[6] We necessarily provide our own coloring to the debate by rereading our own texts and contexts into the tumultuous textual war of the 1790s. Thus, to write about the Revolution is inevitably to implicate ourselves in an ongoing intertextual war, which is, of course, the ongoing writing and revision of a revolution that still reverberates in our language. Two centuries after Burke and his principal respondents acquired Manichean, mythic status, we continue to absorb and to be reabsorbed by both.

1

Hic mulier, Haec vir: Wollstonecraft's Feminization of Burke in *The Rights of Men*

Mary Wollstonecraft published *A Vindication of the Rights of Men* at the end of November 1790 in response to Edmund Burke's *Reflections on the Revolution in France*, which had appeared on the first of the same month. Although less known than *A Vindication of the Rights of Woman* (1792), her first *Vindication* is, in many ways, its ideological precursor, for it is as much about a revolution in sexual identity as it is a defense of the French Revolution. Specifically, Wollstonecraft subverts Burke's explicit sexual values in both the *Reflections* and his earlier work, *A Philosophical Enquiry into the Origin of our Ideas of the Sublime and Beautiful*. In the latter, Burke had distinguished the sublime from the beautiful in terms of conventional masculine and feminine characteristics. Ronald Paulson notes that Burke's political categories "were essentially his own aesthetic ones in the *Enquiry*,"[1] but it remains to be shown precisely how Wollstonecraft's textual war against Burke's *Reflections* is a simultaneous effort to invert the patriarchal values of the *Enquiry*: Wollstonecraft subverts Burke's authority by describing him and the political order he defends in the "feminine" language of the beautiful, while she describes both the Revolution and herself in the "masculine" language of the sublime. But in doing this, Wollstonecraft begins to resemble Burke, as she enacts linguistically the very criticisms she ascribes to him. In addition, her feminized Burke also resembles, inter alia, Mary Wollstonecraft, in one of the most complex role reversals in the language. In chapter 1, I explore how Wollstonecraft's feminization of Burke provides the suppressed "terms" to begin rereading *The Rights of Men* and how the distinction she emphasizes begins to resemble a similarity between herself and Burke. In chapter 2, I analyze Wollstonecraft's intertextual war with the language of Burke's *Enquiry*, focusing on how her deconstruction of the *Enquiry*'s opposed values (the sublime and beautiful) and hence the distinction between Burke and herself turns into the very contradiction she erases only to reinscribe with finality. Finally, in chapter 3, I return to the resemblance between Burke and Wollstonecraft and its significance for Wollstonecraft's representation of the Revolution.

I

It is a commonplace that Burke's distinction between the sublime and the beautiful in the *Enquiry* centers on traditional differences between the sexes. In a footnote to an essay ("A Brief Appraisal of the Greek Literature") published in 1838, Thomas De Quincey noted that "the Sublime *by way of polar antithesis to the Beautiful*" was "an idea altogether of English growth. . . . [T]he Sublime . . . in contraposition to the Beautiful, grew up on the basis of *sexual* distinctions—the Sublime corresponding to the male, and the Beautiful, its anti-pole, corresponding to the female."[2] Thus, in the *Enquiry*, Burke associates the sublime with terror, pain, astonishment, majesty, violence, ruggedness, vastness, power, and punishment. The sublime virtues are "fortitude, justice, wisdom, and the like" (110). In his *Speech on American Taxation* (1774), he had observed that "the great and masculine virtues" are "constancy, gravity, magnanimity, fortitude, fidelity, and firmness." Hence it is not surprising that, in the *Reflections*, these aesthetic and moral values are political as well, since the British commonwealth is also based on "sublime principles" (189).

In contrast, the beautiful, in the *Enquiry*, is associated with pleasure, pity, sympathy, tenderness, smallness, smoothness, delicacy, timidity, and weakness. The softer feminine virtues are "easiness of temper, compassion, kindness, and liberality"—virtues that "engage our hearts" but "are of less immediate and momentous concern to society" than the sublime virtues that preserve it (111). Hence, according to Burke, we admire the masculine sublime while we love the feminine beautiful: "We submit to what we admire, but we love what submits to us" (113).

Although Wollstonecraft often uses the conventional vocabulary of the sublime and beautiful with reference to nature, these and other passages in the *Enquiry* angered her, and so she begins *The Rights of Men* by describing Burke in the "weaker" language of the beautiful while she uses the "stronger" language of the sublime for herself. Although the cultural language of masculinity and femininity permeates Western discourse, Wollstonecraft was responding to Burke's ideological use of it in both the *Reflections* and the *Enquiry*. But this created a series of problematic ironies, since Wollstonecraft could only use the available categories and language of the time: thus, she implicitly valorized the language she resented by inverting the sexual clichés in terms of the "stronger" masculine woman and the "weaker" feminine man. Since Burke was associated with a series of liberal causes, she textually turned him into a dark reactionary and an effeminate wit. She employed a psychological reading of Burke's public life in order to portray his true private self. Wollstonecraft's subversion of Burke allowed her to recreate him in her own image, that is, as she reconceived him. The creation of contradictory Burkes complements her thesis that Burke's thought and life is a series of glaring contradictions.

Wollstonecraft begins *The Rights of Men* with a linguistic role reversal by attributing fancy and wit to Burke—qualities often associated with traditional femininity—and reason and judgment to herself—qualities traditionally associated with masculine thought.[3] In her opening address, she distinguishes "a flight of fancy" from "truth," which "in morals," is the "essence of the sublime," while "in taste, simplicity [is] the only criterion of the beautiful" (*WMW*, 5:7). Having established that the language of Burke's *Enquiry* (which opens with a section on "Taste") will figure in *The Rights of Men*, Wollstonecraft informs Burke that she will provide "a manly definition" of the rights of men, even though he has distorted the phrase through "flimsy ridicule" and a "lively fancy." In contrast to her own reasonable judgment, Burke possesses a suggestively feminine sensibility: he has a "lively imagination" that often spills over into "vagaries," a "teeming fancy" (cf. *WMW*, 5:135) untamed by "ripening judgement" (*WMW*, 5:8, 15, 9). In Samuel Richardson's *Clarissa* (1748), the female protagonist observes that "the liveliness of [women's] imaginations" distinguishes their writing.[4] In Wollstonecraft's posthumously published "Hints," she noted that it "is generally supposed, that the imagination of women is particularly active, and leads them astray" (*WMW*, 5:271).

In *The Rights of Men*, she continually refers to Burke as a man of wit who, "like a celebrated beauty," tries to attract attention to himself (*WMW*, 5:8), and she principally uses *wit* in its eighteenth-century sense of the mental faculty associated with quickness and variety, producing resemblances, "thereby to make up pleasant pictures and agreeable visions in the fancy," as Locke puts it in *An Essay Concerning Human Understanding*.[5] *Wit* of course had its principal semantic significance (via Locke) in its contradistinction to *judgment*: the former fabricates resemblances and similarities; the latter focuses on distinctions and differences and was generally, since it was associated with "clear reason," considered the higher faculty.[6] Locke associates wit with metaphor and allusion, with entertainment, so that the "pleasantry of wit . . . strikes *lively* on the *fancy*, and therefore is so acceptable to all people, because its *beauty* appears at first sight, and there is required *no labour of thought* to examine what truth or reason there is in it."[7] Burke, in the *Enquiry*, had discussed Locke's distinction between wit and judgment with approval, associating wit with the beautiful and judgment with the sublime (17–18).[8] Wollstonecraft skewers Burke with his own aesthetic values by depicting him as an effeminate man of wit and hence an admirer and practitioner of beauty—an effeminate man whose addiction to "spurious, sensual beauty" has "long debauched" his "imagination" (*WMW*, 5:48).

She emphasizes his superficial verbal wit and his facility for saying "brilliant or sparkling things," since *wit* had been traditionally "opposed to *wisdom* or *judgement*" (*OED*, meaning #7). Burke pours forth "a torrent of shining sentences" bearing no resemblance to reason (*WMW*, 5:59). By extension, she makes the *Reflections* a superficial work of Burke's effeminate imagination—an imagination that spurs him "to shine in conversation," anxiously causing him to support that "shining character" that prevents him from ever obtaining any profound "metaphysical passion" nourished by "reflection" (*WMW*, 5:8, with a punning allusion to his own shallow *Reflections*). The references to Burke's desire "to shine" emphasize his "effeminate" vanity. Referring to women who "coquet" with "fine gentlemen" who do the same, Wollstonecraft laments the lengths "this desire of shining" has carried them (*WMW*, 5:23). The feminine connection is even clearer in *The Female Reader* (1789), an anthology edited by Wollstonecraft for the edification of young women. In an essay "On Politeness," Catherine Talbot stresses "elegance of taste" that "represses the desire of shining alone" (*WMW*, 4:133). In an "Essay on Talkativeness," Edmund Rack quotes a friend who observes "that persons who possess most sense and knowledge" seek "not to shine out of their proper sphere" (*WMW*, 4:151). In a "Portrait of a Modern Fine Lady," the anonymous author warns against the "intoxications of female vanity" and the "fine lady" whose "only study is to glitter or shine" in order "to swell her own pomp and importance" (*WMW*, 4:318).

Wollstonecraft was, in effect, reproducing the conventional sexual stereotypes and ascribing feminine characteristics to Burke and masculine ones to herself. In 1777, the conservative writer Hannah More summarized what were believed to be the intrinsic differences between the sexes in a language that Wollstonecraft reverses but later valorizes:

Women have generally quicker perceptions; men have juster sentiments. Women consider how things may be prettily said; men, how they may be properly said. In women (young ones at least), speaking accompanies and sometimes precedes reflection; in men, reflection is the antecedent. Women speak to shine or to please; men, to convince or confute. Women admire what is brilliant; men what is solid. Women prefer an extemporaneous sally of wit, or a sparkling effusion of fancy, before the most accurate reasoning, or the most laborious investigation of facts. In literary composition, women are pleased with point, turn, and antithesis; men, with observation, and a just deduction of effects from their causes. Women are fond of incident, men, of argument....

In short, it appears that the mind in each sex has some natural kind of bias, which constitutes a distinction of character, and that the happiness of both depends, in a great measure, on the preservation and observance of this distinction.[9]

Wollstonecraft incorporates all these gendered clichés into her critique of Burke while reformulating the "distinction" that both More and Burke affirm.

In contrast to Burke's sparkling femininity, Wollstonecraft repeatedly emphasizes her own sober "reflection" and "the operations of that reason" that Burke supposedly condemns "with flippant disrespect" (*WMW*, 5:40). By employing a series of empowering distinctions, she depicts herself as a person of judgment, a person whose "sober manliness of thought" is superior to the "finical man of taste, anxious only to secure his own private gratifications, and to maintain his rank in society." This Burkean man of taste is then linked to women on-the-make, since both are produced by the same social system—women who "marry to settle themselves in a superior rank, and coquet, without restraint"—women whose "desire of shining" corrupts them (*WMW*, 5:40).

II

The feminization of Burke and his *Reflections* continues in other ways, but it often results in unwitting resemblances between Burke and Wollstonecraft herself. For instance, Wollstonecraft delights in connecting Burke's "ornamental feelings" with both the "fashionable world" and the fashionable ladies who find a sentimental book (Burke's *Reflections*) amusing. These ladies enjoy repeating Burke's "sprightly sallies" and retelling "in theatrical attitudes many" of his "sentimental exclamations." Indeed, since "sensibility is the *manie* of the day" (*WMW*, 5:8), Wollstonecraft suggests that the *Reflections* is a work of insincere, sentimental fiction, implying that Burke manipulates the emotions of his aristocratic female readers with "a sentimental jargon, which has long been current in conversation" (*WMW*, 5:30). Later, in *The Rights of Woman*, she noted that "feminine weakness of character" has been "very properly termed *sentimental*" (*WMW*, 5:255). In this context, Christopher Reid argues that, in depicting the beleaguered French queen in the *Reflections*, Burke drew upon the new, sentimental conventions of eighteenth-century drama, with its emphasis on the plight of "virtuous" female "distress," and that Wollstonecraft astutely recognized Burke's sentimental source.[10]

Wollstonecraft, however, describes Burke publicly in the very language she uses to describe herself privately. For instance, while she disdains Burke's "sprightly sallies," she had written an emotional letter to her sister, Everina, on 11 May 1787, complaining that she succumbs "to whim—and yet when the most sprightly sallies burst from me the tear frequently trembles in my eye and the long drawn sigh eases my full heart. . . . I am *tied* to my fellow creatures by partaking of their weaknesses—I rail at a fault—sicken at the sight—and find it stirring within me—new sympathies and feelings *start* up—I know not myself" (*Collected Letters*, 151). Wollstonecraft was a woman of strong emotions, and throughout her life she struggled with the conflict between her feelings and her ideas; thus it is more than interesting that she often describes Burke in a language that documents what she felt to be her own "weaknesses" (see, for instance, her letter to Joseph Johnson in late 1792, *Collected Letters*, 220–21). Given the gender pressures and biases of the eighteenth century, her effort to portray herself publicly as a woman of calm reason and sober judgment was, understandably, an endeavor to create a persona of what she desired to be, a public persona in *The Rights of Men* at odds with her private self as revealed in biographical passages and private correspondence. Similarly, in her psychological reading of Burke she purports to reveal the contradiction between his public image and his "real" private self. Her frequent depictions of herself, in contrast to the flighty and emotional Burke, as a person of reason and judgment, were ways in which she tried to assert a formal control of herself that she lacked in both her private and public lives. In fact, she seems to reverse the process that she describes in the letter and projects the weaknesses that she discovers in herself onto Burke. It is, as will be seen, a suggestive psychological exorcism of private doubts and demons.

For instance, her reference to Burke's "sprightly sallies" repeated by fine ladies who find a sentimental book "amusing," now that "sensibility is the *manie* of the day" (*WMW*, 5:8), is reflexively ironic, since Wollstonecraft herself had published in 1788 *Mary, a Fiction*—"a sentimental novel, largely about herself."[11] Her disdain of "sensibility" also clashes with her many positive references to it in her letters and works. In *The Cave of Fancy* (1787), *sensibility* is affirmatively defined by the sage Sagestus as "the result of acute senses, finely fashioned nerves, which vibrate at the slightest touch, and convey such clear intelligence to the brain, that it does not require to be arranged by the judgement" (*WMW*, 1:201). In *Mary* (1788), it is "the most exquisite feeling of which the human soul is susceptible" (*WMW*, 1:59); indeed, if Wollstonecraft's readers were indulgent, the author would "go on and tell them such tales as would force the sweet tears of sensibility to flow in copious showers down beautiful cheeks, to the discomposure of rouge. . . . Nay, I would make it so interesting, that the fair peruser should beg the hair-dresser to settle the curls himself, and not interrupt her" (*WMW*, 1:8). This, ironically, follows a pejorative description of Mary's mother's enjoyment of silly romantic novels, for here is the very language of sensibility as well as fine ladies reading sentimental novels that Wollstonecraft later rejects.

It is true that Wollstonecraft sometimes distinguished between true and false sensibility and that, in *The Rights of Men*, her attacks on Burke's "pampered sensibility," his "infantine sensibility," and his shameless "parade of . . . sensibility" (*WMW*, 5:9, 58, 18) are often in the context of his false sensibility, specifically a "sensual" Edmund Burke hiding beneath the language of feeling. Her comment in a letter to Eliza W. Bishop (27 June 1787) is pertinent to her criticism of Burkean sensibility: "I am sorry to hear a man of sensibility and cleverness *talking* of sentiment sink into sensuality—such will ever I fear be the case with the inconsistent human heart when there are no *principles* to restrain and direct the wayward impulses of it" (*Collected Letters*, 155). The attack on sensibility culminates in *The Rights of Woman*, where Burkean "men of lively sensibility" justify unjust social distinctions (*WMW*, 5:82), but the emphasis throughout is on how the cult of sensibility weakens women, turning them into creatures of feeling rather than rational human beings. Categorically rejecting Samuel Johnson's definition of *sensibility* in his 1755 *Dictionary* ("quickness of sensation [def. #1]; quickness of perception" [def. #2]), but adding "delicacy," erroneously suggesting that it is part of Johnson's definition, a definition similar to her own affirmative one in *The Cave of Fancy*, she concludes that it lacks even "a trace" of God's image (*WMW*, 5:132).[12]

In *The Female Reader*, Mrs. Chapone, in an essay titled "False Sensibility," warns "vain" young women against believing that "tenderness and softness is the peculiar charm of the sex—that even their weakness is lovely," for they will soon start exaggerating their sensibility and hence selfishly refuse to relieve or succor those in real distress (*WMW*, 4:135). In the subsequent essay, "False Notions of Sentiment," taken from the Edinburgh journal *The Lounger*, the "separation of conscience from feeling is a depravity of the most pernicious sort" (*WMW*, 4:136). In *The Wrongs of Women: or, Maria* (1797), Wollstonecraft asserts that women's "boasted sensibility is often stifled by false delicacy." True sensibility is "occupied with the feelings of others," rather than "its own sensations" (*WMW*, 1:163). In *The Rights of Woman*, she despises the "exquisite sensibility" that is supposedly characteristic "of the weaker vessel"; she deplores women who are the slaves of their senses, "delicately termed sensibility, and are blown about by every momentary gust of feeling," in a world where "feeling" is "the only province of women." She laments that "women are supposed to possess more sensibility" (*WMW*, 5:73, 129, 189, 260). Sensibility, in the eighteenth century, was a gendered phenomenon, specifically associated with women.[13] In this context, Wollstonecraft's emphasis on Burke's emotional sensibility enmeshes him in a phenomenon associated with pronounced "feminine" feeling, although it had long been fashionable for both sexes to culticate their sensibility in public displays of sentiment. But the displays of masculine sensibility resulted in a correspondent "preoccupation with the dangers of 'effeminacy,'"[14] and Wollstonecraft continually evokes this cultural anxiety. In contrast, as we have seen, Wollstonecraft associates herself with linguistic categories that are recognizably patriarchal, describing herself as a person of reason and judgment. It is perhaps telling that the first edition of *The Rights of Men* did not carry her name, and she does not refer to her gender. Indeed, she identifies herself with mental qualities traditionally associated with maleness.[15]

Alluding to the *Enquiry* (110–11), Wollstonecraft tells Burke that since he has "informed us that respect chills love, it is natural to conclude that all your pretty flights arise from your pampered sensibility" (*WMW*, 5:9). Here and throughout *The Rights of Men*, she paints Burke with dainty feminine adjectives, suggesting he has a feminine sensibility and wit bordering on madness. Burke fosters "every emotion till the fumes [cf. *Reflections*, 159], mounting to" his "brain, dispel the sober suggestions of reason" (*WMW*, 5:9). The imagery refers to the body vapors commonly believed to rise to the head, causing melancholic madness or hypochondria, the mental "disease" of females.[16]

Margaret Tims notes, however, that in Wollstonecraft's description of Burke, there is again "an echo of herself, and there is something faintly

comic in this highly emotional woman accusing the worldly-wise
politician of letting his feelings outrun his judgement."[17] Indeed,
Wollstonecraft so often describes Burke in terms applicable to herself
that charges of hypocrisy or contradiction miss the larger point: Burke
not only resembles the private Mary Wollstonecraft, but Wollstonecraft
resembles the public Edmund Burke.

This sustained role reversal results in a thematic illustration of textual
castration. Wollstonecraft distorts Burke's "masculine" life and works;
she uses rumor, insult, and innuendo to reduce him to a vulnerable
cardboard caricature of effeminacy. She accuses him of boasting of his
political "virtue and independence" and then "enjoying the wages of
falsehood" in a "skulking unmanly way"—wages he acquired by secur-
ing, through political favor, "a pension of fifteen hundred pounds per
annum on the Irish establishment" (*WMW*, 5:13)—a malicious allegation
that had been circulating since spring 1790. In Wollstonecraft's reading
of Burke, he is cowardly, insincere, weak, and manipulative—using his
wit and wiles in ways similar to the weak women she deplores in both
Vindications. Even as a whimsical *"gentleman* of lively imagination"
(*WMW*, 5:13), he is an unauthentic man, since Wollstonecraft asserts his
effeminacy within feminine categories that are, as Cora Kaplan notes,
pejoratively ideological.[18]

Referring to the "drapery" of Burke's "fancy" (*WMW*, 5:15), Wollstonecraft alludes to his famous lament for forsaken queens and obsolete
chivalry in the *Reflections*: "All the decent drapery of life is to be rudely
torn off. All the super-added ideas, furnished from the ward-robe of a
moral imagination . . . necessary to cover the defects of our naked shivering nature . . . are to be exploded as a ridiculous, absurd, and antiquated
fashion" (171). Wollstonecraft delights in tearing off Burke's "veils" and
"drapery," exposing him for the effeminate impostor she insists he is.
Just as Burke and other counterrevolutionary writers used metaphors of
clothing for the cultural "ward-robe" covering man's fallen being—"the
defects of our naked shivering nature"—Wollstonecraft and the revolutionaries used metaphors of unveiling—of stripping off the deceitful
clothes that disguise and mask counterrevolutionary man. Focusing on
the Burkean vocabulary of veils and drapery in the *Reflections*, Wollstonecraft intends to "undress" Burke and hence to demystify the
ideology of beauty through which he celebrates European institutions and
traditions.

Indeed, Wollstonecraft wishes "to hunt" his "pernicious opinions . . .
out of their lurking holes" and "to show" Burke to himself, "stripped of
the gorgeous drapery in which" he wraps his "tyrannic principles"
(*WMW*, 5:37). She engages in a rhetorical stripping of Burke's language,

tearing away the gorgeous "robes" and "drapery" disguising his oppressive ideology; thus her own imagery suggests she is "revealing" the
"real" Burke both to himself and to the world. In addition, the language
of stripping evokes Burke's defense of civilization's cultural clothing and
his preoccupation with a revolutionary criticism that views an object, "as
it stands stripped of every relation, in all the nakedness and solitude of
metaphysical abstraction" (*Reflections*, 90).

The linguistic stripping of Burke also conjures up his supposed
"stripping" of George III during the Regency Crisis; for, according to
Wollstonecraft, Burke, "with unfeeling disrespect, and indecent haste,
wished to strip him of all his hereditary honours" (*WMW*, 5:27). In this
parodic Burkean sentence in which Wollstonecraft disguises herself as
the indignant defender of royal honor, she subjunctively performs the
very stripping Burke supposedly desires. Later, referring to Burke's
contradictory anguish in seeing "the gorgeous robes" of the monarchy
"torn off" by the Revolution and religion "stripped of its gothic drapery"
(*WMW*, 5:58, 48), Wollstonecraft also evokes the suggested stripping of
Marie Antoinette, who flees, in the *Reflections*, "almost naked," from
murderous, revolutionary "ruffians" who pierce her bed with a series of
phallic plunges (164). Similarly, in another Wollstonecraftian reversal,
she hunts Burke down à la the revolutionary pursuers, making him
vulnerably exposed and "beautiful," like the beleaguered Marie
Antoinette. Indeed, as she inverts the values of both the *Enquiry* and the
Reflections, she beautifies Burke while she sublimes herself. Threatening
"to strip" him of "his cloak of sanctity," she has her way with Burke's
books, becoming the masculine ravisher of his feminized texts. In
contrast, she "clothe[s]" herself with the "garment" of her "own
righteousness" (*WMW*, 5:26, 35).

Wollstonecraft's endeavor to strip Burkean beauty and to reveal the
mystifying ideology that psychologically enslaves women coincides with
her attack on masculine, chivalric traditions as "gothic notions of beauty"
(*WMW*, 5:10). But Wollstonecraft also imprisons Burke in the language
of his own gothic categories, making him the proverbial "damsel in
distress." In a fundamental sense, the *Reflections* is a defensive chivalric
text through which Burke contests what he contends is a rapacious,
misogynistic revolution. In lamenting swords that fail to appear in
defense of a distraught queen now that "chivalry is gone" (*Reflections*,
170), Burke presents himself as the last knightly defender of beleaguered
beauty and damsels in distress, for, as he noted in the *Enquiry*, "beauty in
distress is much the most affecting beauty" (110). But Burke's
description of himself fighting the revolutionary demons confronting
civilization's imperiled beauty resembles Wollstonecraft's battle against

the feudal forces of the *ancien régime* embodied in Burke's text. And Wollstonecraft's caricature of this "manly" battle reinforces her endeavor to masculinize *The Rights of Men* while she feminizes the *Reflections*.

For instance, she belittles Burke by telling him that "it would be some-thing like cowardice to fight with a man who had never exercised the weapons [consistency and reason] with which his opponent chose to combat" (*WMW*, 5:10), for "in controversy, as in battle, the brave man wishes to face his enemy, and fight on the same ground" (*WMW*, 5:29). Declaring victory by default against her unworthy and unmanly oppo-nent, she uses the connotative language of chivalry, conjuring up knightly jousts and duels, but, in doing so, she uses the very "gothic" language she deplores in Burke. She begins resembling the "male" Burke she insistently denies, while emphasizing his fragile femininity.

After asserting that she will provide "a manly definition" of "the *rights of men*," she contrasts Burke's "confined understanding" with the "sublime" character "that acts from principle" (*WMW*, 5:7, 8). She continues emphasizing the sexual distinction between the beautiful and the sublime in the *Enquiry*. Although she often makes her thematic contrasts as generic comparisons, the distinction is usually implicit with regard to a weak Burke and a strong Wollstonecraft, as in her implied masculine "vigor" versus his "feverish eccentricities" (*WMW*, 5:8). Burke, not surprisingly, has "a mortal antipathy to reason," while she follows "unerring *reason*" (*WMW*, 5:10, 34, Wollstonecraft's emphasis).

Contemptuously conscious of Burke's delicate feminine sensibility, she addresses him with superior hauteur, sounding very much like a smug, condescending male: "If I were not afraid to derange your nervous system by the bare mention of metaphysical enquiry, I should observe . . . that self-preservation is . . . the first law of nature" and the care of the body is "the first step to . . . inspire a manly spirit of independence" (*WMW*, 5:16)—a "manly spirit" Burke notably lacks. Wollstonecraft's reference to his squeamish nervous system suggests Burke's "hysterical" reaction to the "metaphysical" reasoning excoriated in the *Reflections*, or what she sarcastically calls "the impertinent enquiry of philosophic meddling innovation" that sets Burkean "teeth on edge" (*WMW*, 5:52).[19] Burke's "feminine" *hysteria*—the "female" mental and emotional disorder traditionally believed to be caused by "uterine displacement" (see Samuel Johnson, 1755 *Dictionary*, "Hysterick," meanings #1 and 2)—would be especially suggestive to her audience, since hysteria, in the eighteenth century, was primarily seen as a female problem, since women's nervous systems were supposedly more delicate than men's.[20] Indeed, there was an "association between a gendered sensibility and nervous disorders."[21]

In the eighteenth century, Dr. George Cheyne's *The English Malady* (1733) was a standard book on nervous and mental disturbances. According to Cheyne, the English were afflicted with an epidemic of "nervous disorders," especially those people "who had a great Degree of Sensibility . . . and are of most lively imagination." Women, Cheyne seemingly implied, were naturally more sensitive and vulnerable to diseases of the nerves.[22] Wollstonecraft, as we have seen, emphasizes Burke's feminine sensibility, his fragile nerves, and his "lively imagination" (*WMW*, 5:6). All this, along with Burke's correspondent lack of judgment, were standard characterizations of nervous insanity in the eighteenth century.[23] The pejorative nexus of femininity and insanity has been explored by Elaine Showalter in *The Female Malady*. Wollstonecraft, in effect, stigmatizes Burke with characteristics conventionally ascribed to women, making him both feminine and insane. In doing this, however, she validates a pejorative cultural association that typifies her ambivalent, misogynous perspective.

Her reference to "metaphysical enquiry" (*WMW*, 5:16) alludes to Burke's own *Enquiry*, which she is rewriting in terms of the beautifully feminine Burke and her sublimely masculine self. Thus, when she refers to Burke's delicate feminine nerves that the strain of "reasoning" undoes, she is also alluding to the *Enquiry*, where Burke notes that "an air of robustness and strength is very prejudicial to beauty"—beauty needs the appearance of delicacy: "The beauty of women is considerably owing to their weakness or delicacy, and is even enhanced by their timidity, a quality of mind analogous to it" (*Enquiry*, 116)—a statement she was still allusively attacking in *The Rights of Women* (see *WMW*, 5:98, 116, 145).

In the *Analytical Review* (November 1790), Wollstonecraft quoted with approval Catherine Macaulay's observation that women's "system of nerves is depraved" from a "false notion of beauty and delicacy" (*WMW*, 7:314). In this context, Burke's delicate "nervous system" suggests again his overwrought "sensibility"—a word, as we have seen, that she uses selectively, depending on the context. In *Letters on the Female Mind* (1793), Laetitia Matilda Hawkins—a conservative, antirevolutionary writer—notes that "irritable nerves" are intrinsic to the female constitution.[24] Wollstonecraft, in short, continually reproduces and reverses conventional feminine sexual stereotypes, ascribing them to Burke.

Wollstonecraft herself, however, suffered neurasthenic attacks at various points in her life, and her reference to Burke's delicate "nervous system" and his suggestively feminine sensibility reflexively resembles her private descriptions of herself. For instance, in a letter (14 March

1787) to her sister, Everina, she had complained of her "lowness of spirits":

> Don't smile when I tell you that I am tormented with *spasms*—indeed it is impossible to enumerate the various complaints I am troubled with; and how much my mind is harassed by them. I know they all arise from my disordered nerves, that are injured beyond a *possibility* of receiving *any* aid from medicine—There is no cure for a broken heart! . . . The nervous fever I am subject to has increased my natural sensibility to such a degree—I may with reason complain of the irritability of my [nerves]. (*Collected Letters*, 142–43)[25]

This suggests that Wollstonecraft again projects her own sense of weakness onto the feminized Burke in *The Rights of Men*, for as she begins to resemble the public Burke, she makes him resemble the private Wollstonecraft.

She continues to validate Burke's distinction between the sublime and the beautiful in terms of her masculine strength and his feminine weakness. In opposition to his deceptive volubility, she speaks to him with "manly plainness"; Wollstonecraft "exercises" her mind—an activity and end that is "one of the strongest arguments" for both the soul's immortality and her own superiority to Burke. In contrast, "weak minds are always timid" (*WMW*, 5:36, 16, 47)—an allusion to the *Enquiry* and the "beauty of women" that is "owing to their weakness" and "enhanced by their timidity, a quality of mind analogous to it," (*Enquiry*, 116). Burkean "lovers of elegance and beauty" are hence constitutionally incapable of creating the Constitution of France (*WMW*, 5:47).

Indeed, Burkean "counterrevolution" becomes the feminine "Other" that Wollstonecraft contrasts with masculine revolutionary reason. Burkeans who "endeavor to make unhappy men resigned to their fate" engage in a "tender endeavor of short-sighted benevolence," while those who "labor" to make mankind happy by "extirpating error" exercise "a masculine godlike affection" (*WMW*, 5:53). Similarly, the French National Assembly's "active exertions" are opposed to the Burkean status quo, since the former "were not relaxed by a fastidious respect for the beauty of rank" (*WMW*, 5:47).[26]

It can be argued, of course, that Wollstonecraft is merely using the cultural language of the time and that she is consequentially a prisoner of the patriarchal language permeating Western culture.[27] This is, to some extent, true. In *The Rights of Men*, there are many examples of her sympathetic identification with the empowering masculine language of

European culture, as in her rhetorical question that if we doubted our sanity "when all the faculties are mixed in wild confusion," we would fearfully "ask if we are yet men?—if our reason is undisturbed?—if judgement hold the helm?" (*WMW*, 5:27). It is notable, however, that she frequently uses *men* as an indefinite pronoun to refer to humanity instead of the collective noun *man* (the former usage was already rare in the eighteenth century, the Declaration of Independence notwithstanding). The result is to make us all "men," except, of course, the counterrevolutionaries she transforms into the "weaker" sex.

In *The Rights of Women*, Wollstonecraft seems more conscious of linguistic sexual biases, yet she can still reflexively ask, "where shall we find men who will stand forth to assert the rights of man [?]" (*WMW*, 5:114; cf. 5:266 and 5:7). Having already written *The Rights of Men*, her self-fulfilling question alludingly asserts her manly answer. Mary Poovey notes that in Wollstonecraft's usage of the nouns *men* and *mankind*, the "terms used may pass as generic nouns and pronouns, but they most frequently designate males."[28] Thus, while Wollstonecraft uses the ubiquitously available patriarchal language of her culture, she also alludes repeatedly to the gendered language of Burke's *Enquiry*, since she realizes that it reappears politically in the *Reflections*.

However, instead of rejecting Burke's language and categories, she selectively applies them to Burke himself in order to hoist him on his own ideological petard. She inverts the *Enquiry*'s sexual aesthetic by, in a sense, dressing (and undressing) Burke with his own "beautiful" clichés. Thus, while Wollstonecraft simultaneously empowers herself textually through the masculine language of the sublime, she ironically endorses Burke's distinction between masculinity and femininity that she later, in the same text, attacks—only to reaffirm it again with finality. It is in this context that I want to explore extensively her critique of Burke's *Enquiry* in *The Rights of Men*.

2
Intertextual War: Wollstonecraft and the Language of Burke's *Enquiry*

Burke's language in the *Enquiry* and *Reflections* permeates *The Rights of Men*, where many of his arguments reappear in a new revolutionary context. In the *Enquiry*, Burke had maintained that any work associated with *difficulty* suggests the power and grandeur of the sublime (77). In contrast, he argued that "rest and inaction" produce both mental and physical disorders and that, consequently, "labor" is "a thing absolutely requisite to make us pass our lives with tolerable satisfaction; for the nature of rest is to soften all the parts of our bodies to fall into a relaxation," resulting in bodily weakness and frayed "nerves" producing "melancholy, dejection, despair," and sometimes suicide. Hence the "best remedy for all these evils is exercise or labour; and labour is a surmounting of *difficulties*" (135, Burke's emphasis; cf. *Reflections*, 139–40, 143–44, 278–80). Frances Ferguson notes that, for Burke, the sublime excites "passions of self-preservation," making us fear death and causing us to labor against it, while "the beautiful leads us toward death without our awareness"—beauty dazzles and beguiles, evoking Eve's temptation of Adam and hence the necessity of labor, a consequence of the Fall.[1]

In Wollstonecraft's rewriting of the *Enquiry*, she informs Burke that "a manly spirit of independence" is absent in the aristocrat who, as a pampered baby, is treated "like a superior being" and who will probably grow up lacking "sufficient fortitude either to exercise his mind or body to acquire personal merit." Indeed, the "exercise of our faculties is the great end," although the affluent "supinely exist without exercising mind or body" and have hence "ceased to be men" (*WMW*, 5:16, 10). This language reappears in *The Rights of Woman*, where weak, pampered, aristocratic females are continually falling into enervating states of "relaxation" and "softness" (see *WMW,* 5:98, 111, 112–13, 130–31, 136, 145, 165, 191, 199, 208, 212, 215, and 243: "relaxed beauty"). In both books, effeminate aristocrats and weak women are metaphorically equated with Burkean beauty. Burke, we will remember, is associated in *The Rights of Men* with *wit,* whose "beauty," according to Locke, in *An Essay Concerning Human Understanding,* requires "no labour of thought."[2]

Throughout *The Rights of Men,* Wollstonecraft reworks the *Enquiry's* terms to beautify aristocratic men, connecting them, on one level, to a kind of political and social infantilism—an arrested state she also associates with weak women, although the latter are more pointedly enervated by enslaving concepts of beauty. Burke's allegory of the Fall in the *Enquiry*—in which seductive beauty beguiles man into feeble softness and relaxation—a "fall" that must be resisted by arduous exercise and labor, becomes, in Wollstonecraft's version, a fall into social and political femininity. In contrast, the explosive energy of the National Assembly is equated with the sublime: its "active exertions" were "not relaxed by a fastidious respect for the beauty of rank" (*WMW,* 5:47). Her emphasis on effeminate, aristocratic culture and sensual, decadent monarchy is in the conventional language of the seventeenth-century Commonwealthmen's concern over the effeminacy of men degraded by antirepublican institutions.[3] "Distrust of women," as Alan Craig Houston notes, "and of the moral and psychological qualities associated with them is at the heart of republican theories of virtue."[4] Wollstonecraft repeatedly incorporates a variety of misogynous languages into her critique of Burke and the old order.

It is not surprising, then, that effeminate "men of lively fancy" neglect the "exercise of reason"—"an arduous task"—finding it "easier to follow the impulse of passion" (*WMW,* 5:31): the "fanciful" and emotional response conventionally attributed to women. As Meena Alexander notes, "Burke the patriarch is given to the feminine play of feeling and hence not to be seriously considered, while [Wollstonecraft] takes the more virile 'masculine' intelligence based on reason." The result is a "symbolic cross-dressing" of Burke.[5] Wollstonecraft inverts the conventional cultural clichés by reversing the stereotypic gender roles assigned to Burke and herself. More pertinently, by relentlessly characterizing Burke in the pejorative language of feminine vulnerability and weakness (imagination, sensibility, and hysterical madness), Wollstonecraft suggests that Burke's emotional, fanciful account of the Revolution is a tissue of illusions and lies, while her own masculine representations (based on personal strength, labor, reason, and judgment) reflect truth and reality.

She lectures her timidly traditional Burke on enlightened "enquiries" into the revolutionary subjects he fears, since a rigorous "exercise of the mind" enlarges "the understanding" in "restless enquiries that hover on the boundary, or stretch over the dark abyss of uncertainty" (*WMW*, 5:19–20). She informs Burke that "these lively conjectures are the breezes that preserve the still lake from stagnating" (*WMW*, 5:20), echoing Burke's comment in the *Enquiry* that he published his aesthetic meditations because "nothing tends more to the corruption of science than to suffer it to stagnate. These waters must be troubled, before they can exert their virtues" (54). Wollstonecraft hence opposes revolutionary effort and energy to the sterile "narrow-minded[ness]" of Burkean thought (*WMW*, 5:20).

Similarly, the traditional, aristocratic order that Burke defends is effetely effeminate. Confined, like pampered women, within the debilitated category of beauty, the "man of rank and fortune" has difficulty discovering that "he is a man," since "all his wants are instantly supplied." In contrast, the masculine National Assembly knows "more of the human heart and of legislation than the profligates of rank, emasculated by hereditary effeminacy" (*WMW*, 5:42, 40). Wollstonecraft's attack on the aristocracy complements her attack on prescription, "prejudice," primogeniture, and other institutional ideologies through which the Old Order perpetuates itself. Primogeniture is, for instance, a "barbarous feudal institution, that enables the elder son to overpower talents and depress virtue," fostering "an unmanly servility, most inimical to true dignity of character." Primogeniture produces indolence and hence "luxury and effeminacy," introducing "so much idiotism into . . . noble families" (*WMW*, 5:24).

Gendered language has, of course, always been used to weaken or to belittle an adversary while strengthening and reinforcing an ally, and Burke himself uses it throughout his works. In his *Speech on American Taxation* (1774), Burke ridiculed Charles Townshend by associating his political policies with feminine pleasing ("To please universally was the object of his life") and Townshend himself with a "mincing littleness." In his subsequent, antirevolutionary works, he depicted a weak, effeminate England fearfully shrinking from a strong, masculine France, in an effort to shame the English into national "manhood" and hence into a war of the sublime.[6]

But as the Revolution forced itself onto the European continent and into European consciousness, Burke also depicted the vulnerable, aristocratic order in terms of feminine beauty, and the revolutionary powers aligned against it in terms of rapacious masculinity.[7] He did this to energize a "chivalrous" defense of Europe's beautiful traditions and institutions. As he noted in the *Enquiry*, "beauty in distress is much the most affecting beauty" (110), and so, in the *Reflections*, he turned Marie Antoinette and the beautiful European traditions he believed she represented into the proverbial "damsel in distress." Similarly, in *The Rights of Men*, Wollstonecraft depicts an emotional "Burke in distress," ridiculing his "hysteria over the beautiful, endangered queen of France" and emphasizing his feminine art of pleasing.[8]

Referring to women mentally confined by Burkean notions of beauty, Wollstonecraft informs Burke that "an immoderate desire to please contracts the faculties" (*WMW*, 5:23), implying that Burke tries "to please" the pampered, privileged order that pays him. In the *Enquiry*, Burke argued that men seek women who please, who turn on "reliefs, gratifications, and indulgences," women who are "companions" of men's "softer hours" (111). In *Thoughts on the Education of Daughters* (1787), Wollstonecraft had also observed that a young woman "endeavors to please the other sex . . . to get married, and this endeavor calls forth all her powers" (*WMW*, 4:31). In *The Rights of Woman*, she attacked Rousseau, who, in *Emile*, had contended that woman's principal purpose was to please man, and she also argued that conduct books written by males for females tended to "render women pleasing at the expense of every solid virtue" (*WMW*, 5:117, 91; cf. 123, 126, 147–49, 154, 164, 189, 212, 256, 259–60, 263). Indeed, since the "mighty business of female life is to please," women are "restrained" from more important matters by a system of "political and civil oppression" (*WMW*, 5:256). In a letter to Mary Hays, 12 November 1792, Wollstonecraft had warned that female authors had to endeavor to ignore seductive praise, since "it requires great resolution to try rather to be useful than to please" (*Collected Letters*, 219). In *The Rights of Men*, she continually adorns Burke with phrases associated with traditional femininity. But she also, turns him into a patriarchal indoctrinator.

In another reference to the *Enquiry*, for example, she launches a litany of criticisms against Burke's debased patriarchal values. Accusing aristocratic women of false sensibility, of ignoring real suffering while exercising "their tender feelings by the perusal of the last imported novel," she connects these contrived romances with Burke's *Enquiry*: "But these ladies may have read your Enquiry concerning the origin of our ideas of the Sublime and Beautiful, and, convinced by your arguments, may have labored to be pretty, by counterfeiting weakness" (*WMW*, 5:45). In the *Enquiry*, Burke had written that "beauty" in the "female sex almost always carries with it an idea of weakness and imperfection. Women are very sensible of this; for which reason, they learn to lisp, to totter in their walk, to counterfeit weakness, and even sickness" (110). Seeing Burke's cultural observation as an ideology of female weakness veiled in "beauty," Wollstonecraft links Burke's *Enquiry* and *Reflections* to the fashionable novel-reading that she continually contends distracts and indoctrinates women with enervating ideas: novel-reading inscribes the very terms through which they enact their psychological enslavement (cf. *WMW*, 5:101, 256–58). Even though she seems typically blind to her own ironic position—having already written the sentimental novel *Mary*—her initial attack on Burke reappeared, mutatis mutandis, throughout her oeuvre. Thus, when she writes, in *The Rights of Women*, that "false notions of beauty and delicacy stop the growth of [women's] limbs and produce a sickly soreness" and equates "books professedly written for [women's] instruction" with "Egyptian bondage" (*WMW*, 5:186–87), she is still confronting Burke and other patriarchal bogies.[9]

Hence, while Burke is feminized throughout *The Rights of Men*, she also (*WMW*, 5:45–47) describes him as the chauvinistic indoctrinator of "fair ladies":

> You may have convinced them that *littleness* and *weakness* are the very essence of beauty; and that the Supreme Being, in giving women beauty in the most supereminent degree, seemed to command them, by the powerful voice of Nature, not to cultivate the moral virtues that might chance to excite respect, and interfere with the pleasing sensations they were created to inspire. Thus confining truth, fortitude, and humanity, within the rigid pale of manly morals, they might justly argue, that to be loved, women's high end and great distinction! they should "learn to lisp, to totter in their walk, and nick-name God's creatures." Never, they might repeat after you, was any man, much less a woman, rendered amiable by the force of those exalted qualities, fortitude, justice, wisdom, and truth; and thus forewarned of the sacrifice they must make to those austere, unnatural virtues, they would be authorized to turn all their attention to their persons, systematically neglecting morals to secure beauty. (*WMW*, 5:45)

In her feminist critique, Wollstonecraft anticipates many of the arguments made throughout *The Rights of Women*; in this context, *The Rights of Men* is, I believe, her first great feminist tract—a strong, intertextual work warring against the patriarchal texts that she evokes and revises.

Thus, her disparaging references to *littleness* and *weakness* are feminine qualities that Burke applies to women in the *Enquiry* (113, 116, 156–57) and that Wollstonecraft applies to indoctrinated ladies and effeminate males pampered into "beauty." Since she notes that the enslaving stereotypes of the beautiful confine and belittle women, compelling them to act out their own humiliating imprisonment in the very terms that patriarchal ideology provides them, she illustrates this by suggesting that the arguments she attacks are being paraphrased by "fair ladies" parroting Burke (cf. *WMW*, 5:8: "Even the ladies, Sir, may repeat your sprightly sallies"). If, as Ronald Paulson contends, Wollstonecraft's "central insight" is that "beauty and seductiveness are men's fiction imposed on women to keep them weak and submissive," Wollstonecraft also imposes this fiction on Burke and other traditionalists by describing them with their own confining language.[10]

Her principal intent here (*WMW*, 5:45), however, is to expose an ideology disguised in beautiful Burkean "drapery," so her endeavor to strip Burke coincides with her exposure of his deceptive language—a language that unnaturally segregates the sexes by subsuming the sublime into "the rigid pale of manly morals."

Her strategy is to reappropriate the sublime for "one half of the human species" (*WMW*, 5:45), not as a masculine but as a human possibility, since by exclusively confining "moral virtues" to "the rigid pale of manly morals," men keep women from exercising what Burke had called the "great and masculine virtues" in his *Speech on American Taxation*— virtues similar to the "sublime virtues of fortitude, justice, and wisdom" in the *Enquiry* (110). Wollstonecraft specifically refers to these virtues (*WMW*, 5:45), which she believes Burke distorts into "austere, unnatural virtues" for women who would become "masculine" if they cultivated them. Her reference to these "austere, unnatural virtues" alludes additionally to the *Reflections,* to Burke's celebration of "a more austere and masculine morality," and to those who, according to him, support "all liberal and manly morals" (125, 182). Wollstonecraft's critique is directed against various Burkean texts, and just as Burke is preoccupied with revolutionary language in the *Reflections* and subsequent works, Wollstonecraft is concerned with the patriarchal language prohibiting women from expressing themselves in strong, "sublime" terms. In this context, *The Rights of Men* is a linguistic critique of restrictive patriarchal language and categories, a critique culminating in *The Rights of Woman* with her argument that women should not be kept from imitating the so-called "manly virtues," the "exercise of which ennobles the human character" (*WMW*, 5:74).

Her central thesis in *The Rights of Men*, however, is that *both* the sublime and the beautiful are human qualities and that Burkean separations of them result in the dehumanization of both sexes. She suggests that these artificial separations result in the exaggerated sexual stereotypes that both sexes are compelled to act out. Burkean men who insist on the "eternal distinction" (*Enquiry*, 124) between both sexes through an ideology of the sublime and beautiful engage in psychological blackmail by implying that, to be loved, women must act out their own physical and spiritual debilitation: they must "learn to lisp, to totter in their walk, and nickname God's creatures" (WMW, 5:45). This physical and mental crippling (lisping, tottering, nicknaming), suggesting the infantile regression of learned female behavior, also alludes to two pernicious patriarchal texts: Burke's *Enquiry* (women "counterfeit weakness," learning "to lisp" and "to totter in their walk," 110) and Hamlet's misogynous tirade against women—"You jig, you amble, and you lisp, you nickname God's creatures, and you make your wantonness your ignorance" (*Hamlet*, 3.1.146–48). By sacrificing women to a contrived concept of beauty, men deny them the power and respect of the sublime. Consequently, Burke's "eternal distinction" turns women into vain, pampered creatures—weak women pretending to be little girls who lisp, totter, and nickname their impoverished world.

The allusion to Hamlet's nicknames, also quoted in *The Rights of Women* (WMW, 5:76), suggests that women are psychologically prevented from a complete naming of their world because they are encouraged to speak a curtailed language sanctioned by the patriarchal order. Since they are confined to the infantile language of beauty, they are prevented from expressing themselves in an adult vocabulary. Wollstonecraft was sensitive to the link between language and being, and hence she suggests that women are conditioned to deform themselves linguistically with the tendentious terms provided by patriarchy. Convinced by a kind of psychological blackmail that they will be unloved and unsexed by "male" language (cf. WMW, 5:242), they contribute to their own psychic disfigurement by linguistically mutilating themselves with the truncated language that diminishes them (cf. WMW, 5:185). Wollstonecraft rewrites the Enlightenment insight that psychological liberation precedes political liberation—a liberation from and through language.

Envisioning an androgynous sublime and beautiful ("But should experience prove . . . there is a beauty in virtue, a charm in order") created by the political changes potentially present in the French Revolution—a "glorious change" that "can only be produced by liberty"—she anticipates the eventual linguistic liberation of women bastilled in the language of the old linguistic order (WMW, 5:46). Because she understands that language is power, she wars against a series of confining patriarchal texts that function as expressions of Burkean "tradition" and "prejudice." She sees the sublime as an ideology of male power and the beautiful as an ideology of female weakness.

If, as we have seen, Wollstonecraft feminizes Burke and the *Reflections* by describing them in the language of stereotypic femininity and hence places them in the same confining categories that render women weak and powerless, it is precisely at this point (*WMW*, 5:45–47) that she performs a series of ideological reversals by erasing Burke's "eternal distinction" and suggesting the fusion of the sublime and beautiful in terms of "the cold arguments of reason, that give no sex to virtue" (*WMW*, 5:46)—virtues common to both sexes. She thus subverts Burke's *Enquiry* by criticizing what she believes to be its covert ideology: "To say the truth, I not only tremble for the souls of women, but for the good natured man, whom every one loves. The *amiable* weakness of his mind is a strong argument against its immateriality, and seems to prove that beauty relaxes the *solids* of the soul as well as the body" (*WMW*, 5:46).

Wollstonecraft, the initial disparager of effeminate Burkean males, now ironically defends "the good natured man, whom every one loves"—the suggestively "soft" and "beautiful" man (since the beautiful, in this passage, is also common to the male sex) whose "*amiable* weakness of mind is [according to the *Enquiry*'s logic] a strong argument against its immateriality, and seems to prove that beauty relaxes the *solids* of the soul as well as the body" (*WMW*, 5:46). Besides the pejorative allusion to the *Enquiry* ("beauty relaxes"), the adjective *amiable* is used by Wollstonecraft in its principal eighteenth-century sense of lovely and pleasing (Samuel Johnson, 1755 *Dictionary*, definition 1); hence the "*amiable* weakness" of "the good natural man, whom every one loves." However, Wollstonecraft often associates the word with weak females who are convinced that amiable feminine behavior will make them attractive and beloved by men. Thus Wollstonecraft's critical comment that, according to Burke, no man, "much less a woman," was ever "rendered amiable by the force of those exalted qualities" associated with the sublime (*WMW*, 5:45) will later link her ironically with Burke.

In an article in the *Analytical Review* (vol. 6, 1790), Wollstonecraft associated feminine "sentiment" and male "gallantry" with artificial behavior: "The desire of being thought *amiable* in the circle, soon makes vanity domineer over the more natural and laudable inclinations of the heart" (*WMW*, 7:240). In *The Rights of Women*, she "read with indignation the plausible epithets which men use to soften their insults," asking, "What is meant by such heterogeneous associations, as fair defects, amiable weakness, etc.?" (*WMW*, 5:103). The allusion here is to the two principal patriarchal texts she is attacking: Adam's misogynistic description of Eve as "this fair defect" in *Paradise Lost* (10.891) and Burke's celebration of female "weakness and imperfection" in the *Enquiry*—all of which renders women "amiable" and hence lovable (cf.

Burke's homage to Marie Antoinette in the *Reflections*: "The sex, the beauty, and the amiable qualities of the descendant of so many kings and emperors" [168]). In chapter 4 (of *Rights of Women*), she (mis)quotes another pestiferous text, Pope's *Of the Characters of Women*, 1.43: "Fine by defect, and delicately weak," as "Fine by defect, and amiably weak," (*WMW*, 5:131), adding that since women are "made by this amiable weakness entirely dependent," it is not surprising that they "give their defects a graceful covering" (alluding to the fall of Adam and Eve and Burke's *Reflections*, 171). Later, a child's unreasonable reliance on a parent's opinion is "a weakness . . . though the epithet amiable may be tacked to it" (*WMW*, 5:224–25). Indeed, the adjective is almost always a synonym for female weakness (see *WMW*, 5:136, 166).

Earlier, in *The Female Reader* (1789), she had juxtaposed two "Descriptive Pieces" on Queen Elizabeth (from David Hume) and Mary Queen of Scots (from William Robertson) that contrasted the latter's feminine beauty with the former's masculine temperament. After praising Elizabeth's firm resolution and "the loftiness of her ambitious sentiments," Hume adds that, when contemplating her as a woman, "we are apt to be struck with the highest admiration of her qualities and extensive capacity; but we are also apt to require some more softness of disposition, some greater lenity of temper, some of those *amiable weaknesses* by which her sex is distinguished" (*WMW*, 4:280; my emphasis; cf. *WMW*, 5:98: "In fact, if we revert to history, we shall find that the women who have distinguished themselves have neither been the most beautiful nor the most gentle of their sex").[11] All this impinges on the feminization of Burke in *The Rights of Men* and the "very texture" of his "mind," which Wollstonecraft characterizes as "amiable" (*WMW*, 5:8; cf. "amiable" Burkean "benevolence," *WMW*, 5:52).

Given all this, her sudden defense of the "good natured man" and the "amiable weakness of his mind" (*WMW*, 5:46) and her implicit contention that both men and women are "rendered amiable by the force" of sublime qualities (*WMW*, 5:45) is surprising, since she is attacking Burke's aesthetic ideology (the beautiful feminizes; the sublime masculinizes), which she has used to assert her sublime superiority over Burke's effeminate beauty. Redefining the adjective *amiable* by implying that beauty (like the sublime) is common to both sexes, she apparently rejects the contention that the "amiable weakness" of a man's mind renders him feminine, since she now opposes what she maintains is the covert significance of the *Enquiry*: "Beauty relaxes the *solids* of the soul as well as the body" in *both* sexes (*WMW*, 5:46; cf. *Enquiry*, 149–50: "Beauty acts by relaxing the solids of the whole system"). Indeed, her previous reference to Burke's endeavor to prove "that one half of the human species, at least, have not souls" (*WMW*, 5:45) also applies to those "amiable" men whom Burke, in her reading, would also desoul.

There are two points to note. First, although Wollstonecraft may be suggesting that sexless "intellectual beauty" is common to both men and women, her emphasis on the soft, "amiable weakness" of the good-natured man's mind seems to reappropriate for both sexes those feminine qualities rejected by patriarchal writers as well as by Wollstonecraft herself, as has been seen. Second, since she has pejoratively feminized Burke throughout *The Rights of Men* and characterized the texture of his mind as "amiable" (*WMW*, 5:8), he is suddenly in the same position as the "good natured man," whom Wollstonecraft defends against Burke's *Enquiry*. She hence suggests that Burke's divisions of the sublime and the beautiful into exclusive sexual categories result in exaggerated, self-fulfilling, sexual stereotypes. She attempts to reunite the sublime and beautiful by suggesting that both are naturally available to both sexes, even though Burkean reasoners often succeed in their sexual distortions.

When both are separated, Burkean beauty becomes pampered weakness while sublime qualities are shunned by women as "those austere, unnatural virtues" that might make them masculine. Consequently, they "turn all their attention" egotistically "to their persons, systematically neglecting morals to secure beauty" (*WMW*, 5:45). Wollstonecraft's critique of Burke's aesthetic is that it turns both men and women into prisoners of their inherited patriarchal language—a language that restrictively expresses and defines them. Because both sexes are culturally conditioned to fear turning into the "other," they act out their gender roles in the sexual conventions of Burkean tradition.

But Wollstonecraft's critique contains implosive ironies, since, as we will see, she subsequently turns herself into her opposite, an aggressive Edmund Burke, while remaking Burke into her weaker feminine counterpart. While it can be argued that she linguistically confronts the sexes with their absurd fear of the "other" and hence explodes Burke's sexual conventions, she also reinforces others, specifically her "masculine" superiority to Burke's "feminine" weakness. In other words, Wollstonecraft gets caught in contradictions she has not thought through, for even when she seemingly turns concepts like "masculine" and "feminine" into androgynous human qualities, she subsequently overturns the similarities and reaffirms the distinctions.

In addition, she ascribes to Burke rigid polarities that he himself qualified. Thus, while Burke, in the *Enquiry*, insisted on an "eternal distinction" between the sublime and the beautiful (and by extension the distinctive sexes), he also acknowledged that they could be mixed, even though they must keep their proper identities (124–25, 157). Later, in the

Reflections, Burke argued that chivalry constituted the historical union of the sublime and beautiful: "strength" had formerly oppressed "weakness" until chivalry transformed power into the complementary (and complimentary) defender of "beauty" (see 170–71).

Since Burke presents himself in the *Reflections* as the chivalric defender of beauty, Wollstonecraft transvestizes him into an effeminate reactionary whom no one believes in anymore, except gullible women who read his Gothic romances. Burke, in Wollstonecraft's writing, becomes a manipulated linguistic object like the weak women she contends are worded into obedient beauty in *The Rights of Woman*. In her linguistic crossdressing of Burke, Wollstonecraft is not so much interested in engaging Burke in intellectual combat—something she has already declared he is not man enough to do—as asserting victory over her effeminate opponent. It is precisely because Burke is male that Wollstonecraft's imposed language evokes metaphors of transformation and transgression, of crossed boundaries and deviations into pejorative femininity, into the mockery of chivalry in drag. In this fanciful role reversal, through which Burke becomes what she says he must be, he strangely resembles the humiliated aristocrats in the *Reflections*, transformed by revolutionary oppressors: the "old aristocratic landlords" unrecognizably "displumed, degraded, and metamorphosed." "We no longer know them. They are strangers to us. Physically they may be the same men; though we are not quite sure of that, on your new philosophic doctrine of personal identity" (347). [12]

But Wollstonecraft is also vulnerable to the covert ironies of her own language, and while she degrades her counterrevolutionary opponents with a feminine vocabulary and celebrates herself with masculine imagery (even becoming a self-described caricature of hyperbolic masculinity—the boastful bully), she did not apparently suspect that just as she criticizes Burke for being excessively feminine, she would be accused of being excessively masculine. Indeed, Wollstonecraft often writes in a misogynous vein, as if she were a man, especially in the many passages throughout her oeuvre in which she condescendingly condemns "silly" female weakness. Referring to *The Rights of Men*, Mary Poovey contends that "Wollstonecraft actually aspires to *be* a man, for she suspects the shortest way to success and equality is to join the cultural myth-makers, to hide what seemed to her a fatal female flaw beneath the mask of male discourse." [13] Hence, it was not surprising that her enemies accused her of transgressing sexual boundaries, of blurring sexual identities in her quest to masculinize herself. Various conservative reviewers of *The Rights of Men* "attacked her for transgressing gender boundaries of discourse"; in the late 1790s, she was demonized as an ideologically infected female who wanted to "unsex" other women.[14] Referring to the "rigid, and somewhat amazonian temper" of her second *Vindication*, even William Godwin unintentionally perpetuated counterrevolutionary caricatures of Wollstonecraft: many of the "sentiments" in *The Rights of Woman* "are undoubtedly of a rather masculine description."[15]

Thus, in *The Rights of Woman*, Wollstonecraft was still reacting to Burke's *Enquiry*, but she was also responding to accusations of female "masculinity":

> I know that libertines will also exclaim, that woman would be unsexed by acquiring strength of a body and mind, and that beauty, soft bewitching beauty! would no longer adorn the daughters of men. I am of a very different opinion, for I think that, on the contrary, we should then see dignified beauty and true grace. . . . Not relaxed beauty, it is true, or the graces of helplessness; but such as appears to make us respect the human body as a majestic pile fit to receive a noble inhabitant, in the relics of antiquity. (*WMW*, 5:242–43)

Despite the conservative imagery with which she concludes her sentence, she distinguishes between false Burkean beauty ("relaxed beauty") and a true Wollstonecraftian beauty sublimized with androgynous strength.

Since she imagines Burke's "eternal distinction" ceasing to exist, she suggests that women cannot be "unsexed." In *The Rights of Men*, she also contends that human virtues are sexless (*WMW*, 5:46) and endeavors to rethink virtues arbitrarily assigned to a masculine sublime. In *The Rights of Woman*, women's virtues, the same as men's, are based on the "exercise" of "reason," and "not by an endeavor to acquire masculine qualities." Indeed, women have been seduced out of their true "sphere" (what men arbitrarily call masculine and sublime) by Burkean notions of beauty—"false refinement" (*WMW*, 5:90), so that, according to Burke and "Rousseau's system," such women "can never be reproached for being masculine" or for falling from their "sphere" (*WMW*, 5:118). Thinking perhaps of Dr. James Fordyce (among others), whose writing she criticizes and who had written in *Sermons for Young Women* (1765) that "those masculine women, that would plead for your sharing any part of this province equally with us ["masculine" corporeal and scholastic "exercises"], do not understand your true interests,"[16] Wollstonecraft notes that everywhere she has

> heard exclamations against masculine women, but where are they to be found? If by this appellation men mean to inveigh against . . . the imitation of manly virtues, or more properly speaking, the attainment of those talents and virtues, the exercise of which ennobles the human character, and which raises

females in the scale of animal being, . . . [then all enlightened people should] wish with me that [women] may every day grow more masculine. (*WMW*, 5:74; cf. 5:76: in this context, "*rational* men" will excuse her for persuading women "to become more masculine and respectable.")

Since "masculine" is a restrictive misnomer for qualities or virtues that are human, Wollstonecraft refuses to be intimidated from expressing herself and her sex in the privileged language of patriarchy. Thus, to return to *The Rights of Men*, it is possible that Wollstonecraft empowers herself with "masculine" language because she believes that the qualities it expresses are available to everyone. In doing this, however, she implicitly valorizes its masculine mystique.

The rejoinder to this is that, after teaching Burke a lesson by degrading him with his own beautiful clichés, Wollstonecraft stresses her primary point (*WMW*, 5:45–47) that the sublime and beautiful (and by extension male and female characteristics) belong appropriately to both sexes. Indeed, Wollstonecraft appears to affirm this by redeeming the feminine "beauty" she previously mocked: the "good natured man," whose "amiable weakness of mind" (i.e., his sympathy and love for others) Burkean reasoners would characterize as "feminine," is suggestively a complementary combination of both sexes.

She hence continues her critique of Burkean sexual segregation:

It follows . . . from your own reasoning, that respect and love are antagonistic principles; and that if we really wish to render men more virtuous, we must endeavour to banish all enervating modifications of beauty from civil society. We must, to carry your argument a little further, return to the Spartan regulations, and settle the virtues of men on the stern foundation of mortification and self-denial; for any attempt to civilize the heart, to make it humane by implanting reasonable principles, is a mere philosophic dream. If refinement inevitably lessens respect for virtue, by rendering beauty, the grand tempter, more seductive; if these relaxing feelings are incompatible with the nervous exertions of morality . . . the sun of Europe is not set; it begins to dawn, when cold metaphysicians try to make the head give laws to the heart. (*WMW*, 5:46)

Objecting that the unnatural fragmentation of the sublime and the beautiful renders respect and love "antagonistic principles," Wollstonecraft now focuses on how the segregative stereotype of the "masculine" sublime equally dehumanizes men by denying them beauty, which she is now recovering from patriarchal distortions.

By turning Burke's "argument" into a reductio ad absurdum, she carries ("to carry your argument a little further") it as far as she can by insisting that the banishment of beauty would result in patriarchal dictatorships like Sparta (an admired model for many of the radical revolutionaries)—dictatorships based on the sterile "virtues" of an exclusively masculine sublime, sounding eerily, in retrospect, like the Republic of Virtue that so obsessed Robespierre and Saint-Just. In *The Rights of Woman*, Wollstonecraft criticized Rousseau for celebrating "barbarism" and forgetting that the Romans never extended "the reign of virtue" and that, by apotheosizing "savage virtues," Rousseau "exalts" the "brutal Spartans" (*WMW*, 5:84). Indeed, "in his ardor for virtue," Rousseau "would banish all the soft arts of peace" and "almost *carry us* back to Spartan discipline" (*WMW*, 5:94, my emphasis; Wollstonecraft's quotation is actually cast as an affirmative, rhetorical question). Having previously carried Burke's argument back, accusing him of logically implying that "all enervating modifications of beauty" must be banished "from civil society" and hence that men must "return to the Spartan regulations" (*WMW*, 5:46), the two passages are ideologically and linguistically linked, suggesting, in retrospect, a similarity between Burke and Rousseau, Burke's antagonistic representative of revolutionary madness in the *Reflections* and subsequent antirevolutionary works. Wollstonecraft's attack in *The Rights of Woman* on Burke's ideological enemy in the *Reflections* is pertinent, as will be seen, in the context of Wollstonecraft's own resemblances to Burke in *The Rights of Men*. Her representation of Burke suggests an affinity between Burke and herself (which she declines to recognize) in opposition to Rousseau.

Transformation is, in *The Rights of Men*, one of Wollstonecraft's principal themes, especially transformation into opposition, as in her fruitful point that Burkean logic splits the sublime and the beautiful and hence reinforces the seductive femme-fatale stereotypes that Burkean males criticize: by turning "beauty" into the threatening "tempter" (*WMW*, 5:46), Burkean ideology ironically recreates the very women it deplores. In this context, Wollstonecraft anticipates Frances Ferguson's point that an "implicit Burkean account of the Fall," in the *Enquiry*, "echoes Eve's decision to tempt Adam."[17] Indeed, Wollstonecraft seems to suggest that Burkean males fear a fall into beauty—a beauty that she now defends positively in the feminine language she earlier mocked— "amiable weakness," "enervating modifications of beauty," "refinement," "*relaxing* feelings" (my emphasis)—since men stereotypically equate it with femininity, weakness, and death. It is almost as if a chivalrous Wollstonecraft endeavors to rescue beleaguered beauty from Burke's stereotypes, as well as her own. Wollstonecraft, indeed, has a keen sense of irony that is steadily active throughout *The Rights of Men*.

Her rejection of Burke's distinction makes the beautiful a natural part of the sublime, even though libidinous males prefer their segregation: "But should experience prove that there is a beauty in virtue, a charm in order, which necessarily implies exertion, a depraved sensual taste may give way to a more manly one—and *melting* feelings to rational satisfactions. Both may be equally natural to man; the test is their moral difference, and that point reason alone can decide" (*WMW,* 5:46). Wollstonecraft sees that Burke's "eternal distinction" results in a series of fragmentations of the "natural" world, resulting in exaggerated parodies of the sublime and beautiful in terms of strong masculine conquests of submissive femininity.

But since she is suggesting, in contrast, the fusion of the sublime and the beautiful, she perpetuates the stereotypes she is resisting by again feminizing Burke, who if he were more "manly" would see the errors of his way, and "*melting* feelings" would turn into "rational satisfactions." She alludes to the *Enquiry* and Burke's discussion of "that sinking, that melting, that languor, which is the characteristic effect of the beautiful, as it regards every sense" (123) and, more specifically, love ("woman's high end and great distinction!" *WMW,* 5:45), which causes an "inward sense of melting and languor"—a state of relaxation in which the person in love is said to be "softened, relaxed, enervated, dissolved, [and] melted away by pleasure" (*Enquiry,* 149–50; the last quotation is an affirmative, rhetorical question). In *The Female Reader,* Anna Laetitia Barbauld's poem "A Character" depicts an idealized woman—"The lovliest pattern of a female mind"—with the soft feminine vocabulary that Wollstonecraft now finds objectionable, including "melting tenderness" (*WMW*, 4:305). Indeed, Wollstonecraft's two *Vindications* often seem a psychological exorcism of her earlier reaffirmations of traditional sexual stereotypes and, more interestingly, a projection onto Burke of the very language she formerly used to describe herself. Thus, in correspondence with her sister, Everina Wollstonecraft (9 October 1786), she expressed her gratitude for Everina's "tender unaffected letter": "I wept over it—for I am in a melting mood [cf. *Othello,* 5.2.358]—and should have answered it directly; but . . . [a] whole train of nervous disorders have taken possession of me" (*Collected Letters,* 117–18). In a commendatory review of Helen Maria Williams's book on the French Revolution in the *Analytical Review* (December 1790), Wollstonecraft observed that "the destruction of the Bastille was an event that affected every heart—even hearts not accustomed to the melting mood . . . and every page of Miss W.'s book tells us . . . that her's is true to every soft emotion" (*WMW,* 7:323; throughout the review, Wollstonecraft stresses Williams's "feminine" response to the Revolution, *WMW,* 7:322–23).

Hence, even though she is referring to the "libertine imagination" (*WMW*, 5:46)—the "depraved sensual taste" of Burkean males who keep women sexually vulnerable by, as she puts it in *The Rights of Woman*, subjecting them to "libertine notions of beauty" (*WMW*, 5:76, cf. 5:212: "voluptuous notions of beauty"), the Burkean male is a weak male, who may some day acquire "a more manly" taste (*WMW*, 5:46). She implicitly connects male libertines with the weak females who succumb to "*melting* feelings," since they both are creatures of sensual stimuli. She focuses on the covert resemblances of apparent opposites—opposites that ironically mirror each other.

While suggesting that the sublime and beautiful "may be equally natural" to both men and women, she continues to denigrate Burke in the language of beauty. By making Burke both the libidinous male indoctrinator who promotes an ideology of female weakness as well as the effeminate male who falls into his own beautiful clichés, Wollstonecraft scores a facile polemical point but blurs her larger argument that Burkean distinctions fragment the world she wants to restore. By engaging in the same stereotyping, she seems to resemble and even identify with the Burkean "other." She reinforces the very stereotypes she resists, for even when she inverts them, they still have the force of stereotypes.

For instance, when she momentarily seems to distinguish between true and false versions of the sublime and beautiful—envisioning the former as a kind of androgynous fusion that is paradoxically sexless, since virtue is also sexless (*WMW*, 5:46)—she soon returns to the patronizing language she believes men use to word women into submissive beauty.

Just after arguing that virtue is genderless and that inequalities of rank vitiate "the mind that submits or domineers," after suggesting that the sublime and beautiful are coherently combined and potentially common to both sexes in an androgynous world of equality, "a glorious change" that "can only be produced by liberty" (*WMW*, 5:46), and hence anticipating *The Rights of Woman*, where she wishes that Burke's eternal distinction between the sexes be "confounded" (*WMW*, 5:126)— propositions also aimed at the *Reflections* and Burke's apprehension that "all orders, ranks, and distinctions" are being "confounded" by the French Revolution (144; cf. 153 and 170)—after rejecting the separation of thought and feeling and all other Burkean fragmentations of the world and hence minimizing "difference" as she opposes Wollstonecraftian wit to Burkean judgment (the "eternal distinction" between the sublime and the beautiful and all this entails)—after all this, Wollstonecraft begins an ideological turn that reverses her revolutionary argument.

She begins this turn, responding to Burke's attack on the National Assembly in the *Reflections* (130, 138), by ironically alluding and

reverting to the disparaged language of the *Enquiry*: "You must allow us
to respect unsophisticated reason, and reverence the active exertions that
were not relaxed by a fastidious respect for the beauty of rank, or a dread
of the deformity produced by any *void* in the social structure" (*WMW*,
5:47; cf. *Reflections*, 245). She equates the revolutionary assembly with
the sublime (reason, reverence, and "active exertions") and contrasts it
with the Old Order's beauty ("relaxed," "beauty of rank"). She, in effect,
returns to old Burkean distinctions in order to banish Burke with his own
values. Thus, Burke's criticism of "the coarse vulgarity" of the National
Assembly's "proceedings" proves by his "own definition of virtue" its
"genuineness" (*WMW*, 5:47)—that is, its authentic sublimity.

By subliming the Revolution and herself and by beautifying Burke and
her enemies, she continues to valorize Burkean stereotypes rather than to
reaffirm a "true" or corrected notion of the sublime and beautiful, which
she had previously suggested. By empowering revolutionary forces with
the appropriated language of the old patriarchal order, she also suggests
that the Old Order's authority is based on illusory power: stressing the
femininity of the oppressor, she suggests that people have been exploited
and manipulated by the Old Order's "feminine" wiles—a people
conditioned by traditional Burkean ideology to pay chivalric homage to
traditional, prescriptive beauty—a kind of feudal homage to beauty
disguised as the sublime. In other words, Wollstonecraft inscribes a
contradiction that is characteristic of the revolutionary thought of the
time: the real, repressive power of the Old Order (the conspiratorial
union of church and state) is simultaneously a covert myth, revealed by
enlightened men and women who rip away the "masks" and "veils"
concealing the oppressive order's deceptive power (its ideologies and
"superstitions"). By suggesting that oppressed people, like women, have
been deluded and tricked into thinking they are powerless—conditioned
into "counterfeiting weakness" to please the "superior" orders—
Wollstonecraft makes an ideological connection between the social status
of women and the political condition of the "common" man.

Since she has been arguing against the distinctions on which this
political and social order are based, it can be contended that, in returning
to the polarities of the sublime and the beautiful, Wollstonecraft
redescribes the fragmentation of this order—a fragmentation resulting
from the arbitrary distinctions between men and women, the rich and the
poor, and all the other unnatural divisions of the Burkean world. In this
reading, the irony again resides in Burkean clichés turning into their
opposites: the celebrator of a sublime patriarchal order becomes, in
Wollstonecraft's formulation, the effeminate glorifier of clichéd beauty.
Burke becomes the unwitting perpetrator of the sublime in drag. This

would perhaps make sense if Wollstonecraft continued stressing a "truer" androgynous or sexless social aesthetic potentially possible in the liberating energies of the French Revolution. But this she does not do.

For instance, toward the end of *The Rights of Men*, she seems to return initially to a criticism of Burkean distinctions, specifically the distinction between wit and judgment (emphasized in the *Enquiry*), a distinction she had used to beautify Burke and sublime herself: "Some celebrated writers have supposed that wit and judgement were incompatible; opposite qualities, that, in a kind of elementary strife, destroyed each other: and men of wit have endeavoured to prove that they were mistaken" (*WMW*, 5:54). The opening clause initially moves the reader to anticipate that, although "some celebrated writers" (i.e., writers like Burke) "have supposed" that wit and judgment are incompatible, Wollstonecraft will contradict this, as she seemed to do previously. But the reference to "men of wit" who endeavor to prove the opposite qualifies our anticipation because Wollstonecraft has repeatedly described Burke as a man of wit.

Indeed, Wollstonecraft suddenly returns to her posture as a superior writer of judgment, insisting on proper distinctions: "From experience, I am apt to believe that they [wit and judgment] do weaken each other, and that quickness of comprehension, and facile association of ideas, naturally preclude profundity of research" (*WMW*, 5:54). The participle *weaken* contradictorily evokes her argument against what she previously contended was Burke's distinction between the sublime and the beautiful—*weakness* is "the essence of beauty"; "beautiful weakness" is "interwoven in a woman's frame," and hence "respect and love" (like judgment and wit) are "antagonistic principles" that should not be "tinctured" together (*WMW*, 5:45–46). She subverts her former argument regarding the complementary similarities of the sublime and beautiful and begins resembling the Edmund Burke who also insists on the very distinctions she is now making.

Her discriminatory language now sounds hauntingly similar to her earlier indictment of Burke's distinctive language and the men who try to convince women that nature never intended them "to exercise their reason to acquire . . . virtues that produce *opposite*, if not *contradictory*, feelings" (*WMW*, 5:45, my emphasis). It sounds similar to her indictment of Burkeans who argue that nature "has made an eternal distinction between the qualities" dignifying "a rational being" and "animal perfection"—that "respect and love" are antagonistic principles" and that, consequently, "relaxing feelings are incompatible with the . . . exertions of morality" (*WMW*, 5:46). This counterrevolutionary language reflects the distinctions she now reaffirms: wit and judgment are "incompatible; opposite qualities, that in a kind of elementary strife destroy each other"

(*WMW*, 5:54). The contrast turns her back into a writer of judgment and reason: wit is "often a lucky hit; the result of a momentary inspiration. We know not whence it comes, and it blows where it lists," whereas the "operations of judgement . . . are cool and circumspect; and coolness and deliberation are great enemies to enthusiasm" (*WMW*, 5:54). (On the penultimate page, she informs Burke that "depth of judgement is, perhaps, incompatible with the predominate feature of your mind. Your reason may have often been the dupe of your imagination" [*WMW*, 5:59].) Since the "cultivation of reason damps fancy," we must choose between them "if we wish to attain any degree of superiority, and not lose our lives in laborious idleness" (*WMW*, 5:54; cf. *Reflections*, 201: the "overlaboured lassitude of those who have nothing to do"). Consequently, we must "learn to distinguish" between what is possible and what is imaginary—a very Burkean point that seems to negate her previous anticipation of a "glorious change" in a world without distinctions of sex, rank, and the sublime and beautiful (*WMW*, 5:46).

In the end, she returns to distinctions and differences, becoming again the cool writer of judgment confronting a confused man of wit. Informing Burke that there "are times and seasons for all things," an observation she dismisses in *The Rights of Woman* as "mere declamation" (*WMW*, 5:175–76), she associates fancy and wit with youth and judgment and reason with age; thus the "gaiety of youth" should not be "confound[ed]" with the "seriousness of age; for the virtues of age look not only more imposing, but more natural, when they are rigid" (*WMW*, 5:54).

There are several things to note here. First, Wollstonecraft's use of the verb "confound" evokes Burkean echoes not only from the *Enquiry* but from the *Reflections*, where he warns against "distinctions" being "confounded" and writes against Englishmen who were "confounding" the French Revolution with the Glorious Revolution (144; 99–100). Second, she alludes to the language of the *Enquiry* and the association of the sublime with tension and rigidity and the beautiful with relaxation and falling. She hence suggests that Burke has confounded "the eternal distinction" by falling into beauty in his declining years, since wit is more appropriate to youth. Third, her comment that "the virtues of age" (i.e., reason and judgment) look "more imposing" and "natural" when "they appear rather rigid" conjures up her earlier condemnation of Burkeans who confine the "virtues" of "truth, fortitude, and humanity, within the *rigid* pale of manly morals" (*WMW*, 5:45, my emphasis). Her subsequent language seems to affirm the distinctions she earlier argued against, positioning her linguistically within that rigid pale of language she had previously confined Burkean males.

Wollstonecraft concludes by asserting that

he who has not exercised his judgement to curb his imagination during the meridian of life, becomes, in its decline, too often the prey of childish feelings. Age demands respect; youth love: if this order is disturbed, the emotions are not pure; and when love for a man in his grand climacteric takes place of respect, it, generally speaking, borders on contempt. (*WMW*, 5:54–55)[18]

Aside from suggesting that love and respect are often mutually exclusive, as she does throughout *The Rights of Woman*, where women who put all their efforts into "beauty" and "love" are consequently held in contempt by condescending males (thus returning Burke to his feminine role of pleasing readers who now patronize but do not "respect" him), there are a series of subversive contradictions that unravel what previously appeared to be the book's moral center (*WMW*, 5:45–47).

By associating wit and fancy with youth and judgment and reason with age and then accusing the sixty-one-year-old Burke of confounding the distinction by becoming an aged man of wit, the thirty-one-year-old Wollstonecraft again becomes a writer of judgment in the "meridian of life," reestablishing the very distinctions she tried to destroy when she was a celebrator of wit, when she argued for *similarities* rather than differences (*WMW*, 5:45–47). Her affirmative distinction between respect and love ("age demands respect; youth love") harkens back to a pejorative distinction she previously insisted Burke had made in the *Enquiry*: Burke "informed us that respect chills love" (*WMW*, 5:9). More pertinently, Wollstonecraft's distinction contradicts her previous indictment of Burkean distinctions: "It follows ... from [Burke's] reasoning, that respect and love are antagonistic principles; and that if we really wish to render men more virtuous, we must endeavour to banish all enervating modifications of beauty from civil society" (*WMW*, 5:46). Since she now (*WMW*, 5:54–55) reaffirms a distinction she had previously denied (as an unnatural separation of the sublime and the beautiful and hence the creation of artificial male and female roles and categories), she unwittingly subverts her celebration of the French Revolution and the possibility of a world without these distinctions—"a glorious change" that "can only be produced by liberty" (*WMW*, 5:46).

Indeed, as she begins to sound like a cautious conservative or, from a revolutionary perspective, a reactionary inventing excuses about why progress is not possible ("If we mean to build our knowledge or happiness on a rational basis, we must learn to distinguish the *possible*, and not fight against the stream" [*WMW*, 5:54]), her language becomes reminiscently Burkean: distinctions and "order" should not be "disturbed" (*WMW*, 5:54)—an order she earlier suggested consisted of fused similarities in a world where "there is a beauty in virtue, a charm in order, which necessarily implies exertion" (*WMW*, 5:46). In addition, her observation that "when love for a man in his grand climacteric takes place of respect, it, generally speaking, borders on contempt" (*WMW*, 5:55) evokes and subverts her earlier "trembling" concern "for the good natured man, who every one loves," when Burke's "eternal distinction" erroneously suggested that "the *amiable* weakness of his mind" causes it to fall into feminine beauty (*WMW*, 5:46)—a criticism of Burkean distinctions that she now seems to affirm, since Burke now resembles the amiable man loved but not respected for his "beauty."

Moreover, her comments that the "virtues of age" should appear "rigid," that the man who "has not exercised his judgement" during "the meridian of life" becomes in his "decline" the "prey of childish feelings" and that, consequently, "love" for such a man "in his grand climacteric [i.e., in his sixty-third year] . . . borders on contempt" (*WMW*, 5:54–55) refer to a passage in the *Reflections*, specifically Burke's insistence that he would "preserve something of the stiff and peremptory dignity of age," and that even though revolutionaries deal in "regeneration" (a crucial word in the revolutionary lexicon), he refuses to yield them his "rigid fibers" or in his "grand climacteric, to squall in their accents, or to stammer" in his old age ("my second cradle") "the elemental sounds of their barbarous metaphysics" (338). Through the allusion, Wollstonecraft reduces Burke to the senile childhood he rejects.[19]

Thus, while she delights in turning Burke into what he deplores and suggesting that the "rigid" patriarchal ideology he embraces creates the very things he opposes, Wollstonecraft also turns into her opposite by adopting the Burkean categories she formerly rejected. Although she wins a polemical point by reducing Burke to the categories of his own restrictive language, she herself resembles Burke in reinforcing these restrictions with this climactic clincher: "Judgement is sublime, wit beautiful; and according to your own theory, they cannot exist without impairing each other's power. The predominancy of the latter, in your endless Reflections, should lead hasty readers to suspect that it may, in a great degree, exclude the former" (*WMW*, 5:55). In deconstructing Burke's ideology, her own witty language entangles her in reflexive contradictions, as the deconstructor, in effect, deconstructs herself. Her remark that "hasty readers" will suspect that there is more wit than judgment in Burke's *Reflections* makes Wollstonecraft one of these "hasty readers," since she has argued this throughout *The Rights of Men*. Indeed, from the beginning she has unwittingly raised the possibility of her own hasty reading of the *Reflections*. In the "Advertisement" that precedes the text, she notes that she read the *Reflections* "more for amusement than information" and that the "pages of the following letter were the effusions of the moment," and since she had neither "leisure or patience to follow this desultory writer," she "confined" her "strictures" to "the grand principles at which he has levelled many ingenious arguments in a very specious garb" (*WMW*, 5:5). Toward the end of the book, she takes "a retrospective view" of her "hasty answer," "casting a cursory glance" over the *Reflections* and various "reprehensible passages" that she "marked for censure when I first perused it with a steady eye" (*WMW*, 5:58).

Indeed, her subsequent reference to the numerous passages in the *Reflections* that contradict each other (*WMW*, 5:58) echoes her earlier comment that Burke "affirm[s] in one page" what he "den[ies] in another" (*WMW*, 5:10)—a good representation of what she does throughout *The Rights of Men*, so that the condemnatory sentence exists as a reflective description of her own covert resemblance to the Burke she describes. It is this resemblance that I now address.

3

Reflected Resemblances: Wollstonecraft's Representation of Burke in *The Rights of Men*

We have seen that just as Wollstonecraft makes a series of canny connections between Burke's *Enquiry* and the *Reflections*, there are also linguistic resemblances between *The Rights of Men* and the Burkean books she excoriates. By capturing Burke in his own categories and transvestizing him into a weak woman, she engages in the very acts of linguistic distortion that she accuses Burke and other reactionary males of performing, although she does this ostensibly to reaffirm her distinction between Burkean fancy and revolutionary reality. As Burke is turned into a metaphoric woman, Wollstonecraft begins resembling the patriarchal oppressor of frivolous women condemned in both her *Vindications*.

There are other resemblances. Like the *Reflections*, Wollstonecraft's book is presented as an extended letter to an apostrophized person, and just as Richard Price's anniversary sermon initially provoked Burke's response, so the *Reflections* provoked Wollstonecraft's reply. Both Burke and Wollstonecraft respond to a specific antitext, and while there are the obvious differences between them, both select Richard Price as an object of defense or attack. Indeed, Price's appearance in *The Rights of Men* evokes Burkean resemblances in a text in which transformation seems to be a thematic and structural principle.

Early in *The Rights of Men*, Wollstonecraft accuses Burke of launching an ad hominem attack on Price:

In reprobating Dr. Price's opinions you might have spared the man; and if you had had but as half as much reverence for the grey hairs of virtue as for the accidental distinctions of rank, you would not have treated with such indecent familiarity and supercilious contempt, a member of the community whose talents and modest virtues place him high in the scale of moral excellence. (*WMW*, 5:18)

Wollstonecraft is strangely blind, however, to the fact that her indictment of Burke mirrors precisely what she does to him throughout *The Rights of Men*.

Wollstonecraft does not "spare" the "man," and her argument is, on one level, an extended ad hominem attack against Burke: from the beginning, she treats him with "indecent familiarity," informing him that it "is not necessary . . . to apologize to you for thus intruding on your precious time" (*WMW*, 5:7); she transforms him into an effeminate hypocrite, chastises him for his many contradictions, and asserts that if he had been a Jew at the time of Christ, he would have wanted Him crucified (*WMW*, 5:14). She notes that his veneration for "antiquity" makes a good argument for slavery (*WMW*, 5:14), which he opposed, and that if he had been born a Frenchman, he would probably have been "a violent revolutionist," or if the French Revolution had been, in general, "reprobated" by the English, "he would have stood forth alone, and been the avowed Goliath of liberty" (*WMW*, 5:44; Burke's earlier support of the Americans is dismissed as a clever way of drawing attention to himself). She "shrewdly suspects" that he opposes Price and hence the Revolution out of "envy" or as a way of energizing his flagging reputation (*WMW*, 5:44). She turns Burke into a sniveling, hypocritical reactionary; thus she is "led . . . to doubt" his "sincerity" and "to suppose that [he has] said many things merely for the sake of saying them well" (*WMW*, 5:29). After "observing a host" of Burkean "contradictions," she informs him that "it can scarcely be a breach of charity to think that you have sacrificed your sincerity to enforce your favourite arguments" (*WMW*, 5:50), since, in the *Reflections*, "the most just and forcible illustrations are warped to colour over opinions *you* must *sometimes* have secretly despised" (*WMW*, 5:59).

The viciousness of Wollstonecraft's attack has long been noted by her admirers. Her husband, William Godwin, later referred to it as "contemptuous and intemperate"; Eleanor Flexner observes that "she fell back repeatedly on namecalling, innuendo, and, on occasion, even slander."[1] Referring to Wollstonecraft's comment that only Burke's "personal pique and hurt vanity could have dictated such bitter sarcasms and reiterated expressions of contempt," the editors of her collected

Works note that "in fact Burke's attack on Price never stoops to the kind of personal abuse that Wollstonecraft levels at Burke" (Todd and Butler, *WMW,* 5:44 n. #b).

It is, again, not merely a matter of Wollstonecraft's own implosive hypocrisy but her thematic blindness to the very contradictions she creates. Thus, in performing a *psychological* reading of Burke's life and text, in boasting "to strip" and reveal his real secret motives, Wollstonecraft herself begins to resemble her antagonistic opposite. For instance, in her defense of Price, whom she knew and considered a friend, the thirty-one-year-old Wollstonecraft rebukes the sixty-one-year-old Burke for not respecting Price's age, for having no "reverence" for his "grey hairs of virtue" (*WMW,* 5:18; cf. *Reflections:* "We procure reverence to our civil institutions on the principle upon which nature teaches us to revere individual men; on account of their age" 121). In doing this, Wollstonecraft was, as Eleanor Flexner observes, "berating a man . . . who—given any degree of fairness—might also have claimed the distinction of a few 'grey hairs of virtue.'" Although Flexner also thinks Wollstonecraft "was apparently oblivious that she was berating a man only six years younger than Price,"[2] Wollstonecraft was, in fact, conscious of Burke's age, referring earlier to his "sixty years" (*WMW,* 5:9) and later to "his grand climacteric" (*WMW,* 5:55). If Wollstonecraft is "oblivious" here, she is also consistently oblivious throughout *The Rights of Men*, and it is her blindness to the beam in her own eye (an allusive metaphor, Matthew 7:3, that she applies to Burke, *WMW,* 5:26) that contributes to a series of situational contradictions and ironies.

By doing to Burke what she says he does to Price (disrespect of age, "indecent familiarity and supercilious contempt") and by defending Price as "a member of the community whose talents and modest virtues place him high in the scale of moral excellence"—a phrase equally applicable to Burke—she enacts precisely what she says Burke does in the *Reflections* and hence puts both herself and Burke in the same ironic position: she suddenly resembles Burke attacking the venerable Price, and Burke suddenly resembles the victimized Price of the *Reflections.* In addition to the various metaphoric equations through which she transforms Burke into his opposite, she simultaneously places herself in a series of compromising positions that revealingly remind the reader of her resemblance to her own representations of Edmund Burke. Given all the thematic transformations and role reversals in a text that boasts of stripping and hence revealing an adversarial text, Wollstonecraft's own thematic exposures reflexively mirror what she claims to be revealing.

The point, again, is not merely that Wollstonecraft commits the very errors and contradictions with which she charges Burke but that these contradictions underscore the covert resemblances that invert her text. It is more than interesting that a writer as intelligent as Mary Wollstone-craft could not see that she was enmeshing herself in a series of Burkean resemblances even as she emphasized the differences between them. It is almost as if her text is haunted by Burke's authoritative language—a language she excoriates but does not exorcise. Thus she informs Burke that, given Price's virtues and goodness, if she were him, she "should touch" Price's "errors with a tender hand when I made a parade of my sensibility" (*WMW*, 5:18). Although Wollstonecraft is again distancing herself from Burke by distinguishing how she would have linguistically handled Price when parading her "sensibility" (with respect and veneration versus Burke's "supercilious contempt"), the distinction is partially subverted by the comparison, even though it is subjunctively hypothetical. Moreover, her language ("I should touch his errors with a tender hand") is reminiscent of Burke's admonition, in the *Reflections*, that we should approach "the faults of the state" as we would "the wounds of a father, with pious awe and trembling solicitude" (194; but cf. *WMW*, 5:228).

In addition, Wollstonecraft's defense of Price is reminiscent of Burke's defense of Marie Antoinette in the *Reflections*. Both pieces are presented as "visions" of Virtue maligned. Here is Wollstonecraft's vision:

> I could almost fancy that I now see this respectable old man, in his pulpit, with hands clasped, and eyes devoutly fixed, praying with all the simple energy of unaffected piety; or, when more erect, inculcating the dignity of virtue, and enforcing the doctrines his life adorns; benevolence animated each feature, and persuasion attuned his accents; the preacher grew eloquent, who only laboured to be clear; and the respect that he extorted, seemed only the respect due to personified virtue and matured wisdom. (*WMW*, 5:18–19)

Since "the world is not yet sufficiently civilized to adopt" Price's "sublime system of morality" (*WMW*, 5:18), Price is sublimized ("respect due ... virtue and ... wisdom"), and Wollstonecraft's epiphany is presented as an allusive contrast to Burke's vision of Marie Antoinette: an old, venerable Price, reanimated by "a glimpse of the glad dawn of liberty" versus a reactionary Burke blinded by the queen's beauty (*WMW*, 5:18; see *Reflections*, 169–70).

But as she emerges as Price's textual defender, dismissing Burke's "unmanly sarcasms" and convicting him of "willful misrepresentation and wanton abuse" (*WMW*, 5:19), she resembles Burke defending the queen's honor now that "the age of chivalry is gone" (*Reflections*, 170).

Moira Ferguson and Janet Todd note that Wollstonecraft's "rhapsody on Price is certainly as emotionally rhetorical as Burke's on the French queen, and its purpose is similar." Mary Poovey also sees the similarity between both passages: "If Edmund Burke elevates Marie Antoinette to the stature of a maternal guardian of culture, Wollstonecraft answers with her veneration of the paternal religious figure, Dr. Richard Price," presenting him "as a larger-than-life figure, much like Burke's idealization of the French queen."[3] The contrast—the vision of Price's kindled "glimpse" versus Burke's blindly enraptured vision—again contains occult similarities.

But it is in her continual criticisms of Burke's "inconsistencies" (*WMW*, 5:14, 20, 26, 29, 37, 44) and "misrepresentations" that these resemblances are most faithfully reflected: the nature and pattern of these inconsistencies textually align and identify her with the antagonist she tries to exorcise. Wollstonecraft, for instance, is especially effective in pointing to Burke's own inconsistencies by noting that the defender of beleaguered kings had himself attacked George III during the Regency Crisis, when he had, in effect, tried to have the king cashiered on grounds of insanity. (Both Wollstonecraft and Burke were interested in and had researched the subject of madness.) Wollstonecraft contended that this was a self-serving plot by Burke and the Portland Whigs to take power. During the Regency Crisis (1788–89), Burke had shocked many people by publicly asking whether parliamentary members recollected "that they were talking of a sick King, of a monarch smitten by the hand of Omnipotence, and that the Almighty had hurled him from his throne."[4]

Referring to this incident and responding with indignation to Burke's insensitive treatment of the king's "madness" (modern research suggests that the king actually had a rare blood disease; at any rate, he recovered in 1789), Wollstonecraft directly addresses Burke:

> In this state was the King, when you, with unfeeling disrespect, and indecent haste, wished to strip him of all his hereditary honours. You were so eager to taste the sweets of power, that you could not wait till time had determined, whether a dreadful delirium would settle into a confirmed madness; but prying into the secrets of Omnipotence, you thundered out that God had *hurled him from his throne*, and that it was the most insulting mockery to recollect that he had been a king, or to treat him with any particular respect on account of his former dignity. And who was the monster whom Heaven had thus awfully deposed, and smitten with such an angry blow? Surely as harmless a character as Lewis XVIth. (*WMW*, 5:27)

In her account, Wollstonecraft notably neglects to mention that Burke had used the same language in the *Reflections* with reference to Louis

XVI: "Because when kings are hurl'd from their thrones by the Supreme Director of this great drama, and become the objects of insult to the base, and of pity to the good . . . [w]e are alarmed into reflexion; our minds . . . purified by terror and pity" (175). Moreover, Wollstonecraft had herself used the throne image in the *Analytical Review* (vol. 3, 1789), writing that the king's "dreadful malady" was a reminder "that the grand privilege of our nature is so dependent on the body, as to be shook from its throne by disease as well as outrageous passions" (*WMW*, 7:97).

But in quoting Burke against himself, Wollstonecraft's claim that his disrespectful language belies his selective veneration of kings is, at best, disingenuous, since Burke sees the fate of both kings as God's fait accompli, rather than his own. Moreover, her selective paraphrase distorts what he was actually saying by suggesting a tone of disrespect and a meanness of disposition that begrudged the king "any particular respect on account of his former dignity" (*WMW*, 5:27). In addition, the imagery of the king being hurled from his throne echoed the official announcement of the king's "madness": his reason had fled its throne (1989 *Encyclopaedia Britannica* [vol. 5], "George III," 195). Wollstonecraft herself occasionally used the imagery of toppled thrones, and in a letter to William Godwin (15 September 1796), she wrote, "I want to have such a firm *throne* in your heart, that even your imagination shall not be able to hurl me from it, be it ever so active" (*Collected Letters*, 352). As in other instances, the language with which she attacks Burke publicly or, as in this case, Burke's own language often appears in her private correspondence: Godwin's "imagination" appears as a kind of Burkean "Omnipotence" (or impotence) unable to unthrone Wollstonecraft.

In addition, Wollstonecraft's defense of George III is rather disingenuous, since she had already debunked the British constitution and the English kings who were either ambitious or weak (*WMW*, 5:11–12; cf. 20); her contempt for kings in general is reflected throughout her works (see, for instance, *WMW*, 5:85–86, 106, 111). But, more pertinently, her defense of the beleaguered king resembles Burke's defense of the same king against Price's assertion that kings could be "cashiered" by the people (see *Reflections*, 99 ff.) or "hurled" from their thrones ("The question of dethroning, or if these gentlemen like the phrase better, 'cashiering kings,' will always be . . . wholly out of the law" [*Reflections*, 116]). Thus, while Wollstonecraft is shedding crocodile tears over Burke's treatment of the king, coming forth as the outraged defender of aggrieved royalty, there is a sub-rosa link between Burke and herself and Burke and Price.

Even her language, at this point, sounds sarcastically Burkean: "Impressed as *you are* with respect for royalty, I am astonished that you did not tremble at every step, lest Heaven should avenge on your guilty head the insult offered to its viceregent" (*WMW*, 5:28; here she makes Burke a believer in the divine right of kings—a doctrine he had dismissed in *Reflections*, 111). She says this, of course, with mock horror, but the Burkean echoes compromise her revolutionary persona. Indeed, in her defense of the king, she out-Burkes Burke, emerging as the upholder of regal tradition: "In this state was the King, when you, with unfeeling disrespect, and indecent haste, wished to strip him of all his hereditary honours" (*WMW*, 5:27).

On 9 February 1789, in the House of Commons, William Pitt, the prime minister, had responded to Burke and the Portland Whigs, who wanted the king replaced by the Prince of Wales, by rhetorically asking if the assembled members "ought . . . in the earliest moments of his Majesty's illness, to be eager to strip him of every mark of dignity, in order to deck out the Regent with unnecessary powers."[5] Burke repeated Pitt's question and then made his controversial "hurled . . . from his throne" comments. Wollstonecraft alludes to Pitt's suggestion that Burke and the opposition wanted "to strip" the King of every dignity. Her sentence additionally mimes Burke's lament in the *Reflections* that the revolutionaries want to do precisely the same to representatives of the ancien régime, and perhaps there is an allusion to Burke's theatrical account of the potential "stripping" of Marie Antoinette (see *Reflections*, 164). In a text in which Wollstonecraft herself threatens to strip Burke of his "gorgeous drapery" and "show" him naked to himself (*WMW*, 5:37), she engages in a rhetorical "stripping" resembling Burke's supposed stripping of the king, while Burke, in her account (*WMW*, 5:27), resembles the irreverent revolutionaries who strip away the "hereditary honors" of the Old Order.

In fact, Wollstonecraft suggests that Burke has perpetrated revolutionary attacks against the king and queen of England: "When, on a late melancholy occasion . . . with what indecent warmth did *you* treat a woman, for I shall not lay any stress on her title," and when "you descanted on the horrors of the 6th of October, and gave . . . a most exaggerated description of that infernal night, without having troubled yourself to clean your palette, you might have returned home and indulged us with a sketch of the misery you personally aggravated" (*WMW*, 5:26). Burke, in Wollstonecraft's version, suddenly resembles the revolutionary persecutors of Marie Antoinette—performing his own version of the "October Days," when the queen's chamber was invaded and the royal family was forcibly returned to Paris. But what had Burke done with such "indecent warmth" to Queen Charlotte, the wife of George III, to warrant such an extravagant comparison? Todd and Butler suggest that Wollstonecraft alludes to parliamentary efforts to grant the queen an allowance following her husband's supposed insanity, an allowance that Burke had opposed (*WMW*, 5:26 n. c).

Objecting to the terms of the regency bill that vested the queen, instead of the Prince of Wales, with responsibility for the care of the king and for the government of the royal household, Burke (in a speech to the House of Commons on 6 February 1789) warned that her control of the king's privy purse for the duration of his illness could become a source of improper political influence and that Pitt would find it easy to manipulate the queen and, through her, use the money to "create a fund for bribing members of Parliament."[6] This is, depending on motives, petty at worst, but Wollstonecraft orchestrates the imagery to suggest that Burke callously exceeds the revolutionary excesses of 6 October, which he had, in any case, "exaggerated": "What a climax lay before you. A father torn from his children,—a husband from an affectionate wife,—a man from himself!" (*WMW*, 5:27; the sentence, in retrospect, ironically prefigures the fate of the French royal family in 1793). As Wollstonecraft conflates and equates Burke's treatment of the English royal family with the humiliation of the French royal family, she places Burke in the same metaphoric position of the revolutionary mob in the *Reflections*, and her characterization of Burke's "exaggerated description" resembles her own exaggerated portrayal of Burke's "attack" on the royal family and the "misery" that he "personally aggravated" (*WMW*, 5:26).

In attacking Burke's "revolutionary" assault on the British monarchy, Wollstonecraft includes a series of allusions to *Paradise Lost* and to Satan, whom God had "Hurl'd headlong flaming from th' Ethereal Sky" (1.45; cf. 2.180, 374; 10.636). Wollstonecraft turns Burke into Satan, for like the latter he was "prying into the secrets of Omnipotence" (*WMW*, 5:27; cf. *Paradise Lost* 1.655; 9.159) when he had "thundered out that God *had hurled* [the king] *from his throne*" (*WMW*, 5:27). Does the sentence also allusively suggest that Burke has turned the king into Satan ("And who was the monster whom Heaven had thus awfully deposed, and smitten with such an angry blow?") hurled from heaven, or is it that the sentence subverts Wollstonecraft's defense by turning the king into Satan? In either case, there is yet another connection between the king and Burke, whom Wollstonecraft "hurls" from his "throne." Her sarcastic rebuke to Burke, accusing him of demonizing the king ("And who was the monster whom Heaven had thus awfully deposed, and smitten with such an angry blow?"), is complicated by her demonization of Burke: Burke becomes a "maddened" Satan.

As Wollstonecraft lectures Burke on the meaning of madness and the sympathy we should have for the insane (*WMW*, 5:27–28), it soon becomes clear that she is only ostensibly referring to the king's "madness" (ironically underscoring it by repeated references) but is primarily interested in suggesting that Burke is himself mad—hence placing him in the ironic position of being like the king she accuses Burke of so insensitively attacking. After alluding to Burke's own research and visits to madhouses during the Regency Crisis (to educate himself on the subject of insanity) and to the language he had used in a speech to the House of Commons on 11 February 1789 ("those dreadful mansions where these unfortunate beings are confined"),[7] Wollstonecraft informs him that "madness is only the absence of reason. The ruling angel leaving its seat, wild anarchy ensues" (*WMW*, 5:28). Since Wollstonecraft has repeatedly told Burke he lacks reason and has attacked him for disrespectfully "hurling" the mad king from his throne, she also hurls Burke from his throne ("seat," see *OED*, def. 8; cf. *WMW*, 5:8—Burke's "vanity" forces him to be always on "guard to secure his throne") by suggesting that he is equally insane.

For instance, she paraphrases Burke's description of the Revolution as a strange chaos of levity and ferocity inciting "the most opposite passions . . . in the mind" (*WMW*, 5:28; see *Reflections*, 92–93) and hence uses Burke's own language as the descriptive paradigm of insanity and hence Burke's "madness": "This is a true picture of that chaotic state of mind, called madness; when reason gone, we know not where, the wild elements of passion clash, and all is horror and confusion" (*WMW*, 5:28; the next sentence links Burke's mad language with an absence of logical reason). Wollstonecraft turns Burke's description of the Revolution into an "insane" response and the *Reflections* into an insane book.

The ensuing imagery, initiated by the "ruling angel" leaving his "seat," allusively equates Burke's uncontrolled imagination with satanic flights of fancy: "The uncontrouled imagination often pursues the most regular course in its most daring flights" (*WMW*, 5:28). In *Paradise Lost*, Satan also pursues a series of daring flights, whether making his way, in his "solitary flight" (2.632), up through Chaos "audacious" (2.931), "insatiate to pursue / Vain War with Heav'n" (2.8–9) or trying to wing "his way" into heaven's light (3.87–88), which the Miltonic narrator also revisits "with bolder wing" (3.13).

There are other echoes of *Paradise Lost* in the "wild anarchy" that Wollstonecraft informs Burke results in madness, once the "ruling angel" vacates its seat (*WMW*, 5:28). In the war in heaven, Christ routs fallen angels who fall "Through . . . wild anarchy" (*Paradise Lost*, 6.873); when Satan escapes hell, he encounters "Eternal Anarchy" in Chaos (2.896; cf. 10.283), and in *Paradise Regained*, Christ tells Satan that he who does not rule himself is "Subject . . . to Anarchy within" (2.471).

The fact that the "ruling angel" that Wollstonecraft refers to actually represents *reason* subverts the sentence by entangling it with unintended satanic associations. But Wollstonecraft's language continuously turns back on itself.

Hence when she is supposedly explaining the meaning of insanity to Burke in context of his "unfeeling" (*WMW*, 5:27) attack on the precarious king, informing him that the "uncontrolled imagination" reigns "when judgement no longer officiously arranges the sentiments" (*WMW*, 5:28), the reader remembers that Wollstonecraft has contended throughout that Burke's imagination has usurped his judgment. In addition, her references to Burke's "sparkling" wit are behind her allusion to his insane language: "You might have heard the best turned conceits, flash following flash, and doubted whether the rhapsody was not eloquent, if it had not been delivered in an equivocal language, neither verse nor prose, if the sparkling periods had not stood alone, wanting force because they wanted concatenation" (*WMW*, 5:28). All this culminates in Wollstonecraft's "proverbial observation" that "a very thin partition divides wit and madness" and that Burke is the practitioner of a bastard style of writing incarnating the false "romantic spirit" of "modern poetry" into prose—"a mixture of verse and prose producing the strangest incongruities" (*WMW*, 5:28–29), reflecting the jumbled chaos of Burke's deranged mind.

There are, in addition, other allusions to Burke's supposed madness in context of Wollstonecraft's references to Burke's *Enquiry*: "sublime" strength and rigidity versus "beautiful" softness and relaxation. For instance, in Wollstonecraft's deceptive defense of the "*amiable* weakness" of the "good natured" man's "mind" against Burke's sublime, which seemingly proves "that beauty relaxes the *solids* of the soul as well as the body" (*WMW*, 5:46), the informed eighteenth-century reader would have recognized a standard description of insanity.[8] Michel Foucault's study of the central Western texts dealing with insanity in *Madness and Civilization* places this in perspective. Foucault notes that, in classic studies of madness, "Tension and release, hardness and softness, rigidity and relaxation, congestion and dryness—these qualitative states characterize the soul as much as the body, and ultimately refer to a kind of indistinct passional situation, one which imposes itself on the concatenation of ideas, on the circulation of ideas, on the course of feelings, on the state of the fibers, on the circulation of fluids." Thus, there was a mechanistic conception of madness in which "the softening of the fibers and the relaxation of the mind" deranges the imagination, producing insanity.[9]

In the *Enquiry*, Burke notes that "melancholy" results from the "relaxation" of the "vigorous tone of fibre" that is "requisite" for

"carrying on the natural and necessary [bodily] secretions";
consequently, "in this languid inactive state, the nerves are more liable to
the most horrible convulsions, than when they are simply braced and
strengthened. Melancholy, dejection, despair, and often self-murder, is
the consequence of the gloomy view we take of things in this relaxed
state of body" (135; cf. 132). As the mechanism of madness was further
developed in the eighteenth century, a distinction between melancholy
and mania or delirium began to emerge. The theory of humors or animal
spirits producing a personality type was replaced "by the image, more
strictly physical . . . of a tension to which nerves, vessels, and the entire
system of organic fibers were strictly subject. Mania was thus a tension
of the fibers carried to its paroxysm, the maniac a sort of instrument
whose strings, by the effect of an exaggerated traction began to vibrate at
the remotest stimulus." The madman formerly believed to be melancholic
either "because his fibers" were "relaxed or because they had been
immobilized by too great a tension" was now considered melancholic if
"only a few fibers vibrate," while the maniac responded "to any and
every stimulus."[10] Burke's language of vigorous fibers relaxed and
nerves agitated with "horrible convulsions" accords with contemporary
discussions of melancholic madness, although "virtually all the
physicians of the eighteenth century acknowledged the proximity of
mania and melancholia."[11] In *Letters on the Female Mind* (1793),
Laetitia Matilda Hawkins noted that "nervous disease" affects the body
and mind and that unrelieved relaxation results in "confused intellects
and a disturbed imagination."[12]

Wollstonecraft thus uses the recognizable language of "relaxed" or
"insane" beauty in Burke's *Enquiry* to suggest that his aesthetic
categories turn the "amiable" man into an insane man, and she
contradictorily applies these categories to Burke's mental weakness in
which the feminization of his mind is equated with insanity. When she
patronizes Burke by telling him that she fears "to derange" his "nervous
system by the bare mention of a metaphysical enquiry" (*WMW,* 5:16),
she is also alluding, as we have seen, to his putative "feminine" hysteria.

Finally, in all her voluminous allusions to Burke's madness, there is
another covert, contextual resemblance. During various crises in her life,
Wollstonecraft felt that she was going insane. Virginia Sapiro notes that
Wollstonecraft "personally feared" madness throughout her life.[13] In a
letter to Henry Dyson Gabell (16 April 1787), Wollstonecraft fears her
"reason has been too far stretched, and tottered almost on the brink of
madness." In a letter to her sister Everina (11 May 1787), she refers to
her madness ("I then am mad"), describing her contradictory behavior
and the "sprightly sallies" and nervous disorders she later ascribes to

Burke (*Collected Letters*, 150–51). Roy Porter notes "the identification" that Wollstonecraft "makes in her novels between the plight of the mad and the condition of women," but there is, in addition, a complex identification between Burke and herself in *The Rights of Men*.[14] (Before, but especially after, his public opposition to the Revolution, Burke's enemies had represented him as insane.)

The emphasis on Burke's supposed madness suggests that he mistakes illusion for reality, but Wollstonecraft simultaneously engages in the very thing she accuses Burke of doing and hence creates one of those situational ironies so characteristic of *The Rights of Men*—she resembles both the "unfeeling" Burke insensitively mocking the king's madness and the reactionary Burke who defends obsolete kings in the *Reflections*. Likewise, Burke suddenly resembles the beleaguered king she supposedly defends, just as he earlier resembled Richard Price, whom he callously attacks. As she creates for herself a series of contradictory personae—the indignant revolutionary raging against Burkean fragmentations and the Burkean reactionary reinforcing these fragmentations—she simultaneously dethrones Burke, the king, and herself.

II

This process of transforming herself into Burke is illustrated again in her attacks on Burke's "misrepresentations": pejorative representations of the "other" mirror unwitting representations of the writer. After castigating Burke with scores of offensive adjectives and asking him how he dared attack Richard Price with "so many opprobrious epithets," she closes "this part" of her "animadversions" by convicting Burke of "willful misrepresentation and wanton abuse" (*WMW*, 5:19). She contends that Burke intentionally distorted the meaning of Price's 1789 anniversary sermon but also engages in some distortions of her own.

She begins her attack by formulating Burke's misrepresentation:

> You further proceed grossly to misrepresent Dr. Price's meaning and with an affectation of holy fervour, express your indignation at his profaning a beautiful rapturous ejaculation, when alluding to the King of France's submission to the National Assembly; he rejoiced to hail a glorious revolution, which promised an universal diffusion of liberty and happiness. (*WMW*, 5:25)

In the *Reflections*, Burke had objected to Price's allusion to the *Nunc Dimittis* (Luke 2:25–30) by which Price apparently compared his approval of Louis XVI's humiliation on 6 October 1789 (when the captive royal family was forced to return to Versailles) with Simeon's happiness in seeing the child Jesus at the Temple. But in her text and footnote (n. 7), Wollstonecraft claimed that Price was actually referring to July 1789, when the king "first submitted to his people; and not the mobbing triumphal catastrophe in October, which . . . [Burke] chose, to give full scope to [his] declamatory powers" (*WMW*, 5:25 n. 7).

It is not surprising that Wollstonecraft does not quote the disputed passage from Price, since the reader, like Burke, would assume that Price was referring to the events of 6 October, not July 1789. Here is Burke's quotation of Price in the *Reflections*:

> What an eventful period is this! I am *thankful* that I have lived to see it; I could almost say, *Lord now lettest thou thy servant depart in peace, for mine eyes have seen they salvation*. I have lived to see a *diffusion* of knowledge which has undermined superstition and error. I have lived to see the *rights of men* better understood than ever; and nations panting for liberty which seemed to have lost the idea of it. I have lived to see *Thirty Millions of People*, indignant and resolute, spurning at slavery, and demanding liberty with an irresistible voice. Their *King led in triumph, and an arbitrary monarch surrendering himself to his subjects.* (157; except for the second sentence and "*Thirty Millions*," Burke's emphases)

Since Price gave the traditional anniversary sermon on 4 November 1789 (the day on which the London Revolution Society commemorated the Glorious Revolution's centennial), almost one month from the day the king was forced to return to Paris and at a time when the October Days (5 and 6) were the talk of Europe, it would have been a most unfortunate choice of words ("Their King led in triumph" by an "indignant and resolute" people) if he were referring to the events of July, since most people would assume that his words referred to the king's forced return to Paris in October—the only time in 1789 in which he had been "led in triumph."

Wollstonecraft claims that Burke "grossly" misrepresents "Dr. Price's meaning" and suggests that the passage in question clearly refers to "a glorious revolution" that transpired in July—a revolution "which promised an universal diffusion of liberty and happiness" (*WMW*, 5:25). But this is neither the primary nor the contested part of the passage she chooses not to quote. Wollstonecraft had, in fact, reviewed Price's *Discourse on the Love of our Country* in the *Analytical Review* (December 1789) where she quotes, inter alia, the disputed passage approvingly (see *WMW*, 7:187). In addition, by referring to the French

Revolution as "a glorious revolution," she connects this revolution with the British Revolution of 1688 (something Burke denied throughout the *Reflections*) and hence suggests that the French Revolution was a traditional *revolution* that restored ancient rights and liberties to the French people. The salient point, however, is Wollstonecraft's selective reference (alluding only to the second and third sentences) and the flagrant suppression of the part of Price's text that Burke specifically contests (see *Reflections*, 157–59), as well as her insinuation that its contents contain her representation rather than Burke's. In doing this, Wollstonecraft grossly misrepresents Burke, suggesting that he has deliberately distorted what Price actually said, and hence she places herself again in the position of "writing out" precisely what she accuses Burke of doing: she now resembles her own representation of the Burkean distorter of Price's sermon.

Price himself had felt the force of Burke's criticism, since he felt compelled in the preface to the fourth edition (Burke had quoted from the third edition) to insist that he was actually referring to the fall of the Bastille on 14 July and to the king's subsequent, albeit voluntary, submission to the will of the people.[15] Wollstonecraft may have read Price's explanation, or she could have received it from Price himself, since she was a friend of his, even though she would probably have informed the reader had Price, in fact, told her. In a letter (17 December 1790) first cited by Gary Kelly, Price, writing in the third person, compliments Wollstonecraft on her book and suggests that he did not initially know her identity.[16]

By being specifically vague in her reference to the events of July and then neglecting to quote or refer to the principal phrases that had provoked Burke and to which he was referring, Wollstonecraft misrepresents him by suggesting that Price's intended meaning was presented clearly in the text she chooses not to quote. But this is also disingenuous, since her explanation of Price's real meaning does not correspond to the way the reader understands or experiences Price's own words. Indeed, she misrepresents these words by suggesting they are solely about "a glorious revolution, which promised an universal diffusion of liberty and happiness," and hence she resembles the Burkean distorter of "Dr. Price's meaning."

In addition to these textual ironies, Wollstonecraft's linguistic entanglements also compromise her text, as when she tells Burke that since he was "on the watch to find fault, faults met your prying eye; a different prepossession might have produced a different conviction" (*WMW*, 5:53). Wollstonecraft is, however, consistently blind to her own linguistic resemblances to the Burke she describes, since she is also on the "watch to find fault" with Burke's life and *Reflections* (cf. *WMW,* 5:44, where she reads the *Reflections* "warily over").

After informing Burke that he had, in effect, already prejudged the Revolution pejoratively and that if he had an open mind "a different prepossession might have produced a different conviction" (*WMW,* 5:53), she adds the following commentary:

> When we read a book that supports our favorite opinions, how eagerly do we suck in the doctrines, and suffer our minds placidly to reflect the images that illustrate the tenets we have previously embraced. We indolently acquiesce in the conclusion, and our spirit animates and corrects the various subjects. But when, on the contrary, we peruse a skil[l]ful writer, with whom we do not coincide in opinion, how attentive is the mind to detect fallacy. And this suspicious coolness often prevents our being carried away by a stream of natural eloquence, which the prejudiced mind terms mere declamation—a pomp of words! We never allow ourselves to be warmed; and, after contending with the writer, are more confirmed in our opinion; as much perhaps, from a spirit of contradiction as from reason. A lively imagination is ever in danger of being betrayed into error by favorite opinions, which it almost personifies, the more effectually to intoxicate the understanding. Always tending to extremes, truth is left behind in the heat of the chase, and things are viewed as positively good, or bad, though they wear an equivocal face. (*WMW,* 5:53)[17]

This remarkable passage, in which Wollstonecraft seems to distinguish initially between superior and inferior "readings," is paradigmatic of the contradictory readings she offers throughout *The Rights of Men.*

Her description of the passive reader who merely absorbs doctrines is, of course, pejorative, for there is the judgmental distinction between weak readings that merely "reflect" the prejudices of unexercised minds, minds that "indolently acquiesce" in receiving what pleases them (cf. *WMW,* 5:19), and the strong readings that contend against an antagonistic text. Both readings are significantly in the value-laden language of the sublime and beautiful, suggesting the superiority of strong, "sublime" readings to weak, "beautiful" readings.

In this context, Wollstonecraft seems to suggest that her own reading of Burke ("a skil[l]ful writer, with whom we do not coincide in opinion") is strongly sublime, since her judgment prevents Burke's beautiful "prejudices" from warming the "lively imagination." Thus, the "suspicious coolness" (on the next page [*WMW,* 5:54], the "operations of judgement . . . are cool and circumspect; and coolness and deliberation are great enemies to enthusiasm") of her judgment enables her to resist the "stream of natural eloquence" of Burke's *Reflections*. But, at this point, the distinction curiously implodes, for both readings end in reconfirming what the reader previously thought: the beautiful reading reconfirms our "favorite opinions," and the sublime reading results in our being "more confirmed in our opinion." In addition, her prior reference to Burke's proclivity "to find fault" matches her description of the critical reader, whose mind is attentive "to detect fallacy."

If, however, her point is that Burke is the critically sublime reader alert to discover flaws, her apparent criticism of this reader resembles what she herself has done, since the "stream of natural eloquence, which the prejudiced mind terms declamation—a mere pomp of words!" echoes her own "prejudiced" denunciations of Burke's language. Earlier, she had referred to his "declamation" (*WMW*, 5:13) and remarked that Burke's "tears" were reserved "for the declamation of the theatre" (*WMW*, 5:15). She informed him that members of Parliament were "tired of listening" to his "declamation" (*WMW*, 5:43), and two paragraphs prior to her reference to "the prejudiced mind" that dismisses as "declamation" what it dislikes, she had referred to Burke's "vague declamation of sensibility" (*WMW*, 5:53). Her contrapuntal sentence complicitly indicts her own "prejudiced" language.

Since both readers (passive and active) appear ultimately pejorative, what is the point in contrasting them, unless Wollstonecraft is applying both readings to Burke and hence having it both ways? Thus, the Burkean reader passively sucks in doctrines that placidly "reflect" the images of his own mind while reading the events of the Revolution pejoratively. But such a reading applies equally to Wollstonecraft, who passively affirms her own prejudices in her reading of the Revolution, Price's sermon, and the "Declaration of the National Assembly" (the "Declaration of the Rights of Man") with which she initiated the distinction between her superior reading and Burke's critique—"on the watch to find faults" (*WMW*, 5:53). Similarly, if she uses the Revolution to "illustrate the tenets we have previously embraced," she also resembles the critical Burkean reader, "On the watch to find faults," since this is a judicial description of what she does to both Burke and the *Reflections* throughout.

Even if she had provided a tertium quid—an alternative reader or reading that replaces both extremes—which she does not, the ironies of her hostile pronouncements would still abound. The last two sentences do, on one level, appear to reject both kinds of readers: "A lively imagination is ever in danger of being betrayed into error by favorite opinions, which it almost personifies, the more effectually to intoxicate the understanding. Always tending to extremes, truth is left behind in the heat of the chase, and things are viewed as positively good or bad, though they wear an equivocal face" (*WMW*, 5:53). But these sentences are also equivocal enough to suggest that the passive reader, the reader with a "lively imagination," tends to both "extremes"—seeing things as either "positively good, or bad," since Wollstonecraft had previously referred to Burke's "lively imagination" (*WMW*, 5:15), and the sentence is also a good description of the Manichean worlds of both *The Rights of Men* and the *Reflections*. (In *The Rights of Women* [*WMW*, 5:137], she makes a similar point about the two "extremes" represented in writers.) At any rate, her earlier description of the effect of Burke's language— "Words are heaped on words, till the understanding is confused by endeavoring to disentangle the sense, and the memory by tracing contradictions" (*WMW*, 5:50)—revealingly replicates the experience of reading *The Rights of Men*.

Thus, if Burke is supposed to be the partisan reader of both tradition and revolution and if Wollstonecraft rejects both passive and resistive readings, which she appears to do, she proceeds to reaffirm implicitly (on the next page [*WMW*, 5:54]) the superiority of the latter by stressing the superiority of judgment over wit, which, as has been seen, constitutes a thematic contradiction in *The Rights of Men*.

The superiority of judgment (critical distinction) to wit (fanciful resemblance) is in the imagery with which she had described the critical reader: this reader focuses on detecting "fallacy"; his "suspicious coolness" prevents his being "carried away" (*WMW*, 5:53); likewise, the superior "operations of judgement . . . are cool and circumspect; and coolness and deliberation are great enemies to enthusiasm" (*WMW*, 5:54; cf. *WMW*, 5:43—"cool judgement"). Similarly, the "lively imagination" of the passive reader "is ever in danger of being betrayed into error by favorite opinions," and the man of fanciful wit will not be able "to discover that raptures and ecstasies arise from error" (*WMW*, 53, 54). The cumulative effect is to subvert Wollstonecraft's initial rejection of both readings (passive and critical) by reaffirming the superiority of judgment and hence critical readings that distinguish between illusion and reality (*WMW*, 5:54). As she contends against Burke, she resembles the critical reader "contending with the writer . . . as much, perhaps, from a spirit of contradiction as from reason" (*WMW*, 5:53).

A final example of how Wollstonecraft's contradictions turn into what she opposes occurs toward the end of *The Rights of Men*, when she mockingly informs Burke that, in minds like his, "there is often something disgusting in the distresses of poverty, at which the imagination revolts, and starts back to exercise itself in the more attractive Arcadia of fiction" (*WMW*, 5:56). Wollstonecraft suggests again that the escapist, "aristocratic" Burke disdains the facts of poverty, and that his imagination revolts against both reality and reason, preferring the illusions of beauty—"the more attractive Arcadia of fiction" or the world of grace and light that Burke contends the Revolution is destroying in his "fictional" *Reflections*. Wollstonecraft then proceeds with a vision of a progressive, utopian reformer (promoter of mankind's happiness, protector of the poor) who suddenly resembles Richard Price, whom Wollstonecraft earlier saw in a similar vision. Referring to Price, she previously wrote, "I could almost fancy that I see this respectable old man, in his pulpit, with hands clasped, and eyes devoutly fixed, praying with all the simple energy of unaffected piety" (*WMW*, 5:18), and this is reflected in her subsequent vision of the imaginary revolutionary reformer: "I could almost imagine I see a man thus gathering blessings as he mounted the hill of life" (*WMW*, 5:56; cf. her vision of the feminist heroine in *WMW*, 5:119).

Likewise, Wollstonecraft's reverie of a reformed revolutionary world (the happy, protected poor, rich estates broken up into "decent farms" where "plenty smile[s] around" [*WMW*, 5:56–57]) is also reminiscent of Richard Price's "Utopian reveries"—a "sublime system of morality" that "the world is not yet sufficiently civilized to adopt" (cf. *WMW*, 5:56: "What salutary dews might not be shed . . . if men were more *enlightened*")—"reveries" that could only proceed from "a benevolent mind" (*WMW*, 5:18). And these shared utopian reveries are, in turn, reminiscent of Burke's Arcadian fictions. Thus, after accusing Burke of squeamishly rejecting the "distresses of poverty" for the imaginary "Arcadia of fiction," Wollstonecraft proceeds to imagine the possibility of her own utopian Arcadia, "if men were more *enlightened*!":

A garden more inviting than Eden would then meet the eye, and springs of joy murmur on every side. The clergyman would superintend his own flock, the shepherd would then love the sheep he daily tended; the school might rear its decent head, and the buzzing tribe, let loose to play, impart a portion of their vivacious spirits to the heart that longed to open their minds, and lead them to taste the pleasures of men. Domestic comfort, the civilizing relations of husband, brother, and father, would soften labor, and render life contented. (*WMW*, 5:56)

Earlier, Wollstonecraft had informed Burke that she was not "hailing a millennium, though a state of greater purity of morals may not be a mere poetic fiction; nor did my fancy ever create a heaven on earth, since reason threw off her swaddling clothes" (*WMW*, 5:33). But she does just that in her imaginary description of "a garden more inviting than Eden"

(*WMW*, 5:56). By envisioning her enlightened utopia, she subverts her reference to Burke's "attractive Arcadia of fiction," for her own "poetic fiction" is also attractively Arcadian.

Indeed, her description of this happy rural scene is, in some ways, a reactionary pastoral world where everyone functions harmoniously in his hierarchic place—the clergyman superintending his "flock"; the "shepherd" (and clergyman) lovingly attending his "sheep"; the teacher longing to lead his "buzzing tribe" to the intellectual "pleasures of men." In fact, women are conspicuously absent in this Arcadian fiction of the future—there are no Eves or other feminine presences, only sexless schoolchildren ("the buzzing tribe"), the clergyman, the shepherd, husband, brother, and father in a patriarchal world in which "domestic comfort" implies, at best, woman as the soft and silent comforter.

Wollstonecraft presents her Arcadian faith in response to Burke's comment, in the *Reflections*, that he who deprives the poor of religious consolation, specifically the expectation of a heavenly future world, is, in fact, their "cruel oppressor" (372). But in Wollstonecraft's reading of Burke, he is the cruel oppressor, promising the poor "Arcadian fictions," since they suffer "the distresses of poverty," while she and Price are messianic liberators, laboring to set man free. But Wollstonecraft's vision of "paradise" is also projected into a promised future, and her resemblance to Burke, at the end, becomes reified in her rebuking reminder that he blindly refuses to see faults, even though she wonders if his conscience occasionally caused him to recollect his "own errors, before he lifted the avenging stone" (*WMW*, 5:59).[18]

III

In retrospect, *The Rights of Men* is an illustrative political text that turns into a reflection of what it resists. Wollstonecraft's critique of Burke mirrors her own contradictions and misrepresentations. She reinscribes and validates the opposition she rejects. It is not merely the text's contradictions that subvert the superior position out of which Wollstonecraft writes, but the way in which these contradictions become structural, thematic statements of her representation of Burke's *Reflections*. As she repeatedly enacts the linguistic processes she criticizes, she resembles Burke at the very instant she endeavors to expose or exorcise his pernicious presence.

On one level, her exposé of Burke is psychological, and this seems to coincide ironically with her obsessive pursuit of Burke, a pursuit that continues into subsequent works, where she is still warring with his palpable presence. But she also seems to be at war with herself (cf. *Collected Letters*, 110, l. 26), and if her own text is, at times, haunted with Burkean echoes, she also seems to attribute and to project onto him what she believes are her own "feminine" weaknesses. Her strategy of feminizing Burke while empowering herself with "masculine" language transforms *The Rights of Men* into a strong, sublime text that overwhelms Burke's weak, sentimental "novel." In doing this, she reinforces traditional sexual stereotypes, even as she resists them, by suggesting the superiority of the "masculine." She correspondingly degrades the category of the feminine by subjecting Burke's transvestized text to misogynous ridicule—the transformation of a masculine text into a feminine reading is clearly meant to be humiliating. Even though she, at one point, argues for sexless virtues, she subverts this theme by accepting the denigration of character traits traditionally associated with femininity and hence implicitly endorses the suggested superiority of traditional masculinity.

If there are a series of distinctive Wollstonecrafts in *The Rights of Men*, there are, similarly, a series of protean Burkes: an unmanly Burke, a hysterical, feminine Burke, a Wollstonecraftian Burke resembling private descriptions of herself, a slavish, self-serving Burke; a Burke who is a deliberate distortionist, a libertine Burke who linguistically enslaves women, as well as a reactionary Burke who defends oppressive power. It is perhaps significant that Wollstonecraft seems to resemble Burke most not when she is demeaning him but when she is replicating her own representations of his twisted language, turning him into the weaker Richard Price so egregiously "defamed" in the *Reflections*.

Moreover, her Burkean resemblance curiously illustrates one of the central themes of the *Reflections*: that it is the nature of revolutionary ideology to turn into its opposite.[19] Hence, according to Burke, the revolutionary government resembles the demonized order it excoriates; a Catholic nation is turned into a militant anti-Christian state, a self-proclaimed democratic republic into a "democratic tyranny." Burke contends that such a revolution is doomed to repetition and distortion as it replicates the Manichean divisions used to define the demonic "other"—thus revealing its secret attraction to the power it supposedly opposes. It is perhaps too subtle to suggest that Wollstonecraft also applies Burke's insight to himself—seeing his own Manichean ideology recreate its opposite—or that she oedipally becomes the "father" she has killed, but it is clear that whenever she tries to "hold up the glass" and "show" Burke to himself (*WMW*, 5:18, 37), she seems revealingly to reflect herself as well.

In *The Rights of Men*, Wollstonecraft portrays Burke's *Reflections* as an exercise in reductive ideology, and Frances Ferguson contends that Wollstonecraft, in "one of the shrewdest insights of late eighteenth-century writing," links Burke's politics in the *Reflections* with his aesthetic position in the *Enquiry*:

> Burke's account of what is *naturally* pleasing in women involves, [Wollstonecraft] argues, the same kind of tendentious statement about women's nature that leads him repeatedly to define nature and natural rights in terms of property and the holding of real estate. For Burke's entire tendency in the *Reflections* is to make all individuals epiphenomena of property in land and to minimize individual rights while maximizing an individual's responsibilities to represent his land. And if this involves making property in land look like nature, Burke is entirely happy to do so.

In Ferguson's reading, Wollstonecraft, while manifesting "a naive" yet admirable "faith in reason," attempts to transcend cultural and sexual divisions represented as "natural" by reconceiving fragmented, conventional reason ("a version of identification with forces superior to oneself") and pity ("a version of identification with forces inferior to oneself")—and arguing instead that "reason should learn to imitate pity, should learn to read the similarities of reason that link men and women."[20] Wollstonecraft, however, also valorizes what she believes is natural (enlightened opinions and sentiments in a new egalitarian world based on nature and reason) and opposes it to the "unnatural" counterrevolutionary world. In her reading of Burke, she also identifies and reifies ideology as "nature."

Ironically, the criteria she establishes for "stripping" and revealing Burke to the world by exposing his femininity, his contradictions, and his distortions mirror her own representations of herself. By continually placing herself in positions resembling public (often hostile) representations of Edmund Burke, she enmeshes herself in a series of self-representations that subvert the empowering distinction between Burke and herself: her climactic insistence on her superior *judgment* turns into pejorative resemblances of the "feminine" *wit* that she attributes to Burke. In addition, Burke's fashioned resemblance to the private Wollstonecraft revealed in her correspondence—a representation not available to the eighteenth-century reader—suggestively evokes the issue of disguise raised by Wollstonecraft, contra Burke, in *The Rights of Men*. That her covert identifications with her counterrevolutionary enemy are often misrepresentations suggests that she engages in elaborate rituals of self-deception. Both revolutionary and antirevolutionary writers frequently engage in misrepresentations of the "other," but their self-fashioning ideologies reproduce the repression of the other as a subversive resemblance. It is as if, within their mutually repetitive systems of binary representation, their language mimetically mirrors the opposition that they resist and reproduce. The demonization of the "other" seems inevitably to reproduce suppressed (and repressed) similarities—complementary textual terms that are re-presented as "difference."

The hostile terms that Wollstonecraft ascribes to Burke—insanity, theatricality, and contradiction—were underscored by Burke himself in the *Reflections*, in his condemnation of the Revolution that she represents. Wollstonecraft, in effect, reverses Burke's representation and attributes it to the nascent counterrevolution, but this, in turn, reillustrates a contradiction inscribed in classic revolutionary texts: Wollstonecraft and other revolutionaries replicate the representations that they resist— they are profoundly implicated in the system of representation that they reject. They hence produce readings hauntingly similar to the ones they rebel against. Preoccupied with revealing and annihilating a counterrevolutionary "other," they magnify those binary oppositions they oppose and hence must eliminate or erase. Their antithetical emphasis on resemblance and similarities—the pristine dream of a unified republic of virtue and reason—clashes against "counterrevolutionary" contradiction and difference—a difference that is doubly written "out"—erased and exposed. Thomas Paine, as we will now see, reillustrates this ironic intertextual war.

Four months after the publication of Wollstonecraft's *The Rights of Men*, Paine produced the first part of *Rights of Man*, exposing Burke's contradictions in ways that resemble his own representations of the Revolution. Paine continued Wollstonecraft's opposition of revolutionary reason to Burke's counterrevolutionary imagination, and he pursued an allegation that Wollstonecraft had first made in *The Rights of Men*: Burke was the recipient of a secret pension and hence had no moral authority to criticize the Revolution. In subsequent publications, Paine continued to elaborate on this allegation and, in doing so, projected onto Burke a series of Painean resemblances, similar in kind to those of Wollstonecraft. Likewise, Paine cited a Burkean text that he produced to reveal Burke's private, "secret" self: mercenary, hypocritical, and mendacious. He thus continued to document the contradictions and discrepancies between Burkean "appearance" and the reality that supposedly belied it.

4

Paine and the Myth of Burke's Secret Pension

In the eighteenth century, it was a common practice for the Crown to award pensions and sinecures for a variety of reasons and purposes. It was also common for people to denounce these pensions and sinecures as corrupting agents, while they themselves sought them. It was even more common to exploit the opprobrium attached to Crown awards to discredit political enemies. During the French Revolution, for instance, Burke's opponents attacked his moral credibility by accusing him of receiving a secret pension that accounted for his opposition to the Revolution and that revealed his hypocrisy, since Burke had publicly opposed pensions and places that were intended to corrupt the independence of Parliament. Burke's character was hence made an issue, and the case against him seemed especially damning, since Burke had, it was alleged, been on the take even before the Revolution began. Thomas Paine provided the primary intertextual reading of Burke's "secret" pension, and the significance of that reading needs to be first contextualized with the following background.

Throughout his political life, Burke's opponents had periodically tried to discredit him by spreading rumors about a pension that he had supposedly received secretly. In 1774, there had been a flurry of such stories—the most common story was that he had received a secret pension from the marquess of Rockingham, Burke's patron and friend. In the next decade, he was again accused of being a recipient of a secret pension—a pension that seemed especially compromising, given Burke's endeavors in the House of Commons: in 1782, when the Rockingham Whigs took office, Burke, in his position of Paymaster-General, had helped promote the abolition of pensions and sinecure appointments that the Crown had used to influence Parliament. Although Burke's principal reform bill, the Civil List Act, had been rejected on two previous occasions by Parliament, a modified version of the bill finally passed into law on 11 July 1782. Bills were subsequently passed in 1783 reducing pensions and emoluments of the Exchequer and, with Burke's assistance, the office of Paymaster-General.

Eight years later, when Burke had stated publicly his opposition to the French Revolution and announced his intention to publish his *Reflections on the Revolution in France*, he was again accused of being a secret pensioner—of receiving covertly the kind of pension he had earlier opposed. Burke, however, had never opposed pensions per se, insisting on various occasions that people who had given years of valuable public service should be appropriately rewarded. He had no objections to pensions for life, which made men independent. He felt the same way about patent offices, which served for the same purpose. In fact, he felt he deserved one or the other and was disappointed that he had not received one. He did, however, object to secret pensions and offices at pleasure, which were used for influence. Thus, the rumor that he was receiving a secret pension suggested that he was actually a hypocritical opportunist.

Paine was among the first to circulate what was, in essence, a malicious rumor. In his private journal, William Godwin, another of Burke's political enemies, recorded a conversation with Paine, in which Paine recounted a conversation he had purportedly had with Burke:

> Paine and Burke talking together observe what a government of pensions and corruption ours is—and distributed by such a fool said Paine—I wish, however, said Burke, this fool would give me one of his places. Paine communicated intelligence to B. respecting Nootka Sound [a dispute between Britain and Spain over claims to the northwest coast of North America in 1790]—You must carry this, said B., to Grey [Charles Grey, liberal aristocratic Whig aligned with Charles James Fox and other Whig supporters of the Revolution]; I cannot bring it into Parliament, I am at this moment negociating with Pitt respecting the impeachment of [Warren] Hastings.[1]

Although the date of the purported conversation is not recorded in Godwin's journal, the reference to Nootka Sound indicates it transpired in spring 1790, when Paine returned to London. It also appears that Paine was privately suggesting that Burke was hypocritically hoping for a place or sinecure and hence could be bought.

Two years later, in 1792, Paine publicly referred to his conversation with Burke in his *Letter Addressed to the Addressers*:

> I was in England at the time the bubble broke forth about Nootka Sound: and the day after the King's message, as it is called, was sent to Parliament [6

May 1790], I wrote a note to Mr. Burke, that upon the condition the French Revolution should not be a subject (for he was then writing the book I have since answered) I would call upon him the next day, and mention some matters I was acquainted with, respecting the affair [Nootka Sound] . . . .

When I saw Mr. Burke, and mentioned the circumstances to him, he particularly spoke of Mr. Grey, as the fittest member to bring such matters forward; "for," said Mr. Burke, "*I am not the proper* person to do it, as I am in a treaty with Mr. Pitt about Mr. Hasting's trial." (*CW*, 2:497–98)

Paine's italicized quotation of Burke underscores his irritation that Burke did not convey the information about Nootka Sound and hence, according to Paine, was shirking his responsibility as a member of Parliament.

It is not clear why Burke would have agreed to meet with Paine, since he had declared publicly (9 February 1790) in a speech that was later published the same month that he would break with any friend who supported the Revolution. The editors of Burke's *Correspondence* accept that the meeting between the men took place on 7 May 1790—a little over a month since Paine arrived in London, specifically to reply to Burke's forthcoming *Reflections* (6:76).

There is, however, a notable discrepancy between Godwin's account of what Paine privately told him and Paine's public account: in the latter, there is no mention of Burke's wish that the regal "fool" would give him "one of his places"—a curious, uncharacteristic admission for Burke, who knew he was speaking to an admirer of the Revolution who intended to reply to his *Reflections*[2]—and a doubly curious omission for Paine, since he accuses Burke of being a secret pensioner in the same work (*Letter Addressed to the Addressers*, in *CW*, 2:501–2). At any rate, the rumor that Burke was a secret pensioner surfaced precisely when he had announced publicly his opposition to the Revolution.

The rumor had, in fact, already appeared in Wollstonecraft's *The Rights of Men* (November 1790). For Wollstonecraft and other of Burke's political enemies, the issue was not only Burke's errant hypocrisy but the blatant betrayal of his previous progressive values: Burke, the enlightened supporter of the Americans, the Irish, and the people of India, had sold himself to please powerful people hostile to the Revolution—the secret pension he was receiving causally complemented his reactionary opposition to the French Revolution. Wollstonecraft accused Burke of boasting of his "virtue and independence" while "enjoying the wages of falsehood"; she questioned his moral consistency in receiving secretly "a pension of fifteen hundred pounds per annum on the Irish establishment"—a pension that was nominally in "the name of *another*" (*WMW*, 5:13). The reference to the pension on the Irish Establishment (which was separate from Britain and not restricted by British law) was, in fact, the basis of the allegation. It was also based on a hypothetical half-truth.

During the Regency Crisis (1788–89), when it appeared that the Portland Whigs would soon take power, the duke of Portland had made tentative plans to help Burke with his financial problems once the Prince of Wales replaced George III. Burke's friend, Sir Gilbert Elliot, was present when plans for Burke's assistance were being discussed. In a letter to his wife, Elliot noted that, in addition to helping Burke's brother, Richard, Portland planned to assign Burke the office of paymastership (at £4,000), but since this would not be a permanent position, Portland proposed to grant Burke, on the Irish Establishment, "a pension of £2000 a year clear for his own life, with the reversion of half of it to his son for life, and the other half to Mrs. Burke for her life. This will make Burke completely happy by leaving his wife and son safe from want after his death if they should survive him."[3] But in February 1789, the king recovered and the plan was discarded: the Portland Whigs did not take power, and Burke never received the pension.

Portland's aborted plan probably became known to Burke's political enemies. Two more entries in Godwin's journal, however, suggest that Burke's enemies, in 1790, were focusing on an earlier economic explanation for Burke's political apostasy. In an undated entry closely preceding Paine's 1790 conversation with Burke, Godwin notes that "Lord Lansdown[e] says he was desired by Fox to delay entering upon the treasury two days, which was spent in granting pensions and reversions to the party, particularly to Burke's cousin and son, one of which L Lansdown negatived, in 1782."[4] In conjunction with Paine's report that Burke was hoping for a "place," the inference is that Burke vindictively opposes the French Revolution because Shelburne (William Petty Fitzmaurice, second earl of Shelburne, created marquess of Lansdowne in 1784), presumably in his role of prime minister, a position he assumed when Rockingham died in July 1782, denied a pension to one of Burke's kinsmen. Later, as Lord Lansdowne, he became an aristocratic patron of bourgeois radicalism and an avid supporter of the French Revolution, forming the "Bowood Circle"—a group of liberal and revolutionary sympathizers (including Richard Price and Joseph Priestley) who met at Bowood House, Lansdowne's Wiltshire country seat near Calne. Rockingham and Burke had long been bitter political enemies of Shelburne, which in Burke's case was further exacerbated by his support of radical intellectuals. Godwin, however, alludes to a personal financial motive to explain Burke's hostility.

Godwin's economic explanation of Burke's defection from the Revolution's "sacred cause" is consummated in his subsequent journal entry: "Mr. Moore, private secretary of Lord Holland, offers to sell a pension of £1,500 per annum on the Irish establishment—confesses that it stands in his name, but is the property of Mr. Burke, granted in 1782."[5] This undated entry was written about the same time as Paine's account of his talk with Burke in May 1790, when Burke's opposition to the Revolution had been publicly established, and it accords with Wollstonecraft's public allegation that Burke was secretly receiving a £1,500 pension on the Irish Establishment "in the name of *another*." Although the allegation was false, it quickly became a fanciful "fact" repeated by Burke's revolutionary enemies.[6]

All of Godwin's private sources were, not surprisingly, hostile to Burke. For instance, the claim that Shelburne had denied a pension to Burke's kinsman was attributed (by Godwin in his journal) to Richard Price—the dissenting minister whom Burke ridicules in the *Reflections*.[7] Apparently Lansdowne told Price, who, in turn, told Godwin. Similarly, Godwin's source for the allegation that Burke was receiving a pension on the Irish Establishment was Mr. Moore, whom Godwin identifies as the private secretary of Lord Holland (Henry Richard Vassall Fox)—another aristocrat sympathetic to the Revolution and the nephew and principal disciple of Charles James Fox—leader of the Whigs, whom Burke later broke with (May 1791) over the issue of the Revolution.[8] In the spring and summer of 1790, Paine had been meeting with the Revolution's Whig supporters.

It remains obscure why Burke would have kept a pension in the name of Lord Holland's secretary (especially as, in this case, secretaries sometimes "confess") or why Moore would have tried to sell a pension that was not legally his. It is striking that Godwin and the rest of Burke's accusers never publicly disclosed the name of the person supposedly concealing Burke's pension. A public name, of course, would have made it possible to verify the allegation. While the concealed name, as in this case, undoubtedly passed by word of mouth and was recorded privately, it was never, as far as I know, made the basis for a public allegation. Although some of Burke's enemies sincerely believed or wanted to believe the dubious rumor they were circulating, their wishful writing never resulted in a bill of specifics. For instance, just as the secret name concealing Burke's pension was never publicly revealed, so the mysterious date initiating the pension was never publicly disclosed: both the name and the date would help to either substantiate or discredit the allegation. The details of the rumor are now in place: aborted proposals floated in 1782 and/or 1788 to obtain a pension for Burke became, in 1790, the basis of a rumor masquerading as a fact.[9]

It was Paine, however, who made the most out of the allegation and who was credited with unmasking Burke as a secret pensioner. In the first part of *Rights of Man* (March 1791), he notes that the "report" of Burke's pension "has been some time in circulation, at least two months" and that he only mentions it so that Burke "may have an opportunity of contradicting the rumor, if he thinks proper" (*CW*, 1:246). Later in the same work, Paine again alludes to the rumor, claiming that Burke is accustomed "to kiss the aristocratic hand that hath purloined him from himself" (*CW*, 1:260). In the second part of *Rights of Man* (February 1792), he claims that Burke "is a stickler for monarchy, not altogether as a pensioner, if he is one, which I believe, but as a political man" (*CW*, 1:366). More emphatically, he refers to "a certain transaction known in the City, which renders him suspected of being a pensioner in a fictitious name" (*CW*, 1:320). Thus, as late as February 1792, Paine had no proof that the rumor of Burke's pension was true, even though he believed it was.

By May 1792, however, he was more confident. In a public letter to the British attorney-general, Paine promised to show, in a future publication, that Burke had "been a masked pensioner at £1500 per annum for about ten years" (*CW*, 2:445). The reference to a secret pension originating in 1782 accords with Moore's allegation, which Godwin had recorded in his private journal, and it was apparently this rumor that Paine was prepared to substantiate.

In a published letter to Onslow Cranley, lord lieutenant of the County of Surrey (21 June 1792), Paine boasted that "the signature of *Thomas Paine* has something in it dreadful to sinecure placemen and pensioners" (*CW*, 2:461)—a comment he undoubtedly believed would terrify Burke. Paine finally produced the evidence of Burke's pension in a *Letter Addressed to the Addressers*, probably written in the summer of 1792. After mentioning Burke's successful efforts to circumscribe places and pensions in 1782, "toward the end of Lord North's administration," he quotes a clause in what was "generally known as Mr. Burke's Reform Bill," stating that no single pension exceeding £300 or additional pensions exceeding £600 annually would be awarded to anyone and that "the *names of the persons*" granted pensions would "be laid before Parliament in twenty days after the beginning of each session" (*CW*, 2:501, Paine's emphasis).

Mr. Burke's Reform Bill was, in fact, the Civil List Act of 1782 (22 Geo. III, c. 82), which Burke did write and which Paine is quoting.[10] Having shown that pensions had to be publicly revealed, Paine then quotes a "provisory clause" that was "afterwards added": "That it shall be lawful for the First Commissioner of the Treasury, to return into the Exchequer any pension or annuity, *without a name*, on his making oath that such pension or annuity is not directly or indirectly for the benefit, use, or behoof of any member of the House of Commons" (*CW*, 2:501, Paine's emphasis).

Paine, however, engages in a series of deliberate misrepresentations, for he does not say that the "provisory clause" is in context of a separate category of pension (article 21, actually referred to as a "secret pension"), while the article (#17) stipulating the revelation of names is in context of public pensions.[11] By suggesting that the so-called "provisory clause" relates to and follows the article dealing with the mandatory revelation of names, Paine clearly implies that Burke "afterwards added" the clause so that he could draw a secret pension "without a name." But in addition to quoting out of context and running two articles together (17 and 21), Paine contradicts himself in citing the £600 limit for individuals (a secret pension would be restricted to £300), since, in the following paragraph, he accuses Burke of receiving a secret pension of £1,500 per annum (*CW*, 2:502). Moreover, by citing the necessary approval of the first commissioner of the treasury for receipt of a secret pension (article 20), he makes a conspiratorial connection, since the first commissioner in 1782 (March–June) was the marquess of Rockingham—Burke's patron and friend. But what Paine again does not say is that Rockingham died on 1 July 1782, that his administration (with Shelburne's participation) consequently fell, that the "Bill" was not approved until 11 July and did not go into effect until April 1783 (article 17)—making it impossible for Burke to have received Rockingham's approval. He also does not say that Burke's enemy, the earl of Shelburne, became the first commissioner on Rockingham's death or that the recipient of a secret pension also had to have the king's consent (article 20)—a "consent" that George III had no reason, in Burke's case, to grant, given his dislike of the Rockingham Whigs and given Burke's endeavors to oppose the Crown's influence and, later, given his efforts to replace the king with the Prince of Wales during the Regency Crisis (1788–89).

Although Paine's misrepresentations and contradictions have no bearing on the fact that Burke never received a secret pension, they do reveal Paine's double game, for his account is so filled with discrepancies and suppressions that only those who wanted to believe it could.

There are, for instance, additional inconsistencies in Paine's account: the notorious "provisory clause" that he quotes stipulates that the anonymous beneficiary could in no way be associated with the House of

Commons, but Burke had been a member of the Commons since 1765. According to the clause (article 21) quoted by Paine, Burke could not have drawn the anonymous pension legally. But Paine either misses or ignores the contradiction—otherwise, he would have pounced upon it, since Burke would have, according to the provision, been guilty of drawing a pension illegally.

Paine then proceeds to provide the vague particulars of his insinuatory indictment:

> But soon after [the North] administration ended, and the party Mr. Burke acted with came to power [March–June 1782], it appears from the circumstances I am going to relate, that Mr. Burke became himself a pensioner in disguise; in a similar manner as if a pension had been granted in the name of John Nokes, to be privately paid to and enjoyed by Tom Stiles. The name of Edmund Burke does not appear in the original transaction: but after the pension was obtained, Mr. Burke wanted to make the most of it at once, by selling or mortgaging it; and the gentleman in whose name the pension stands, applied to one of the public offices for that purpose. This unfortunately brought forth the name of *Edmund Burke*, as the real pensioner of £1,500 per annum. When men trumpet forth what they call the blessings of the Constitution, it ought to be known what sort of blessings they allude to. (*CW*, 2:501–2)

The reference to the £1,500 pension alludes to the pension on the Irish Establishment—the £1,500 pension that Wollstonecraft had accused Burke of receiving in "the name of *another*." Paine's account also accords with the various details in Godwin's journal: the North Administration ended in March 1782, the year Moore supposedly tried to sell the pension on the Irish Establishment, but "confessed" that it belonged to Burke, even though it was in Moore's name. There is, however, a new twist in Paine's version: Burke tries to sell or mortgage the pension secretly, not "the gentleman in whose name the pension stands." Aside from this, Paine's account seems based on Moore's private confession, and he could have obtained it from a variety of sources.

The principal problem is Paine's presentation of allegations that were never substantiated. Paine reveals inadvertently the weakness of his case when, after announcing dramatically that he will expose Burke as a secret pensioner, he prefaces his revelation with the modest phrase, "it *appears* from the *circumstances* I am going to relate, that Burke became himself a pensioner in disguise" (*CW*, 2:501, my emphasis). But he then inflates the "circumstances" by baldly stating that Burke was receiving a pension under someone else's name, and the unnamed gentleman who was the nominal holder tried either to buy the pension or to sell it when Burke's name was discovered. The phrase "applied to one of the public offices for that purpose" is ambiguous.

Since "the signature of *Thomas Paine* has something in it dreadful to . . . placemen and pensioners" (*CW*, 2:461), one would also expect Paine to reveal the name of the man whose concealed presence incriminates Burke, the "concealed pensioner" (*CW*, 2:508). But by underscoring Burke's revealed name (*CW*, 2:502), Paine unwittingly underscores the conspicuous absence of the other name: the anonymous "gentleman in whose name the pension stands," for Paine's allegation hinges on also bringing forth this name. Since he is making a public allegation, Paine is obligated to reveal the public name—a source that he does not need to protect or conceal, since, according to him, Burke's name and the "gentleman in whose name the pension stands" had already been "discovered" in 1782. Instead, Paine does exactly what he accuses Burke of doing: he conceals the name and hence hides the identity of the "witness." Moreover, the fact that Paine does not mention the name of the anonymous gentleman, after bringing forth "the [italicized] name of *Edmund Burke* (*CW*, 2:502), underscores ironically the italicized "*without a name*," with which he highlights the notorious "provisory clause" of "Mr. Burke's Reform Bill": the clause allowing a pension to be drawn anonymously (*CW*, 2:501).

Instead of a real incriminatory name, Paine provides a hypothetical example of a pension "granted in the name of John Nokes, to be privately paid to and enjoyed by Tom Stiles"—two fictional names that lawyers traditionally used in actions of ejectment. The fact that Paine mentions neither the real name nor the particular circumstances also underscores the kind of reflexive concealment (and hypocrisy) with which he charges Burke. [12] Indeed, the "gentleman in whose name the pension stands" is hidden under the name "John Nokes": Paine's onomastic example revealingly entangles him in the kind of onomastic deception that Burke supposedly committed. After dramatically announcing previously that he would unmask Burke as a secret pensioner, he can only provide, when the revealing moment arrives, the sound and fury of unsubstantiated rumors. He quickly turns to other matters (see *CW*, 2:502 ff.).

In addition to the ways in which Paine is compromised by his own language, there are implosive ironies in his suggestion that Burke could be secretly bought, for this was the very charge that Paine's enemies had made against him. Likewise, just as Paine accused Burke of receiving a secret pension in the past, so Paine's enemies had accused Paine, during the American Revolution, of receiving a secret pension and hence of being a "bought pen." Paine's biographer, Alfred Owen Aldridge, notes that Paine accepted "clandestine rewards for his propaganda, particularly from both the American government and the French Ministry for his writings on the American Revolution," although he "never ceased alluding to the free bestowal of his services." Referring to Paine's services to the American and French governments, Jack Fruchtman notes that "being a hired pen suited Paine."[13] Paine was naturally always sensitive to charges that his was a "bought pen," and he was equally insistent that his motives were always pure and disinterested. In an article published in the *Pennsylvania Packet* (December 1778), Paine noted (in a comment Burke would have sadly enjoyed) that he knew "that when men get into parties, and suffer their tempers to become soured by opposition, how tempted they are to assign interested reasons for other people's conduct, and to undermine the force of their reasonings by sapping the reputation of the person who makes them" (*CW*, 2:279).

Moreover, Paine, the enemy of pensioners and placemen, sought a pension he believed he deserved for his services to the American Revolution, off and on, for the rest of his life. Conversely, as late as 1802, he was still insisting (this time to the citizens of the United States) that since it was "impossible to discover" any worldly aspirations within him, everything he did should "be ascribed to a good motive": "In a great affair, where the happiness of man is at stake, I love to work for nothing; and so fully am I under the influence of this principle, that I should lose the spirit, the pleasure, and the pride of it, were I *conscious* that I looked for reward" (*CW*, 2:928; my emphasis).

Paine's emphatic insistence on his own disinterestedness stemmed from repeated allegations that he could be bought. In a letter to Benjamin Franklin (4 March 1779), he complained of being set down as a "pensioned writer . . . furiously abused in the newspapers and everywhere else" (*CW*, 2:1168). In 1782, Robert Morris (who had been appointed superintendent of finance by Congress) signed an agreement with George Washington and Robert R. Livingston (the newly appointed secretary for foreign affairs) whereby Paine would receive 800 dollars a year to write for the government. As David Freeman Hawke notes,

> he would be paid from a secret fund that the superintendent of finance could use without the need to give a public accounting. The agreement was to be kept absolutely secret since "a salary publicly and avowedly given for the choice purpose would injure the effect of Mr. Paine's publication, and subject him to injurious personal reflections." However, someone talked. "Your old acquaintance Paine," Joseph Reed told Nathanael Greene, "is a hireling writer pensioned with £300 per annum payable by General Washington out of the secret service money."[14]

Significantly, the year (1782) in which Paine's secret pension was revealed was the same in which, according to him, Burke's was discovered. In the same year (1782), Paine was paid by Robert Morris to defend the Bank of North America, becoming known as Morris's "pensioned pen."[15] John Smilie, a spokesman for the backcountry farmers opposing the bank, referred to Paine as "an unprincipled author, whose pen is let out for hire"—a phrase Paine angrily quoted in a letter (April 1786) appearing in both the *Pennsylvania Packet* and the *Pennsylvania Gazette* (*CW*, 2:421).

The issue, however, is not Paine's hypocrisy in falsely accusing Burke of receiving the kind of covert funds that he himself had actually received but the psychological compulsion to ascribe to Burke the kindred things he himself conceals: onomastic deception, secret payments. It illustrates a characteristic (although it is not uniquely characteristic) of many of Burke's revolutionary enemies—they project onto Burke the very defects and distortions they themselves have or commit. Their distortions of Burke are tellingly thematic, since they entrap and betray themselves in the very language with which they indict their antirevolutionary enemy. The "secret" resemblances between Paine and Burke are similar, for instance, to those that Wollstonecraft projects onto Burke in *The Rights of Men*. In both cases, public documentation of Burke's "lies" and discrepancies reveal resounding resemblances to their own private self-representations.

In the end, however, the myth of Burke's pension became an established fact of revolutionary discourse. (In 1802, Paine was still referring to "the pensioned pen of Edmund Burke" [*CW*, 2:910].) In numerous pamphlets and cartoons, Burke was ridiculed and excoriated as the secret pensioner of the counterrevolution. On 23 March 1791, shortly after the publication of the first part of *Rights of Man*, the pro-revolutionary Society for Constitutional Information voted its "thanks to Paine for exposing the 'Sophistries of hireling Scribblers.'" In 1792, Burke's enemy, Thomas Cooper, referred sarcastically to "the Pension which this disinterested Politician has been so frequently accused of receiving in another man's name, from the Irish Establishment." In early 1793, an effigy of Burke was "hung twenty feet up on a scaffold after being paraded through town [Dronfield, England] with a sign reading 'Edmund Burke the Irish Pensioner.'"[16] Throughout the revolutionary years and beyond, the fiction of Burke's secret pension became a standard explanation of his "real" opposition to the Revolution.

There remained, however, the final irony. After he had retired from Parliament in June 1794, Burke was finally awarded a public pension in recognition of his many years of public service. In August 1794, William

Pitt wrote to Burke, informing him that "a Civil List Pension of £1,200 had been granted him on his own life and that of Mrs. Burke [as Burke had previously requested], but that soon as Parliament reconvened another larger annuity would be proposed by the government, in the form of a parliamentary grant." When Parliament reconvened, however, Pitt "found that Burke's enemies were stronger than he thought," making it difficult "for him to procure the grant in the form he had proposed." Consequently, Pitt abandoned the idea of the parliamentary grant and "instead got Burke two further annuities—totaling 2,500—from the Crown. It was disappointing of course to Burke that the grants should not be from Parliament, but under the circumstances [i.e., Burke's pressing economic problems] he could hardly refuse them."[17] Burke, in fact, did not receive the annuities until 1795, when he quickly sold them so that he could begin paying off his debts.[18]

Burke's enemies, however, used the granting of the public pensions to reinforce the myth of his secret pension: the public pensions finally proved that Burke had been bought, and his price was £3,700. Burke's annihilatory reply to those questioning his pensions, especially the young duke of Bedford and the earl of Lauderdale (whose incomes originated from the Crown), appeared in his *Letter to a Noble Lord* (1796), but the existence of the public pensions awarded after Burke's retirement from the House of Commons (1794) was continually used to imply that the myth of Burke's secret pension was somehow poetically true.[19]

Paine was the crucial, public formulator of the myth, and his allegation dovetailed thematically with the fictions and myths that he accused Burke of creating in *Rights of Man*: anyone who would draw a secret pension would also lie about the French Revolution. In *Rights of Man*, Burke is the mendacious fabricator of counterrevolutionary myths, and Paine contrasts the Revolution's true facts with Burke's theatrical fictions. Focusing on the events of 14 July and the October Days of 1789, Paine distinguishes Burke's counterrevolutionary drama from his own sober history. Illusion and reality was again the major leitmotif of the great intertextual war.

5

Paine's Revolutionary Comedy:
The Bastille and October Days
in the *Rights of Man*

For over two centuries, scholars and critics have generally reaffirmed Paine's contrast in *Rights of Man* between Burke's exaggerated theatrical account of the October Days and his own detailed, historical account of the same event. In numerous commentaries, Paine's critique of Burke's dramatic fiction has been quoted approvingly, even though Paine's narrative, like Burke's, is complicit with the theatrical imagery he criticizes. Paine, in fact, establishes a criterion of historical truth that he subverts with the same theatrical paradigms he applies to Burke, as he creates a dramatic narrative driven by the theatrical tropes he condemns. If Burke writes the Revolution as an antirevolutionary tragedy, Paine rewrites it as a revolutionary comedy—the resolution of conflict and the happy ending of 6 October. Likewise, in his narrative of the Bastille's fall, he highlights the "causes" of Burke's fictional tragedy—the suppression of real causes—to underscore the truth of his superior, factual history.

In *Rights of Man*, Paine's version of the Bastille's fall and the October Days of 1789 comprehends a thematic contrast to the suppressions, distortions, and misrepresentations in Burke's *Reflections*. Like other revolutionary respondents, he focuses on the October Days to highlight the difference between Burkean theater and revolutionary history, and he amplifies Burke's "silence" on the Bastille to show how Burke suppresses inconvenient facts. In addition, he condemns Burke for not dealing with the Revolution's "commencement or progress." This is because, according to him, Burke does not understand the origins of the Revolution; consequently, Burke was astonished when it "burst forth" *idea*

(*CW*, 1:298). In contrast, Paine contends that the Revolution was "the consequence of a mental revolution previously existing in France," and he traces this revolution to "the writings of the French philosophers" and to the American Revolution. He also provides an account of the events leading up to and prefiguring the Revolution—the financial crisis, the Assembly of Notables, the calling of the States General; in short, a series of causal events that Burke fails to mention (see *CW*, 1:290–313).

But Burke had, in the *Reflections*, presented his version of the Revolution's origins and commencement, referring, just as Paine does, to the Enlightenment as an ideological source. In addition, he refers to the growth of "a great monied interest," the economic expansion of the bourgeoisie, as a cause of the Revolution, which, coupled with the influential power of a new class of intellectuals—the "Men of Letters" who revolutionized public opinion by discrediting the institutional values of the Old Order—made the Revolution a reality (209–10, 211–14). He also refers to the class suicide of French nobles who "countenanced too much that licentious philosophy which has helped to bring on their ruin" and to the unnatural separation of new money and old landed wealth, which created unnecessary resentment and distinctions (244–45). He criticizes revolutionaries who cite as "causes" historical injustices that are disguised pretexts for their own injustices (247–48; see 173–74 for other causes). By contending that Burke does not deal with the commencement or the "causes" of the Revolution, Paine misrepresents Burke by suppressing what Burke says these causes are. Both Burke and Paine, of course, select those facts and events that support the thesis they want to push. Burke, not surprisingly, is more interested in enumerating the causes of the Revolution's inevitable failure. Paine castigates Burke for ignoring or suppressing facts or causes because Burke's facts and causes are not his.

Paine focuses on the events of 14 July because, for him, this revolutionary date marks the start of the real revolution prepared by the prior mental revolution. In contrast, he notes that "through the whole of Mr. Burke's book I do not observe that the Bastille is mentioned more than once," except for a couple of slight references that Paine later acknowledges in a footnote (see *CW*, 1:259–60). Burke indeed does not deal with the fall of the Bastille—an event that had immense symbolic significance for revolutionaries. (Paine acknowledges the Bastille's symbolic significance when he writes "the downfall of it included the idea of the downfall to despotism" [*CW*, 1:261].) Before the Revolution, however, it had already been decided that the Bastille was, in effect, useless and needed to be destroyed to make way for urban development. Burke considered the Bastille's fall unimportant. In a letter to an anonymous correspondent, in January 1790, he notes that they both know that "the destruction of the *Bastile*, of which you speak, . . . was a thing in itself of no consequence whatever":

> The *Bastile* was at first intended as a citadel undoubtedly; and when it was built, it might serve the purposes of a citadel. Of late, in that view, it was ridiculous. It could not contain any garrison sufficient to awe such a city as Paris. As a prison, it was of as little importance. Give despotism, and the prisons of despotism will not be wanting, any more than lamp-irons will be wanting to democratic fury. (*Correspondence*, 6:80)

Burke did not deal with the Bastille's destruction because, unlike Paine, he did not consider 14 July the beginning of the real revolution, which he dates 6 October 1789, with the invasion of the king's palace at Versailles and the forced removal of the royal family to Paris (*Reflections*, 175). Burke's symbols and dates are not Paine's.

Paine, nevertheless, dwells on the events leading up to 14 July and focuses on the Bastille to reveal the real reason for Burke's silence: Burke is callously unmoved by despotism's silenced victims—the victims languishing in the prison that the Revolution opens (*CW*, 1:260). He contends that Burke cares only for the theatrical sufferings of anachronistic kings and queens; thus, in his famous aphorism, Burke "pities the plumage, but forgets the dying bird" (*CW*, 1:260). Paine, however, does something characteristic of the revolutionary historiography of the time: he refers to abstract victims without mentioning the real victims; he celebrates the opening of the Bastille and the symbolic fall of despotism without mentioning the specific victims liberated on 14 July. It is not coincidental that Paine is also silent about despotism's flesh-and-blood victims, since there were only seven prisoners when the Bastille was taken: four forgers, tried and convicted, two lunatics, shortly returned to an insane asylum, and one nobleman incarcerated, at his family's request, for libertinism. This fact does not fit Paine's revolutionary script, so after one commiserating glance, he proceeds with his narrative. While he insists that Burke's "hero or heroine must be a tragedy-victim expiring in show, and not the real prisoner of mystery, sinking into death in the silence of the dungeon" (*CW*, 1:260), he himself exploits Enlightenment and revolutionary clichés dealing with the mysterious tragedy victims of the Bastille, silently expiring in despair.

Throughout *Rights of Man*, Paine contrasts "the sober style of history" that he implicitly writes with Burke's "theatrical representation" (*CW*, 1:269, 258). He refers to Burke's "tragic paintings," his artful manipulation of facts to produce "a weeping effect," his demonization of the Revolution through "horrid paintings"—all illustrated in his "theatrical exaggerations for facts" (*CW*, 1:258–59, 267). Burke "should recollect that he is writing history and not *plays*, and that his readers will expect truth, and not the spouting rant of high-toned declamation" (*CW*, 1:259). Burke, in the *Reflections*, had also accused Richard Price and other revolutionary sympathizers of producing melodramatic revolutionary drama: "There must be a great change of scene; there must be a magnificent stage effect; there must be a grand spectacle to rouze the imagination" (156). Allusively contrasting his response with the response of Price exulting over the king's humiliation in the *Discourse*, Burke says he would "be truly ashamed" if he shed tears over the dramatic enactment of "such a spectacle" on stage, while exulting over it "in real life": "I should be truly ashamed of finding in myself that superficial, *theatric sense of painted distress*, whilst I could exult over it in real life" (175, my emphasis). Paine, in effect, ascribes to Burke the very thing Burke rejects: "that superficial theatric sense of painted distress." This suggests that Burke's condemnation of revolutionary drama provided Wollstonecraft, Paine, and others the terms with which they condemn Burke. Since Paine is also selectively rewriting the Revolution so that it accords with his interpretation of facts, the distinction between Burke and himself disappears within the context he himself establishes.

Paine's language, for instance, illustrates that he is also producing drama; the imagery he selects to highlight the significance of the Bastille's fall is both theatrical and artful: "The mind can hardly *picture* to itself a more tremendous *scene* than which the city of Paris *exhibited* at the time of the taking of the Bastille" (*CW*, 1:261, my emphasis). Likewise, "the representative system of government . . . presents itself on the open theater of the world" (*CW*, 1:373). Earlier, referring to the *Declaration of the Rights of Man*, the imagery is equally dramatic: "We see the solemn and majestic spectacle of a Nation opening its commission . . . to establish a scene so new, and so transcendently unequalled by anything in the European world" (*C W*, 1:317). Commenting on this passage, Tom Furniss notes: "That [Paine] repeats precisely what he repudiates Burke for shows how Paine works within the same paradigms as his adversary—especially when he tries to construe the Revolution as good rather than bad drama."[1]

Having accused Burke of selectively emphasizing or suppressing facts, Paine does the same, authoritatively citing the figure of twenty-five to thirty thousand foreign troops that surrounded Paris in July 1789—a figure he had received in a letter from Thomas Jefferson (11 July 1789).

He ignores, however, Jefferson's subsequent account of the events of 12 July (in a letter dated 13 July): a mob threw stones at the "German cavalry," provoking the cavalry to counterattack.[2] In Paine's version, "the Prince de Lambese, who commanded a body of German cavalry . . . insulted and struck an old man with his sword," and the enraged French, "remarkable for their respect of old age," then "attacked the cavalry" with stones (*CW*, 1:263). Paine's preference for the revolutionary version clashes with his previous rebuke to Burke for ignoring the authoritative Thomas Jefferson—"an authority which Mr. Burke well knows was good" (*CW*, 1:261).[3]

Something similar happens in his account of the October Days, for what links his version of the fall of the Bastille and the October Days is his contention that Burke intentionally suppresses the "causes" of both events. He notes that he "cannot consider Mr. Burke's book in scarcely any other light than a dramatic performance; and he must, I think, have considered it in the same light himself, by the poetical liberties he has taken of omitting some facts, distorting others, and making the machinery bend to produce a stage effect" (*CW*, 1:267–68). In the *Reflections*, Burke had accused the Revolution's supporters of producing sensationalist theater, insisting on "a magnificent stage effect" (156), so Paine reapplies Burke's critique to his theatrical *Reflections*. Ignoring the fact that Burke did not deal with the events of 5 October, since they did not figure in his dramatic narrative, Paine refers contradictorily to Burke's "account of the expedition to Versailles" and the omission of "the only facts, which as causes, are known to be true; everything beyond these is conjecture, even in Paris" (*CW*, 1:268). He then reveals the causes that Burke conceals—the causes that provoke the "people" into reacting: "It is to be observed throughout Mr. Burke's book, that he never speaks of plots *against* the Revolution; and it is from these plots that all the mischiefs have arisen. It suits his purpose to exhibit consequences without their causes. It is one of the arts of the drama to do so" (*CW*, 1:268). Since Paine establishes the principal criterion he uses to condemn Burke's book—the concealment of "causes"—he thematically compromises himself by making concealment an issue, since he engages in the very concealments he condemns. Jerome D. Wilson and William F. Ricketson observe that "Paine gives a very detailed account of events that led to the march as well as to the events in Versailles."[4] Paine, however, excludes embarrassing events that contradict his version of "sober" history.

While he concedes that "the expedition to Versailles . . . still remains enveloped in . . . mystery" (*CW*, 1:268), he concentrates on the known causes: the "uneasiness" caused by the king's failure to sanction the

Declaration of the Rights of Man and the August 4th Decrees (*CW*, 1:268–69), as well as secret machinations by the Revolution's enemies to provoke the march in order to use it as a pretext—hoping that the king would flee to Metz, "where they expected him to collect a force" and oppose the Revolution (*CW*, 1:270). In one ambiguous clause, Paine also implies that the patriotic crowd might have been infiltrated by enemies of the Revolution acting as agents provocateurs (*CW*, 1:270; 3rd par.). Although the last "cause" is conjectural, Paine's principal cause, in the revolutionary version he cites, is the trampling of the national cockade by the *Garde du Corps* in the banquet of 1 October (*CW*, 1:269). This, according to him, was the primary reason why the crowd gathered on 5 October—they marched to Versailles "to demand satisfaction" for the insult to the cockade, but "all this Mr. Burke has carefully kept out of sight" (*CW*, 1:269). In the *Reflections*, Burke had argued that the Convention Parliament of 1689 had gone out of its way to keep "from the eye" any hint of radical democracy in the Glorious Revolution (102). Paine suggests allusively that Burke similarly "keeps out of sight" anything embarrassing or inconvenient (see also *CW*, 1:319, 434). But Paine himself keeps out of sight one of the cardinal causes of the march—at least as important as the bruised cockade—the scarcity of bread in Paris. Paine evidently did not want to contend that the scarcity of bread (a glaring omission) was a counterrevolutionary plot (a popular explanation for the "Great Fear" in July 1789) to starve the people, so he suppresses this material cause and concentrates on an indignant people marching to Versailles to vindicate the national cockade and the rights of man. Indeed, the omissions in his account of the Bastille (the actual prisoners) and 5 October (the scarcity of bread) underscore the ideological nature of his narrative, since these facts do not fit the story he is telling. Like Burke, he is often more interested in ideological explanations than in "material" ones.

In his narration of both events, Paine sees the Revolution in terms of its political symbols—the attack on the Bastille is an attack on a symbol of despotism (*CW*, 1:261); the insult to the national cockade constitutes an attack on the Revolution, provoking the march to Versailles. In addition, Paine either misses or keeps out of sight Burke's reason for omitting the events of 14 July and 5 October: dating the Revolution's commencement on 6 October, a revolution "which may be dated from that day" (*Reflections*, 175), Burke is not interested in the events of 14 July and 5 October. These events do not figure in his antirevolutionary script. It would be difficult for Paine to attack Burke's interpretation of when the Revolution actually began (and hence what is really important) because he could only counter with his own interpretation. He hence ascribes motives that explain why Burke really conceals the evidence that he reveals.

In Paine's march to Versailles, there are other omissions that color his narrative. For instance, no one in his revolutionary crowd has any sort of weapon—no pikes, muskets, or cannons—the latter celebrated in contemporary prints commemorating the march. Hence, he does not mention that the "very numerous body of women, and men in the disguise of women, collected around the Hôtel de Ville" (*CW*, 1:270) had also ransacked the Hôtel, coming away with weapons and ammunition. Nor does he mention the forced recruitment of women in Paris and on the road to Versailles.[5]

When he discusses how Lafayette, as commander of the National Guard, "set off after them" (*CW*, 1:270), he fails to mention that Lafayette tried to stall for hours and was reluctantly compelled by his own troops to go to Versailles[6]—another remarkable omission, since Paine cites Lafayette as one of his personal sources (*CW*, 1:270 n. 7). Paine also omits that, once the crowd arrived at Versailles, hundreds of women invaded the National Assembly, creating momentary havoc, nor does he mention the king's meeting with a small delegation of the women, whom he charmed. In Paine's sanitized narrative, all threatening violence is "kept out of sight," so it does not conflict with his version of events.

When he discusses the events of 6 October, there are other glaring omissions. For instance, in his version, a member of the despised *Garde du Corps* appeared at a palace window, early in the morning, and insulted and then fired on the people who remained in the streets below—the cause of the people rushing "into the palace in quest of the offender" and pursuing *Garde* members "to the apartments of the King" (*CW*, 1:271). The crowd, however, had pursued the guards to the *queen's* apartments— the locale where Burke stages his tragic scene in the *Reflections* (164).[7] Moreover, Paine does not mention the bodyguards that were murdered before the mob reached the queen's apartment—something he would obviously have contested if he doubted it (cf. *Reflections*, 164). He again suppresses inconvenient facts contradicting the script he is writing.

The queen and the murdered bodyguards do appear elliptically in the next paragraph: "On this tumult, not the Queen only, as Mr. Burke has represented it, but every person in the palace, was awakened and alarmed; and M. de Lafayette had a second time to interpose between the parties, the event of which was, that the *Garde du Corps* put on the national cockade, and the matter ended, as by oblivion, after the loss of two or three lives" (*CW*, 1:271).

Paine's account of the queen merely "awakened and alarmed," just like everyone else, omits any reference to Burke's account of the queen leaping from her bed and barely escaping as a frenzied revolutionary mob breaks in and pierces her bed with a hundred sharp strokes (*Reflections*, 164). Since Paine is specifically contrasting his representation with Burke's, his silence on Burke's specific representation is again telling, since he evades rather than contests it. In the second part of *Rights of Man*, he takes Burke to task for not refuting the "principles" contained in *Rights of Man*: "I am enough acquainted with Mr. Burke, to know, that he would if he could" (*CW*, 1:349)—a statement that could be appropriately applied to himself. Likewise, he omits the fact that the queen then fled to the king's quarters and that Lafayette (and members of the National Guard) had "interpose[d] between the parties" to prevent the retreating guards from being massacred, not to break up a fight between two contending forces. In addition, the ambiguous allusion to "the loss of two or three lives" is a belated reference to the murdered bodyguards, whose heads were soon affixed to pikes. Paine underscores the silences in his text by having "the matter ended, as by oblivion," after the ambiguous "loss of two or three lives." This "oblivion" corresponds to the suppression of facts and causes that Paine insists Burke keeps "out of sight" (*CW*, 1:269).

Paine's facts are not Burke's facts. But since he makes a thematic issue out of revealing Burke's dishonest "silences" and contesting Burke's fabricated "facts," he exposes his own vulnerable representation to the same criteria. If, according to Paine, Burke suppresses "causes" and emphasizes "consequences," he, himself, does the same. Moreover, by making Burke's suppressions and distortions of facts examples of Burke's intellectual dishonesty, Paine's language betrays itself in acknowledging the forgetfulness, the "oblivion" by which so many details are conveniently changed or forgotten. Indeed, Paine knew that language can betrayingly reveal what is being suppressed or concealed. In an essay on the *Origin of Freemasonry* (1805), he anticipated what later became known as the Freudian slip: "It sometimes happens, as well as in writing as in conversation, that a person lets slip an expression that serves to unravel what he intends to conceal" (*CW*, 2:833–34).

One of the most remarkable omissions in Paine's narrative emphasis on "causes" is the conspicuous absence of the duc d'Orleans, who, it was widely believed, had secretly financed and incited the crowd that marched to Versailles. The official inquiry conducted by the *Châtelet*, published in March 1790, had suggested "a vaguely defined Orleanist plot."[8] Indeed, Lafayette as well as the French court believed this, and,

consequently, the duc d'Orleans was exiled to London (21 October 1789-
July 1790) on the pretext that he was on a secret mission to discover plots
against the king! Lafayette, one of Paine's sources, informed the duke
that he was being exiled. Moreover, Paine had referred to Orleans as a
possible cause in his January (1790) letter to Burke—the letter he
reproaches Burke for not heeding in *Rights of Man* (*CW*, 1:244, 261,
297). In the letter, Paine informed Burke that

> the March to Versailles has yet some mystery in it. I believe the Duke of
> Orleans knows as much of this business as any body knows. It certainly
> produced a Rupture between him and the Marquis de la Fayette. The Truth is
> that the Duke submitted to the proposal made to him of leaving the Kingdom.
> I am in this respect confident of the Authority I speak from. The Duke and
> the Marquis had some interviews . . . and it was agreed to cover his departure
> by an appearance of business. (*Correspondence*, 6:73–74)

Paine's "authority" is Lafayette himself—the restorer of peace and
reconciliation in *Rights of Man*. Orleans's presence, of course, would
have complicated Paine's sanitized account of the patriotic crowd
marching to Versailles to vindicate the national cockade. Thus, two
conspicuous causes are forgotten in Paine's representation: the scarcity
of bread in Paris and the reputed role of the duc d'Orleans.

After the "oblivion" of the palace invasion, Paine proceeds with his
narrative: "During the latter part of the time in which this confusion was
acting, the King and Queen were in public at the balcony, and neither of
them concealed for safety's sake, as Mr. Burke insinuates" (*CW*, 1:271).
But Burke insinuates nothing of the kind, since he refers to the royal
family's "concealment" during the time the revolutionary mob was
rampaging through the palace—not during their subsequent balcony
appearance—a "scene" that Burke dispenses with, moving immediately
to their forced journey to Paris (see *Reflections*, 164–65). Paine, one
would think, could have made a stronger case by stressing that Burke,
once again, conceals causes, since, in Paine's narrative, the balcony is the
scene of reconciliation, where the king freely chooses to return with his
people to Paris. But by having the king and queen appear "in public at
the balcony," Paine also dispenses with the solitary appearance of the
apprehensive queen, who was, during a dangerous moment, compelled
by the hostile crowd to appear alone on the balcony—a moment saved
when Lafayette then appeared, bowed, and, kissing the queen's hand,
won the crowd over.

In Paine's next paragraph, everything is happily resolved: "Matters
being thus appeased, and tranquillity restored, a general acclamation

broke forth, of *Le Roi à Paris* . . . The King to Paris. It was the shout of peace, and immediately accepted on the part of the King. By this measure, all future projects of transporting the King to Metz, and setting up the standard of opposition to the Constitution, were prevented, and the suspicions extinguished" (*CW*, 1:271). In Paine's version, the king chooses freely to return to Paris, urged by the encouraging shouts of the patriotic crowd, rather than the intimidating insistence of the mob yelling, "*Le Roi à Paris.*" Given Paine's emphasis on causes, it is again remarkable that he can suggest that the king's return was not compelled by the insistent crowd that caused it.

In addition, Paine omits the journey from Versailles to Paris, which Burke exaggeratingly highlights in the *Reflections*, where "the royal captives" are slowly led in triumph by a frenzied revolutionary mob (preceded by the piked heads of the murdered guards) for six harrowing hours (165). In one sentence, Paine has the royal family arriving in Paris and greeted "by M. Bailley, the mayor of Paris" (*CW*, 1:271). Shortly after, he refers to the "procession from Versailles to Paris" in which "not an act of molestation was committed during the whole march," even though there were at least three hundred thousand people accompanying the king in the procession (*CW*, 1:272). Since Paine writes his sober history as a comprehensive contrast to Burke's fanciful drama, emphasizing Burke's distortions and suppressions of facts and events, his decision not to contest Burke's exaggerated script indicates that there were enough embarrassing details to compromise his revolutionary comedy—the happy ending of 6 October. For instance, if he had contested Burke's narrative, he would have had to address the guards' decapitated heads "stuck upon spears" (*Reflections*, 164–65)—heads that are "out of sight" in his own narrative. In addition, he would presumably have had to address what the (inflated) crowd of three hundred thousand was doing for six hours, for while there was no physical "molestation" of the royal family, the crowd carried a variety of weapons and sang insulting songs culminating in their cry that they were bringing "the baker, the baker's wife, and the baker's errand boy" back to Paris.[9] Paine consistently omits or forgets any suggestion of intimidation or coercion.

This becomes ironic when he chastises Burke for condemning Jean-Sylvain Bailly for calling 6 October "un bon jour," since, according to Paine, Bailly was referring to the "peaceful termination" of "the arrival of the King at Paris" (*CW*, 1:272). We have seen, however, that Burke's 6 October is certainly not Paine's and vice versa. As Frans De Bruyn notes, "History writing is as much a narrative or dramatic art as the writing of plays"; thus, when Paine assigns "appropriate 'facts' and 'causes,'" he "ineluctably commits himself to his own narrative or version of events. He cannot do otherwise, for the effort to understand discrete historical events inevitably involves him in the articulation of a plot or story."[10]

After closing his "account of the expedition to Versailles," Paine cites the radical prorevolutionary newspaper, the *Révolutions de Paris*, as a principal source for his version of the October Days: "An account of the expedition to Versailles may be seen in No. 13, of the 'Révolution[s] de Paris,' containing the events from the 3rd to the 10th of October, 1789" (*CW*, 1:272 n. 8). One would assume that his source tendentiously confirms the story he tells, and to some extent it does: there is no mention of Lafayette's reluctance to march to Versailles (something Paine could have confirmed from Lafayette himself) or the invasion of the queen's apartment. But it is again precisely what is not seen in Paine's account that is revealing. For instance, *Révolutions de Paris* does mention the lack of food (i.e., flour and bread) as a cause of the march;[11] it mentions the crowd of women who went to the Hôtel de Ville, threatened to hang people from the lamppost, threw stones at the soldiers impotently protecting the Hôtel, soldiers who retired, allowing "our brave amazons" (*nos braves amazonnes*) to enter and ransack the Hôtel, taking away guns, ammunition, and cannons.[12] In Versailles, it reports on a delegation of the women informing the National Assembly of the need of bread and mentions the king's meeting with another delegation and his sad acknowledgment of the lack of food.[13] It reports that two of the king's bodyguards were injured on 5 October in altercations with the National Guard.[14] It reports Lafayette arriving and telling the king that he has been sent to protect the king because he is not safe.[15] On page 20, there is an engraving of the people (armed with pikes and cannon) who surround the royal family just before the latter are forcibly conducted to Paris. In their detailed discussion of the October Days, Darline Levy and Harriet Applewhite reproduce the engraving as well as a translation of the caption accompanying it: "The National Guard of Paris and Versailles, numbering more than 20,000, not counting the more than 12,000 men and women, armed with various weapons, who complained to the King about the lack of bread in the capital, pressing the King to establish his residence in Paris."[16]

The *Révolutions*'s account of 6 October is also telling. In the early morning of that day, it is the crowd gathered outside that provokes a bodyguard inside the palace to fire, killing a National Guard, providing the crowd the opportunity to invade the palace and search for the culprit. Erroneously believing they have found him, they take an innocent man outside, cut off his head, and affix it to a pike that is paraded to Paris. In various other places in the palace, the crowd arrests other members of the bodyguard, and one, trying to calm the crowd, is piked to death. A third bodyguard is killed by a National Guard who is forced by the enraged crowd to decapitate the victim. Another mob ransacks the bodyguards' quarters, while others continue looking for other guards. Later, when the royal family appears on the balcony, the king is so emotionally distressed that he cannot speak. When he does speak, he addresses the crowd with tears in his eyes and begs them to rescue his beleaguered bodyguards.[17] In the very source Paine cites, there appears the causal bread, the intimidating weapons, and the decapitating violence that are all kept out of sight in his march to and from Versailles. By making an issue out of Burke's fabricated drama and his own objective history, the distinction between Burke and himself disappears within this criterion. By showcasing Burke's concealments of details he wants kept out of sight, he reveals his own concealments by ironically making concealment an issue: he exposes his own concealments precisely when he is revealing Burke's.

In one of his mocking condemnations, Paine characterizes Burke's method of producing bad counterrevolutionary drama: "Mr. Burke brings forward his bishops and his lantern, like figures in a magic lantern, and raises his scenes by contrast instead of connection" (*CW*, 1:272). But this is also Paine's method of writing revolutionary drama, for he casts Burke in the role of principal counterrevolutionary villain and proceeds to contrast his reactionary "scenes" with his own progressive ones. Paine's "causes" are counterrevolutionary conspiracies and insults that contrastingly provoke the revolutionary heroes he celebrates: Lafayette, the vanquishers of the Bastille, and the patriotic crowd that marches to and from Versailles. He brings forward his revolutionary heroes, like figures in a magic lantern, and connects his scenes through contrasts.

Like Wollstonecraft's representation, Paine's critique provides the very terms for reading his comedic drama: his representation of the *Reflections* mirrors his own reading of the Revolution—the suppressed origins and causes kept out of sight. His emplotment of revolutionary history as comedy reflexively complements Burke's antirevolutionary tragedy—both write "out" the "other" French Revolution. More fundamentally, Paine's criticism of Burke's critique corresponds to an assault on Burke's "fictional" language, the origin and locus of counterrevolutionary mystification and suppression. The assault on Burke's language is, in Paine's mind, the original equivalent of the assault on the Bastille—the canonical tyranny of Burke's sources and texts, which Paine, as we will now see, storms victoriously.

6

Revolution and the Canon:
Paine's Critique of the Old Linguistic Order
and the Creation of the Revolutionary Writer

In *Reflections on the Revolution in France*, Burke had contested the contention that kings could be elected and cashiered, quoting a series of canonical texts expressing what he maintained were the fundamental principles of the British constitution. Quoting the Declaration of Right and constitutional principles "forever settled," Burke cited the documentary succession of the monarchy and envisioned both the Crown's stability and the people's rights bound textually together through successive documents reaffirming the same fundamental principles (100). Arguing that the English people, through Parliament, had freely renounced any abstract right to change the constitution, Burke contended that such constitutional principles were "binding" (104). Although Burke acknowledged that "the original compact of state" mutually binds both the king and the people only as long as the "terms" are observed and both continue to exist in "the same body politic" (105), Paine criticized Burke's binding quotations, emphasizing Burke's restrictive reading—a reading Paine insisted bound the English people to the obsolete words of the dead.

Paine had also attacked similar binding declarations during the American Revolution, so there was an intertextual context for his attack on Burke. For instance, in the third *American Crisis* (1777), Paine quoted the first paragraph of the Declaratory Act passed by Parliament in 1766—an Act that gave Parliament the right "*to bind the colonies in all cases whatsoever*" (*CW*, 1:76).[1] Paine rejected Parliament's "right" to bind the American people as "slaves" (*CW*, 1:77; cf. 2:217). Thus, there was already a prior context for Paine's contrast between Burke's restrictive reading and his own liberating writing. In *Rights of Man*, Paine endeavored to liberate the English people from Burke's confining canon—all the authoritative documents of the dead that Burke cites in the *Reflections*. In his contemptuous references to traditional clauses and constitutions, Paine engaged in a revolutionary writing and hence a radical reading that broke the traditional terms of Burke's eighteenth-century "text." But Paine was, in many ways, writing within a radical "tradition" and hence replicating prior radical arguments. In this context, I explore Paine's contention that he was writing in a new revolutionary language and presenting a devastating critique of the Old Order. My focus will be on Paine's representation of his autorevolution against the Old Order. While considering his critique of this Order, I will periodically return to the tradition he writes "out"—in the sense of simultaneous exposure and erasure.

Paine's rebellious reading posits a Manichean contrast between Burke's confining documents and the exhilarating documents of the American and French Revolutions—documents liberating people from preconceived linguistic prisons. Paine, in effect, endeavors to discredit Burke's sources and authorities, the traditional canon, while celebrating and legitimizing the new revolutionary canon consisting of, among other things, the French and American Constitutions and, of course, the writings of Thomas Paine himself. In doing this, he commenced a correspondent linguistic revolt against the Old Order's language and canon. Gerald Bruns's comment on "canonization" is pertinent to Paine's critique of Burke's sources: "The whole point of canonization is to underwrite the authority of the text, not merely with respect to its origin as against competitors in the field . . . but with respect to the present and future in which it will reign or govern as a binding text. . . . [T]he theme of canonization is *power*."[2] In this context, Paine and other revolutionaries were engaged in a revolution against the binding texts of the traditional canon: all the confining sources upholding the traditional political order. But their endeavor to formulate an oppositional canon also constituted a series of restrictive readings, for their rejection of the traditional canon was also an exercise in exclusion, just as their reading of world revolution was also an exercise in power.

For instance, after the forceful rejection of the British "reading" of America and the right "to bind the colonies in all cases whatsoever," Paine published, in 1786, his *Dissertations on Government*, insisting that when people "form themselves into a republic," they "renounce not only the despotic form [of government], but despotic principle." Thus, "the citizens of a republic put it out of their power, that is, they renounce, as detestable, the power of exercising, at any future time any species of despotism over each other" (*CW*, 2:372–73). Paine's quoted authority for this binding declaration is the "pledge and compact" contained in the 1776 Constitution of Pennsylvania (*CW*, 2:373)—a Constitution he had been "instrumental in establishing."[3] Since "despotism" is, among other things, the British form of government, Paine's citation of his binding source is reminiscent of Burke's binding quotation of the British Parliament: both sources "renounce" and hence forbid future generations the right of choosing an alternative form of government. Both readings suggest how the new canon often resembles the old orthodoxy.[4]

There was, however, an earlier context for Paine's critique of Burke's canonical sources: his references to textual tyranny and binding proclamations are in the language of seventeenth-century republican discourse, in the works of, among many others, Locke, Sidney, and Defoe, which flow from earlier debates emanating from the English Civil War. Paine's critique of the British government during the American and French Revolutions is in the recognizable language of seventeenth-century radical Puritans and republicans—a language reproduced in the discourse of the eighteenth-century Commonwealth men. Paine may have, for instance, derived his critique of monarchy in *Common Sense* (1776), a critique reiterated in *Rights of Man*, from John Hall's revolutionary civil war pamphlet, *The Grounds and Reasons of Monarchy Considered* (1650, republished in London in 1771).[5] The English Civil War colors the Anglo-American debate over the French Revolution in the 1790s. Both revolutionary and counterrevolutionary writers continually connect both Revolutions.[6] In the 1790s, the language and issues of the 1640s reverberate in both revolutionary and counterrevolutionary discourse. Although Paine often represents himself as commencing an original revolutionary tradition (contending in various publications that he had made the American and French Revolutions possible), he writes within a tradition of prior revolutionary discourse, in which contemporary canonical wars over privileged texts are a continuation and extension of the canonical wars waged in the seventeenth century.

In the French Revolution, the competitive arguments over origins and sources were also an argument over competitive canons—it was an argument over whose privileged reading of the Revolution would dominate discourse. In his *Address to the Addressers* (1792), Paine's challenge to the British government's threatened prosecution of *Rights of Man* is part of this competitive discourse: governmental prosecution is an attack on the people's right to choose the government they wish; therefore, any jury condemning the book would be denying the people's "rights." Such a jury would hence consist of "traitors," and "their verdict would be null and void" (*CW*, 2:489). In *Rights of Man*, Burke's canonical citations are also "null and void" (*CW*, 1:254). Paine thus rejects as "null and void" any counterrevolutionary reading contradicting his own.

In what became a total textual war, both revolutionary and counterrevolutionary writers focused on the meaning of language that either confirmed or contradicted their respective readings of what words and hence the Revolution really meant. In *Rights of Man*, Paine condemns Burke's traditional reading of the British constitution. To Burke this constitution consisted of the British polity's parts (including the monarchy and the two houses of Parliament) and its reconfirming documents—a traditional understanding and meaning encapsulated in Samuel Johnson's 1755 *Dictionary*. Paine, however, refers to a Constitution in its modern sense of a written document that formulates the fundamental laws and principles by which a government is constituted. Hence, he challenges Burke to produce the nonexistent English constitution. Since Paine is attacking the old linguistic order, he pointedly attacks both Johnson's definition and Johnson himself as a source of authoritative meaning: "From the want of understanding the difference between a constitution and a government, Dr. Johnson, and all writers of his description [i.e., Burke], have always bewildered themselves" (*CW*, 1:382). Paine attacks both Burke and Johnson as linguistic Tories who bind the English people to restrictive, repressive meanings. He hence condemns prescriptive meanings embodied in the prescriptive past, in which "precedent, like a dictionary determines every case" (*CW*, 1:387).

But the rebellion against traditional meaning—meaning that constituted a reading of "reality" and the world—was also an endeavor to rewrite traditional meaning and the way people linguistically understood and experienced the eighteenth-century world. In England, in the 1790s, this endeavor culminated in the new dictionaries published by the radical pamphleteers in the London Corresponding Society. *Rights of Man* and other revolutionary works challenging the old, traditional meanings while simultaneously promoting "new" revolutionary understandings were also, in this sense, disguised ideological dictionaries.

The revolutionaries, like counterrevolutionaries in the 1790s, were supremely logocentric. In 1795, Paine, referring to the Terror, contended that, had "a constitution been established two years ago (as ought to have been done), the violences that have since desolated France and injured the character of the Revolution, would, in my opinion, have been prevented" (*CW*, 2:587). Despite the fact that the French Constitutions (of 1791 and 1793) had been either suspended or disregarded by rival revolutionary cliques, Paine still believed that the power and authority of the right words could have somehow prevented the Terror.[7] In the war over meaning, linguistic antagonists focused their attacks not only on what a respective "enemy" text supposedly said, but the way in which it was said.

In *Rights of Man*, for instance, Paine wages a semantic war on Burke's language, even turning their competitive styles into a semantic statement: Paine sets his "transparent" republican style against Burke's covert, "aristocratic" style. Modern criticism has focused principally on the radical implications of Paine's style, emphasizing it as a new, aggressive attack on the traditional order in a language that is assertively "common." Paine's style thus expresses a radical, democratic denial of the Old Order's privileged domination of political discourse. His attack on the style and content of reactionary language complements the style in which it is made.[8] In this reading, *Rights of Man* seems proto-Wordsworthian, a radical critique of language that is abstract, "artificial," and mystified. In contrast, Paine endeavors to locate man's real rights in the real language of men. I will return to this point later, but it is significant that this is also the way that Paine represents both himself and his language: he refers to *Rights of Man* as "a work, written in a style of thinking and expression different to what had been customary in England" (*CW*, 1:348). He sees his book as an act of political and linguistic revolution.

In his *Address to the Addressers* (1792), he notes that the "overthrow" of Burke's "fallacious book was scarcely the operation of a day," allusively equating the overthrow of the Bastille with Burke's despotic *Reflections*. Indeed, Paine "shook the fabric of political superstition" (*CW*, 2:470, 471). In Paine's formulation, Burke's language is part and parcel of the oppressive order's defeat. In the preface to *Rights of Man* (1791), he makes Burke's language a political, linguistic issue, noting that, since Burke's attack on the Revolution "was to be made in a language little studied, and less understood, in France, and as everything suffers by translation, I promised some of the friends of the Revolution in that country, that whenever Mr. Burke's pamphlet came forth, I would answer it" (*CW*, 1:245). Paine suggests that Burke's language is an old, unread language—a dead language like Latin or Greek, "little studied" except by "gothic" monks and reactionary aristocrats (a redundant phrase in Paine's lexicon). Indeed, there is, I suggest, a linguistic link between Paine's representation of Burke's language and his hostility to classical languages in *The Age of Reason* (1794). In the latter, he argues against the study of these dead languages, since "genius is killed by the barren study of a dead language, and the philosopher is lost in the linguist" (*CW*, 1:492). He sees a conspiracy by "the advocates of the Christian system of faith" to prevent the spread of "progressive knowledge" by promoting, in its place, the obsolete, oppressive knowledge contained in the dead languages they celebrate—narrowing man's mind to the confining boundaries of their restrictive vocabularies (*CW*, 1:493).

In *Rights of Man*, Paine poses as an interpreter of Burke's dead language, revealing the real meaning of his "learned jargon" (*CW*, 1:319). He quotes a passage in the *Reflections* where Burke argues that "abstract rights" can be "metaphysically true" but "morally and politically false":

> The Rights of Man in governments are their advantages; and these are often in balances between differences of good; and in compromises sometimes between *good* and *evil*, and sometimes between *evil* and *evil*. Political reason is a *computing principle*; adding, subtracting, multiplying, and dividing, morally and not metaphysically or mathematically, true moral demonstrations. (*CW*, 1:319, Paine's emphases; the passage is slightly misquoted; see *Reflections*, 153)

Paine translates Burke's words in the following way: "The meaning then, good people, of all this, is, that government is governed by no principle whatever; that it can make evil good, or good evil, just as it pleases. In short, that government is arbitrary power" (*CW*, 1:319). His reductive reading of Burke's text is, of course, an ideological distortion that is characteristic of both revolutionary and counterrevolutionary discourse: in the war over meaning, they both invade an enemy text and impose their own meaning and hence control over the text's semantic territory. In this context, Paine enacts what he accuses Burke of doing in the *Reflections*: "he asserts whatever he pleases" (*CW*, 1:272). Likewise, just as revolutionaries and antirevolutionaries engaged in subversive misreadings of enemy texts, they both objected to enemy attacks and misrepresentations of their own texts. Paine's comment in the second *Forester's Letter* (1776), in which he rails against a Tory distortion of *Common Sense*, is also applicable to his own distortions of the *Reflections*: "The explanations which he hath endeavored to impose on the passages which he hath quoted . . . are such as never existed in the mind of the author, nor can they be drawn from the words themselves" (*CW*, 2:67).

This kind of polemical, ideological reading is also characteristic of political discourse in the seventeenth century. In *The First Treatise of Government* (1689), for instance, John Locke engages in a series of reductive readings of Sir Robert Filmer, whom he often quotes, mocks, and then translates into "plain English," in a plain style retrospectively reminiscent of Paine.[9] Filmer and other seventeenth- and eighteenth-century Tories engage in similar rhetorical strategies, so their antagonistic representations often mirror and replicate each other. In his writings, Paine contends that nothing he has ever read has mattered much to him except his own illuminating works, and his self-fulfilling representation spills over into contentions that his writings constitute the founding texts of the modern world. There is a tendency to accept Paine's self-representations and then read them back into a style that radically reflects its content.[10] It is more fruitful, I suggest, to consider how the French Revolution revivified previous ideological battles (authority and tradition, rebellion and self-representation), energizing them with what seemed to be new life. Like his predecessors, Paine sees an oppressive textual tradition embodied in all that he wars against, including Burke's *Reflections*—a book that immediately achieved canonical status and that Paine opposes with his countercanonical *Rights*.

Since Paine and other revolutionaries questioned and challenged the meaning of the traditional European world, the debate over revolution and counterrevolution was often about the very meaning of that world and the language that sustained it. Revolutionary and counterrevolutionary writers realized or intuited this to varying degrees. They knew that the linguistic, ideological war was an extension of the military war—they sensed that language and ideology are intimately intertwined and that whoever controls language controls not only the terms of "war" but the terms of "reality" itself.

In *Rights of Man*, Paine understood that Burke's *Reflections* was, in part, a counterrevolutionary critique of revolutionary language, and he responded by making Burke's language a thematic issue. Referring to Burke's "unprovoked attack" on the Revolution, he asserts that there "is scarcely an epithet of abuse to be found in the English language, with which Mr. Burke has not loaded the French nation and the National Assembly." In his "copious fury," Burke unleashes a "frenzy of passion" (*CW*, 1:249). Like Wollstonecraft, Paine turns the *Reflections* into a crazed assault on liberty and reason by Burke's rabid language—a language reflecting the "madness" of Burke's enraged mind. Inverting a favorite Enlightenment cliché, Paine represents Burke's book as "darkness attempting to illuminate light" (*CW*, 1:254)—the semantic reversal of the genetic revolutionary Word creating light out of darkness.

In *Rights of Man*, the old linguistic order is the source of dark mystification, imprisoning oppressed minds within the semantic prisons it constructs. The person confined by this language "lives immured within the Bastille of a word" (*CW*, 1:287; the person "immured" is also the aristocrat "confined" by his own language). Paine links political liberation to linguistic liberation, and the aggressive allusion to the Bastille suggests that the old linguistic prison must also be stormed and opened before people can be rescued and liberated. Paine, in effect, presents himself as the principal *vainqueur* of despotism's verbal Bastille, assaulting its semantic structure by opening and revealing its dark secrets.

But he also endeavors to demystify the old language by mocking and degrading its traditional meaning. He contrasts this bogey language with the "rational" language producing the revolutionary events he celebrates, insisting that a psychological, semantic revolution preceded the political revolution (see *CW*, 1:298–99, 340). He distinguishes, throughout, between the "reality" of rational, revolutionary language and the "illusion" of irrational, traditionary language that enslaves and mystifies exploited minds. Thus he literally locates the right of the French nation to make war or peace within the French Constitution, which he contrasts with the fantasy language of England, where "this right is said to reside in a *metaphor*, shown at the Tower for six-pence or a shilling a-piece" (*CW*, 1:283). Paine reduces the British monarchy to the metaphoric "crown" and hence to the illusory language that represents it. Later, he asks mockingly, "But, after all, what is this metaphor called a crown, or rather what is monarchy? . . . Doth the virtue consist in the metaphor, or in the man?" (*CW*, 1:325). In his allusion to the exhibition of the "Crown" Jewels in the Tower of London (a practice begun at the Restoration) as well as the exhibition of animals in the Tower's menagerie (like the Crown, "lions" are also shown in the Tower [*CW*, 1:283; cf. 1:385]), Paine showcases the monarchy as a kind of exotic zoo exhibit—wild and entertaining but irrelevant to the new system of politics. Since the "crown" is only a metaphor, it exists as an obsolete linguistic fiction.

But Paine's allusive imagery additionally has several subversive contexts. For an eighteenth-century Englishman or woman, the Tower still had powerful associations, embodying English history and myth. For the English, the Tower was the repository of records and parchments containing the corporate memory of the nation; it was a royal palace, the site of coronation processions, as well as a prison for famous villains and victims, such as Anne Boleyn, Lady Jane Grey, Thomas More, Richard II, Sir Walter Raleigh, and Guy Fawkes. The "princes in the tower" were supposedly murdered there, as were many of the Protestants celebrated in John Foxe's *Book of Martyrs*. Its bloody history, a vivid conglomeration of fact and fiction, reverberated with sinister legends of dungeons and torture chambers, executions and ghosts—Traitor's gate, the Bloody Tower—all pointing back to its origin with William the Conqueror—the founder of the "Norman Yoke" so abhorred by Paine and other radical Whigs. In addition, the Tower was associated with revolt and resistance—with John Lilburne and the Levellers, Wat Tyler and the Peasant Revolt. More importantly, for Paine, it was the prison and place of execution for kings and queens; hence he metaphorically returns the "crown" and, by extension, the monarchy back to and within its oppressive origins.

Moreover, Paine's reference to the Tower had another intertextual dimension, since it was often equated with the Bastille in revolutionary discourse. In 1792, for instance, François Noël, a French spy in London, reported to Pierre Lebrun, the French Foreign Minister, comparing the situation in England with that of France in 1789, seeing the Tower of London as an English Bastille. British revolutionaries such as John Oswald and John Hurford Stone, Paine's revolutionary associates in Paris (1792–93), saw the same connection.[11] In the *Reflections*, Burke had referred to Louis XVI imprisoned in a "Basti..e for Kings" (165), a phrase Paine probably remembered. In this context, Paine, I suggest, does two paradoxical things: he reduces the monarchy's mystique to a metaphoric crown, and he threatens the monarchy with its old imprisoned history as well as the new rebellious history of the Revolution.

But Paine's critique of the Old Order's language ironically redounds upon himself as well. The "crown," we will remember, is a metaphor, "said" to harbor a fictional "right," shown in the Tower. Paine insists on metaphor, even though the crown is a symbol or, more appropriately, a metonymy. He focuses on the "crown" as a source of privileged reference and then makes a metonymical shift to "Tower," which he reads as metaphor, as the key to the English people's usurped and lost "right." Paine reads figurative levels of language back to a pejorative, historical locus, but this is essentially a case of saying makes it so, since his contrast between the French people's "right" to make war and peace and the English people's usurped "right" (lost in abstract, mystified language) is in the language of the French Constitution, where the "real" right is concretely embodied. "The French Constitution says, that the right of war and peace is in the nation. Where else should it reside but in those who are to pay the expense?" (*CW*, 1:283). In revolutionary France, there is, he suggests, a direct correspondence between language and what it represents. But the Constitution that Paine cites as a canonical source of authority was itself nonexistent in March 1791, when the first part of *Rights of Man* appeared. The 1791 Constitution was not completed by the National Constituent Assembly until 3 September 1791 and was not sanctioned by the king until 13 September, when it legally took effect. Paine's prior representation of the nonexistent English constitution now ironically resembles the nonexistent French constitution.

Paine, in effect, paraphrases a previous law pertaining to war and peace that he has been told will eventually appear in the forthcoming Constitution; thus, like the English people, removed from their rights through interposing levels of language, Paine is removed from an original, misplaced source. Although many parts of the 1791 Constitution had been previously enacted by the National Constituent Assembly, Paine, nevertheless, suggests that he is paraphrasing ("The French Constitution says") a completed Constitution rather than a constitution in the making. He misrepresents both his text and his source by stating that the "right" resides in the taxpaying citizens, those who pay the "expense," and hence that there is a direct correspondence between the people and the language that establishes and affirms their rights. The right to make war and peace was, however, a compromise—passed by the Constituent Assembly (22 May 1790) and rewritten into the 1791 Constitution—where the "right" resides in the people's *representatives* in the National Assembly, although the king (suppressed in Paine's representation) proposes and sanctions formal declarations of war.[12] Like contemporary counterrevolutionaries, Paine valorizes a superior representational language that supposedly corresponds to reality and contrasts it with a demonized language of illusion. The contrast, however, is often based on misreadings, misnamings, and misrepresentations—"strong" misreadings and "misprisions" of enemy texts, authorizing the writer to constitute an authoritative text and source.

Paine's assault on the Crown is, in this context, an act of linguistic regicide that allows him to redefine and relocate the people's rights by first destroying the old, oppressive language. Thus he asserts that when "we speak of the Crown, now, it means nothing," even though the "old terms" are still used "to give an appearance of consequence to empty forms" (*CW*, 1:415). As early as *Common Sense* (1776), Paine had symbolically shattered the king's "image": after proposing an iconoclastic ceremony in which a crown is placed on the Bible to show that "in America the law is king," he observes (since there "ought to be no other" king) that the crown should then "be demolished, and scattered among the people whose right it is" (*CW*, 1:29). Similarly, in 1792, Paine congratulated the National Convention for abolishing the French monarchy, contending that it was not enough to "dethrone an idol; we must also break to pieces the pedestal upon which it rested" (*CW*, 2:541–42). Assailing linguistic idolatry, he associates the destruction of the Old Order's significance with the destruction of its mystifying symbols and language.

In *Rights of Man*, Paine redefines the *monarchy* and commences a linguistic revolution overturning traditional meaning: a *republic* "is a word of a good original," but "the word *monarchy* . . . has a base original significance. It means arbitrary power in an individual person; in the exercise of which, *himself*, and not the *res-publica*, is the object" (*CW*, 1:369; cf. 2:1316). The "original significance" of *monarchy*, however, literally means "the rule of one" in ancient Greek, and Paine's definition actually accords with the Greek *tyrant* (*turanuss*) and the resultant pejorative "tyranny." He redefines *all* monarchy to signify despotism. Although there is something amusing about the monolingual Paine providing revisionist etymological explications, his clever use of *base* turns the monarchy upside down: suddenly its *low* origins and *base* etymology signify a linguistic role reversal by which the Old Order's high prestigious vocabulary "falls." In *An Essay for the Use of New Republicans in Their Opposition to Monarchy* (1792), Paine poses as linguistic demystifier, revealing again the covert meaning of *monarchy*:

> Now, what is monarchy? Whatever effort may have been made to conceal its true nature and to familiarize the people with that hateful term, its real meaning cannot be disguised: it signifies *absolute power vested in a single person*, although that person be a fool, a traitor or a tyrant. (*CW*, 2:542)

Paine's attack on the traditional political order was simultaneously an attack on the language that sustained it. Using the conventional revolutionary distinction between an open and transparent republican language and a covert and opaque "feudal" vocabulary, he redefines traditional meaning in an endeavor to change the semantic understanding of the European world. Like other revolutionaries, his linguistic revolt is part of the political revolt he is waging. The break with the Old Order is simultaneously a breaking of its language.

In *Rights of Man*, his attacks on titles is part of this break, but with this difference: when he is redefining traditional power (the monarchy), he reveals its covert, oppressive meaning, but in attacking titles, he degrades the traditional language by ridiculing it. "Titles," for instance, "are but nicknames, and every nickname a title"—a "thing . . . perfectly harmless in itself," but that, nevertheless, diminishes the person to which it is affixed: "It talks about its fine blue *riband* like a girl, and shows its new *garter* like a child." In Paine's caricature of traditional language, titles linguistically diminish *man*, curtailing him within nicknames that feminize and unman him: "It renders man diminuative in things which are great, and the counterfeit of woman in things which are little" (*CW*, 1:286). Making the aristocratic man diminutive and dainty—"the counterfeit of woman," Paine exploits the conventional distinction between powerful "manly" language and pejorative "feminine" words permeating both revolutionary and counterrevolutionary discourse. Indeed, the passage evokes Wollstonecraft's *The Rights of Men*, where she makes a similar point regarding the language and "nicknames" applied to women (*WMW*, 5:45). Like Wollstonecraft, Paine suggests that the aristocratic order is effetely effeminate. He underscores this connection by associating titles with the "fine blue *riband*" and the "new *garter*"—frivolous "feminine" articles as well as pejorative political allusions: Paine alludes to the famous "blue riband" of the Order of Saint-Esprit that Calonne, the former controller general of French Finances (1783–87) and subsequent counterrevolutionary (1790–95), "enjoyed showing off."[13] Likewise, Paine's reference to the garter alludes to the Order of the Garter, England's highest order of knighthood, commonly known as "the blue ribbon." Paine thus allusively associates what he believes is a doomed European political order with its obsolete origins—the chivalric devotion to absolute monarchy and the childish pride in absurd, archaic symbols.

He additionally contrasts France's new political order with the Old Order's political infantilism: "the elevated mind of France . . . has outgrown the babyclothes of *count* and *duke*, and breeched itself in manhood" (*CW*, 1:286). Indeed, Paine seems to be responding to a passage in the *Reflections*, where Burke laments and equates the loss of old names and titles to a loss of political identity: the "old aristocratic landlords" are "so displumed, degraded, and metamorphosed . . . that we no longer know them. . . . They do not even go by the names of our ancient lords" (*Reflections*, 347; cf. 241). In this context, Paine displumes, degrades, and metamorphoses the political language of the Old Order.

In *Dissertation on the First Principles of Government* (1795), Paine traced titles back to their ominous origins: after the Conquest, the Norman invaders concealed their "real names [robbers] under fictitious ones, which they called titles" (*CW*, 2:582).[14] In *Rights of Man*, Paine focuses on the fictitious nature of these titles and hence on the illusory nature of the political order that legitimizes them: "Through all the vocabulary of Adam, there is no such animal as a duke or a count; neither can we connect any idea to the words." Since these words mean "nothing" because the "animal" is nonexistent, Paine denies that they even have the status of mythological fiction (*CW*, 1:287). In denying the reality of the traditional political vocabulary, Paine and others were denying the reality of the established political order. They were, at the same time, attempting to reinforce the new revolutionary order with their new (and old) revolutionary semantics. Their effort to change the meaning of words and names was an effort to rename and reword "reality"—to relanguage the traditional world. Because Paine and other revolutionaries knew that language is intertwined with our perception of reality, they attempted to purge or exploit the contaminated past supposedly carried in the traditional vocabulary. They believed that revolutionary Adams could begin naming a new world into being, even though they themselves frequently rearticulated the language of radical tradition.

Indeed, just as counterrevolutionaries contended that the Revolution constituted a new "fall" of language, the revolutionaries traced the old corrupt language back to a fallen time.[15] In *Rights of Man*, Paine contrasts the "free, bold, and manly" language of the French National Assembly with the "vassalage" language of the British Parliament—a degraded language originating with the Conquest (*CW*, 1:295–96). He suggests a connection between Norman "slavery" and linguistic slavery—between the fall of the English political world and its language. He contends that the Conquest tinctures English parliamentary thought; even the Glorious Revolution, which Burke celebrates in the *Reflections*, was infected with "this vassalage idea and style of speaking" (*CW*, 1:296). Paine hence suggests that the Norman invaders imposed their language on the conquered English people—a linguistic conquest still resonating in deferential parliamentary addresses and petitions to "their Sovereign Lord the King" (*CW*, 1:326).[16] In contrast to the corrupt, servile language spoken by the British Parliament, the French National Assembly's language "cannot debase itself" (*CW*, 1:295).

In connecting the Conquest with the contamination of the English mind, Paine was reproducing a linguistic myth favored by radical republicans and Puritans in the seventeenth century—a myth reverberating in their rebellious readings of history in the 1640s. In addition, Enlightenment criticism had commenced the radical critique of traditional language and the correspondent thesis that political liberation begins with linguistic liberation (with the demystification of the Old Order's superstitions and illusions). The French Revolution consummated this criticism, reenergizing it with a new and vital relevance, with an electrifying sense that the old regimes were collapsing with their mystified languages.

When he returned to America in 1802, Paine was still obsessed with the linguistic origins of despotism, fearing that it would also infect the American mind, especially since American common law had foolishly inherited and adopted the enslaved legal language of England. In his essay *Constitutional Reform* (1805), he notes that many of the "terms used in courts of law" are in Latin and French: "The Latin terms were brought into Britain by the Romans ... from the first invasion of

[Britain] by Julius Caesar. . . . The French terms were brought by the Normans when they conquered England in 1066 . . . and whose language was French" (*CW*, 2:1003). Paine connects these "terms" with foreign invasion and hence linguistic hegemony and domination. He insists that these terms are used "to *mystify*, by not being generally understood," and hence to legitimize what is actually alien law (*CW*, 2:1004). He suggests that America cannot be completely free until it liberates itself from "the terms" of the old imperialist languages. The term "contempt of court," for instance, is "copied from England . . . and is derived from the Norman Conquest of England, as is shown by the French words, used in England, with which proclamation for silence, 'on pain of imprisonment,' begins, 'Oyez, Oyez, Oyez'" (*CW*, 2:1005). Paine continually traces English linguistic tradition back to the oppressive origin of conquest and slavery.[17]

To read Paine historically is to see him confronting old historical forces (monarchy, priestcraft, and the old confining canon) that he believes the Revolution was finally on the verge of destroying. In England, the Glorious Revolution had become an agreeable fiction that religious and constitutional problems and issues had been "forever settled." But the French Revolution raised the old specters (tyranny, popular democracy, Old Corruption, and regicidal republicans) that had haunted revolutionary and counterrevolutionary imaginations for over a century. J. G. A. Pocock has noted that Paine and other revolutionaries were refighting and reformulating battles waged earlier by Lilburne and Overton, but we still need to reconsider these battles within the macrocosmic Revolution of the 1790s.[18] The radicalness of Paine's critique is not his attack on monarchy—hardly a daunting exercise in the late eighteenth century—but his attack on the House of Commons, the "democratic" part of the constitution. But even this was historically grounded in the radical argument that Parliament was of Norman origin.[19]

Paine's representations of himself engaging in a revolutionary war against the Old Order are as historically central to the radicalness of his discourse as any of his arguments. It is the celebratory bravado with which he represents himself assaulting the Old Order that constitutes his true originality: the writer as *ur*-revolutionary.[20] In the ideological wars of the seventeenth and eighteenth centuries, representation, in its many voluminous senses, is a fundamental issue: each side offers a representation of the political, social "world" and insists that it truly reflects "reality." In the French Revolution, revolutionaries and counterrevolutionaries returned to a mythic version of representation as the direct correspondence of signifier and signified in *their* respective language, politics, and economics. In this context, Paine and Burke were waging a continuing war over whose representation would prevail.

In *The Eighteenth Brumaire of Louis Bonaparte* (1852), Karl Marx noted that revolutionaries tend to repeat old revolutionary representations and hence are ironically implicated in a reactionary tradition: "The beginner who has learned a new language always translates it into his mother tongue."[21] Marx's comment compels us to consider whether Paine had learned a "new language" or was repeating revolutionary tradition. More crucially, I think, Marx's text doubles back upon itself and asks whether revolutionary discourse is profoundly implicated in a system of representation it resists, and whether the acrimonious battles over words and canons are a continuation of a previous ideological cleavage in Western discourse and the correspondent dream of unmediated "reality."

Words, texts, and canons are tissues of history—history that is often ironically ambiguous. The word *revolution*, for instance, conveys a semantic doubleness, for if it now suggests an abrupt break with the past and the initiation of a new beginning, its primary meaning is that of restoration or a return to an original point. In this paradoxical sense, Paine's critique is simultaneously a "revolutionary" assault in the language of revolutionary tradition.

In retrospect, we can see that his political critique, like Burke's, was also a linguistic critique—an ideological dictionary complementing the radical dictionaries being published in France and England.[22] In Paine's revolutionary works, the new victorious language dramatically overthrows and defeats despotism's old oppressive language. In *Rights of Man*, he even insists that a linguistic counterrevolution is impossible: "There does not exist in the compass of language, an arrangement of words to express so much as the means of effecting a counter-revolution" (*CW*, 1:320). In saying this, Paine was wishfully declaring the Revolution's linguistic and hence ideological triumph. His endeavor to rewrite the European world was also an endeavor to expunge and erase the traditional meaning of that world—it was an exercise in and about power, since whoever controlled the "terms" of the revolutionary debate would inevitably dominate the "meaning" of political discourse. In the end, Paine's reading also impinged on the new revolutionary canon and the continuation of a radical reading of the European world—a reading that continues to color our own understanding of what that world and the Revolution represent.

In *Vindiciae Gallicae*, James Mackintosh provided another reading of the Revolution and European history, which he opposed to Burke's *Reflections*. Like Paine, Mackintosh contradicted Burke's canonical readings, making the distinction between revolutionary reality and counterrevolutionary illusion the defining test of "true" history. Contesting Burke's reading of the Glorious Revolution, the confiscation of church land, and the significance of revolutionary representation, Mackintosh produced a vigorously sustained critique of Burke and the world he defended.

7

Mackintosh, Burke, and the French Revolution

James Mackintosh is a writer whose fame and memory proceeds from one work, *Vindiciae Gallicae* (1791), a cerebral response to Burke's *Reflections* and a vigorous defense of the French Revolution. Born in 1765, in Scotland, Mackintosh moved to London in 1788 and, after a brief medical career, supported himself writing articles before deciding to become a lawyer. After Burke's *Reflections* appeared, he concentrated on *Vindiciae Gallicae*, published in April 1791 (there were three rapid editions, the second and third appearing respectively in July and August). Among the Revolution's supporters, *Vindiciae Gallicae* acquired immediate canonical status, and Mackintosh acquired instant celebrity. He was lionized as a writer who had met Burke on his own ground and defeated him. In a letter to Mackintosh (23 December 1796), Burke himself noted that "it is in all hands allowed that you were the most able advocate for the cause which you supported" (*Correspondence*, 9:194). In *Letters from France* (1793), Helen Maria Williams observed that Mackintosh "vied with [Burke] in his own manner, and exhibited his eloquence without [Burke's] disorder"; Mackintosh, a young man of twenty-six, had reversed roles and vanquished the sixty-year-old Burke, whose intemperate emotionalism contrasts with Mackintosh's logical maturity.[1]

In the twentieth century, Mackintosh's book is commonly referred to as the best reply of all of Burke's respondents, the most intelligent and the subtlest. In his influential rhetorical study, James T. Boulton acknowledged that Burke had a superior sense of language but added that Mackintosh had surpassed him in his range of knowledge and classical sources. Since Mackintosh, like Burke, wrote "for the intelligent middle and upper classes," Mackintosh's scholarly *Vindiciae* also contrasts stylistically and thematically with Paine's popular *Rights of Man*.[2]

Given the venerable reputation of *Vindiciae Gallicae*, it is notable that there is scant Mackintosh scholarship and only one modern biography (Patrick O'Leary's). In the nineteenth century, his son, Robert, published a useful but biased two-volume biography, which included passages from Mackintosh's journals.[3] Aside from Patrick O'Leary's biography, Leslie Stephen's entry in *The Dictionary of National Biography*, and some new material by Seamus Deane, Mackintosh has inspired little interest.[4] This is partially because he subsequently denounced the Revolution and was denounced in turn as an "apostate" by many of his former friends and admirers. After his recantation, he was rhetorically trounced by a formidable array of revolutionary sympathizers: Coleridge (who repented his attack after his own apostasy), Godwin, James Stuart Mill, and, most memorably, William Hazlitt in *The Spirit of the Age* (1825). Hazlitt's portrayal of Mackintosh as a pedantic plagiarist, erudite—but frigid and unoriginal—a good conversationalist who never (with the exception of *Vindiciae Gallicae*) succeeded in producing anything substantial, a weak ingrate who was overwhelmed by Burke in a personal meeting (winter 1796) and who, Hazlitt suggests, sold out to the establishment, betraying his friends and admirers—still reverberates in twentieth-century accounts of his life. Among critics of the Revolution (who have chiefly ignored him) and its admirers, there has been little abiding interest. Since my focus is on *Vindiciae Gallicae*, I will briefly discuss Mackintosh's life after its publication before refocusing on the book's principal themes.

With the publication of *Vindiciae Gallicae*, Mackintosh was celebrated by prominent Dissenters and Whig supporters of the Revolution, including Charles James Fox, Richard Brinsley Sheridan, William Godwin, Thomas Christie, and the Holland House circle. Mackintosh was also popular in France and seems to have collaborated with other British radicals. In October 1791, the prospectus for the new *Cercle Social* monthly, *La Chronique du Mois*, announced that Mackintosh, Paine, John Oswald, and others would contribute "to eradicate the ancient prejudices which have so long sown discord and rivalry" between France and England.[5] As if to underscore his revolutionary endorsement, Mackintosh, in 1792, became a member of the Society for Constitutional Information (attacked by Burke in the *Reflections*) and honorary secretary of the Friends of the People. Both organizations supported electoral reform and the French Revolution. He also published a letter to William Pitt (1792) accusing him of misrepresenting the Revolution and its British supporters and of trying to disguise his "apostasy"—the word that would be repeatedly hurled at Mackintosh after his recantation.

Fluent in French, Mackintosh traveled to Paris in April 1792, where he had a brief stay. On 26 August, the National Assembly declared him an honorary French citizen, and although it was reported that he had rejected a proposal that he be elected to the French National Convention, he did accept, on his return to England, a certificate of honorary citizenship from the French minister in London.[6] During this time, he was close to Thomas Christie, a fellow Scotsman, whose *Letters on the Revolution of France* appeared on 7 May 1792, shortly after the *Vindiciae*. In late 1792, a British spy-watcher reported on the subversive activities of the British in Paris: "There are . . . 8 or 10 . . . English or Scotch who work with the Jacobins and in great measure conduct their present manoeuvres. I understand these gentlemen at present are employed in writing a justification of democracy and an invective against monarchy which is to be printed at Paris, and dispersed through England and Ireland." The last one mentioned is "Mackintosh who wrote against Burke."[7]

On 1 December 1792, the *Manchester Herald* provided an account of a banquet in Paris (18 November), in which Mackintosh was toasted (in absentia with Sheridan and Fox) by British revolutionaries who extolled them for "propagating the doctrines of the French Revolution." A previous account of the banquet had appeared in the Parisian *Moniteur*, although this account was subsequently denied by John Oswald, a prominent expatriated British radical, in Jacques-Pierre Brissot de Warville's *Patriote français*: "We did not drink those toasts, nor could we do so without falling into signal absurdity. Met to celebrate the rapid progress of the eternal principles of liberty and equality, how could we think of cringing to the heads or tools of any party? How could we pronounce the name of Fox, Sheridan, and Mackintosh?"[8] In other words, the Jacobin Oswald suggested that Mackintosh and the others were compromised Whigs rather than true revolutionaries. Erdman accepts Oswald's denial, even though British radicals in Paris tried to protect revolutionary admirers in England by underplaying or disguising the latter's radical sympathies.[9] Whatever the case, the ensuing uproar (Burke played up the banquet in Parliament) illustrated again the controversial nature of the Revolution. Although Mackintosh probably never engaged in "subversive" activities, his hostility to the British constitution, in *Vindiciae Gallicae*, was as vigorous as Paine's in *Rights of Man*.

Mackintosh continued studying law and writing articles; in 1795 he was called to the bar at Lincoln's Inn. He was, however, having private doubts about the Revolution, doubts that had begun in April 1792 with the murder of Théobald Dillon, a commander of French troops in Belgium. In 1794 Mackintosh ended a moderate critique of Burke and the war against France with an "unbiased tribute of our admiration and thanks to that illustrious statesman":

> The friend of what we must call the better days of Mr. Burke,—whose great talents have been devoted to the cause of liberty and mankind,—who . . . is requited for the calumnies of his enemies, the desertion of his friends, and the ingratitude of his country, by the approbation of his own conscience, and by a well-grounded expectation of the gratitude and reverence of posterity. (*Works*, 465)

Interestingly, the last two clauses crystallized the terms by which Mackintosh would subsequently see himself as well.

In two anonymous reviews (November and December 1796) of Burke's *Letters on a Regicide Peace*, Mackintosh first indicated publicly that he was having second thoughts about the Revolution. He nevertheless refuted Burke's arguments while praising his style. Patrick O'Leary suggests that Burke found out who the author was and let it be known that he respected his talent. Acting on this hint, Mackintosh then wrote to Burke.[10] His son, Robert, suggests that Burke read the anonymous reviews and, correctly surmising that they were written by "his old opponent," contacted Mackintosh and conveyed "flattering expressions," thus opening a correspondence.[11] Robert Mackintosh's account is, however, dubious. On 22 December 1796, James Mackintosh wrote a letter to Burke, admitting that he had been wrong about the Revolution and requesting a subsequent meeting. Telling Burke that he had always admired and studied him, but self-consciously absolving himself of flattery ("I am too proud to flatter even you"), Mackintosh then proceeds to his real point:

> For a time indeed seduced by the love of what I thought liberty, I ventured to oppose your Opinions without ever ceasing to venerate your character. . . . I cannot say (and you would despise me if I dissembled) that I can even now assent to all your opinions on the present politics of Europe. But I can with truth affirm that I subscribe to your general Principles; that I consider them as the only solid foundation both of political Science and of political prudence; that I differ solely as to some applications of them which appear to my poor understanding not entirely accordant to the scheme and Spirit of your System; and that above all if the fatal necessity should arise (which God forbid) there is no Man in England more resolutely determined to Spill the last drop of his blood in defense of the laws and Constitution of our Forefathers. (193)

Since Mackintosh had attacked both "the laws and Constitution" in the *Vindiciae*, as well as Burke himself, his letter is a belated apology and recantation. He then requests a brief meeting and is confident that Burke will not "punish my presumption as to expose me to the sneers of those who are less generous by disclosing any Circumstances of this address" (*Correspondence*, 9:192–94). Mackintosh, in essence, wanted a private understanding with Burke without a public acknowledgment that he had, in effect, recanted his vindication of the French Revolution. Understandably sensitive to the "sneers" of antirevolutionaries and also, one supposes, the sneers of friends who had applauded his attack on Burke, Mackintosh wanted Burke's esteem, but he also wanted to retain his liberal reputation.

Burke had been aware of Mackintosh since 1791, when the *Vindiciae* was published. In a letter to his friend French Laurence (2 August 1791), Burke had "not read or even seen Mackintosh," but his son, Richard, had reported that the *Vindiciae* was "Paine at bottom" (*Correspondence*, 6:312). It is possible that Burke subsequently read the *Vindiciae*, since he complained in the House of Commons (December 1792) that Mackintosh and others had misrepresented him by quoting him out of context. [12]

Burke replied to Mackintosh in a letter dated 23 December 1796. Still devastated by the death of his son, Richard, he dictated a gracious letter, complimenting Mackintosh for having the strength to recognize his errors and inviting him to Beaconsfield (*Correspondence*, 9:194–95). On the same day, Burke wrote his friend French Laurence, enclosing Mackintosh's letter and asking Laurence to accompany Mackintosh to Beaconsfield, noting that the letter came as a surprise, that it was extremely "civil," and that encouragement should be given "to all converts of Talents" (*Correspondence*, 9:197). By 25 December, however, he had second thoughts about Mackintosh's conversion, as he informed Laurence in another letter:

> I forgot to speak to you about Mackintosh's supposed conversion. I suspect by his Letter that it does not extend beyond the interior politicks of this Island, but that, with regard to France and many other Countries He remains as franc a Jacobin as ever. This conversion is none at all, but we must nurse up these nothings and think these negative advantages as we can have them. (*Correspondence*, 9:204–5)

Mackintosh's conversion was, however, privately sincere, and he met Burke at Beaconsfield sometime shortly after. Although we do not know Burke's response to the meeting, Robert Mackintosh says that the visit lasted several days and that his father considered it "as amongst the most interesting of his life." He then reproduces a passage from Thomas Green's *Diary of a Lover of Literature* (published in 1810), in which

Green refers to a conversation he had with Mackintosh on 13 June 1799: "[Mackintosh] passed the last Christmas [of Burke's life] with Burke at Beaconsfield, and described, in glowing terms, the astonishing effusions of his mind in conversation." Green then cites some of the memorable things Burke had said, including this extravagant compliment: "You, Mr. Mackintosh, are in vigorous manhood; your intellect is in the freshest prime, and you are a powerful writer; you shall be the faithful knight of the romance; the brightness of your sword will flash destruction on the filthy [revolutionary] progeny."[13] Whether Mackintosh actually told Green that Burke had said this or whether Green invented the anecdote, it evokes Burke's atypical "chivalry is gone" lament, reversing it with Mackintosh in the inherited role of the new defender of Christendom, drawing his swordly pen to annihilate "the filthy progeny." It comes across like someone imagining what Burke sounds like. It does suggest, however, another Burkean identification and is, in this context, poetically true, even though Mackintosh would not draw his sword for another three years.

Mackintosh did not announce his public repudiation of the Revolution until 1800, continuing to play it safe (a liberal Whig disappointed with the Revolution's course), and hence having it both ways. He apparently did not tell his liberal friends about his meeting with Burke or his doubts about the Revolution, since his public repudiation and "apostasy" came as a startling surprise.

The first public expression of his disenchantment appeared in the thirty-nine lectures on *The Law of Nature and Nations* that he gave at Lincoln's Inn from February to June 1799 and then repeated with variations in 1800. Quoting from a draft of the preliminary lecture, Robert Mackintosh notes that his father was defending "the very foundations of society against the fury of a wild enthusiasm, which usurped the name of reason."[14] In January 1799, a preliminary Introduction to the lectures was published, in which Mackintosh referred to "promulgaters of absurd and monstrous doctrines," "shallow metaphysicians," and "savage desolators"—phrases William Godwin believed were personally directed at him, as he informed Mackintosh in an angry but civil letter on 27 January 1799.[15]

Since the publication of the *Vindiciae*, Godwin and Mackintosh had been political friends. On 22 April 1796, for instance, Godwin had invited Mackintosh to a dinner party, which had included Mary Wollstonecraft. Godwin was thus hurt when he became convinced that his friend was alluding to him in the January publication. After receiving Godwin's angry letter, Mackintosh wrote him, satisfying Godwin that, despite their political differences, Godwin was not the target of the phrases. In the forthcoming lectures, Mackintosh promised to distinguish between individuals and their ideas.[16] Godwin attended several of the lectures but stopped after he became convinced again that Mackintosh's comments were aimed at him. Although Patrick O'Leary believes Godwin read too much between the lines, Hazlitt's account, in *The Spirit of the Age*, is the one remembered by posterity: "Poor Godwin, who had come, in the *bonhommie* and candour of his nature, to hear what new light had broken in upon his old friend, was obliged to quit the field, and slunk away after an exulting taunt thrown out at 'such fanciful chimeras as a golden mountain or a perfect man.'"[17]

A year later, Mackintosh was ready to renounce the Revolution publicly. In a letter to his friend George Moore (6 January 1800), Mackintosh admires Moore's "honesty and magnanimity, in openly professing [his] conversion":

> I think I shall have the courage to imitate you. I have too long submitted to mean and evasive compromises. It is my intention, in this winter's lectures, to profess publicly and unequivocally, that I abhor, abjure, and forever renounce the French revolution, with all its sanguinary history, its abominable principles, and for ever execrable leaders. I hope I shall be able to wipe off the disgrace of having been once betrayed into an approbation of that conspiracy against God and man, the greatest scourge of the world, and the chief stain upon human annals.[18]

Although he had begun his antirevolutionary critique the year before, Mackintosh apparently felt guilty for compromising (for not going public with his personal abjuration) and hoped to imitate Moore's "conversion"—the word Burke had used in his letter (25 December 1796) to French Laurence. James T. Boulton finds it striking that Mackintosh's intention to "profess" and publicly "abhor, abjure, and forever renounce" the Revolution is in the "terminology traditionally associated with the recantation of a heretic." Indeed, it resonates as a kind of expiatory exorcism.[19] Other references to "conversion" and "apostasy" permeating the discourse of the revolutionary era suggest that the Revolution was a transforming event—a crusade of conformable faith.

Mackintosh's conversion was sincere, but he paid a price for his apostasy and "betrayal." He was shunned by many of his former friends and vilified as an "apostate black" like Judas, who at least hanged himself in shame, as Charles Lamb put it in his 1801 epigram, "To Sir James Mackintosh."[20] Mackintosh felt increasingly isolated, although he still had many admirers. In a letter to his friend Richard Sharp

(9 December 1804), he reviewed his career and justified the consistency of his principles. Referring to the lectures at Lincoln's Inn, he conceded that he had overreacted: "I rebounded from my original opinions too far towards the opposite extreme. I was carried too far by anxiety to atone for my former errors. In opposing revolutionary principles, the natural heat of controversy led to excess." He refers to his letter as a "confession."[21]

Mackintosh's letter is crucial for understanding how he saw himself. In 1803 he had been awarded the recordership of Bombay and knighted, providing his enemies with the charge that he had sold out to the powerful, explaining his defection and apostasy. Leslie Stephen, in *The Dictionary of National Biography*, notes that Mackintosh, who had a wife and five daughters, had been anxious to study and write as well as save money: the recordership and a subsequent pension, would, he hoped, make him independent for life (vol. 12, 619). Writing to Sharp from Bombay, Mackintosh self-consciously reviews his life and opinions, contending that he had been consistent with his principles, that the Revolution had changed, not he. Emphasizing that he was young, inexperienced, and naive when he wrote the *Vindiciae* and that he was consequently overwhelmed by a revolution that he had misjudged, Mackintosh believes he was correspondingly misrepresented by partisan factions. Thus, to revolutionary partisans and superficial observers, it appeared that he was an apostate: "But in the changing state of human affairs, the man who is constant will be sometimes thought inconstant to his politics." People who knew him, however, witnessed his "sufferings" as the Revolution degenerated—a process that had started in April 1792.

Obsessed with the Revolution, he realized that his opinions were slowly evolving, but his attachment to the progressive "party" inhibited him from professing his reassessment: "Like most other men, I was not very fond of owning that I had been mistaken, or of contradicting the opinion of those with whom I lived, or of adopting any part of the doctrines of those, whom I had been accustomed to oppose." Because he had erred in waiting too long to break openly with the Revolution, he could be accused of "gross economic motives." He had, however, a clear conscience that he had not intentionally deviated from his fixed beliefs and principles. In the lectures at Lincoln's Inn, he had overcompensated by moving "towards the opposite extreme"—a normal frailty of human nature. Since Napoleon had reestablished "monarchical despotism in France," he perceives the danger of being drawn again to "the democratic [i.e., radical] side of the centre"—a "deviation" he hopes to avoid by seeking a middle point between both extremes. He is, however, confident that he remains the same humane Whig he always was and that he has never fallen "into any slavish principles—any doctrines adverse to the free exercise of reason, to the liberty and the improvement of Mankind." Absolving himself of apostasy, he acknowledges that he had made mistakes and had provided his enemies with the opportunity to misrepresent his motives.[22] Still smarting from his fall from progressive grace, he sees himself as an enlightened Whig whose "deviation" was, nevertheless, consistent with his true principles.

There is, additionally, another dimension of the letter that is pertinent. Commentators have routinely noted the Burkean resonances of his writing subsequent to his meeting with Burke in 1796. Seamus Deane formulates Mackintosh's dilemma in the following way:

> Mackintosh could never free himself from Burke's thrall, even though he knew that his reputation for consistency depended on distinguishing between Burke's liberal position and his own. But he had absorbed Burke more deeply and was closer to him than he seemed to realize. To admit as much was to accept that he had in fact repudiated the ideas of *Vindiciae Gallicae*. He had recanted, but he could not wholly admit this to himself, partly because it had become such a public issue and the subject of so much hostile comment.[23]

This is perceptive, but there are moments (as in the letter to Sharp) when Mackintosh realizes his "closeness" to Burke and identifies with him.

Like the Irish Burke, the Scottish Mackintosh was an outsider who had achieved fame through industry and talent. More pertinently, in contending that he was accused of inconstancy when, in fact, he was consistently true to his principles, he reformulates the political argument of Burke, who was also accused of inconstancy and apostasy, of selling out to the powerful. In the *Reflections* and *Appeal from the New to the Old Whigs* (1791), Burke had also maintained that he was a true Whig whose principles and life were "consistent." Moreover, Mackintosh's reference to his own *deviation* was a key word with which he had twitted Burke in the *Vindiciae* and that Burke had used in the *Reflections* with reference to the temporary deviation of the Glorious Revolution—a subject I will return to later.

Mackintosh continued to identify with Burke and had planned, but never wrote, his biography. In a letter to Burke's old friend William Windham (16 December 1806), Mackintosh notes the "difficulty which the common thinker must feel, in tracing the links of the chain that holds together Mr. Burke's life, as a consistent whole.[24] . . . Every man can see dissimilarity of actions or words; but not many can see how necessarily that may arise, from that very unchangeable identity of principle."[25]

It is also possible that part of the appeal of living in India was, for Mackintosh, the fact that India had been a major priority—some would say an obsession—for Burke. When Mackintosh returned to England and became a member of the House of Commons, he took part in an inquiry into the East India Company's affairs, just as Burke had done several decades before. If Wollstonecraft, at points, ambivalently identifies with Burke, Mackintosh's identifications are more direct. He reads his postrevolutionary life through Burke's.

Mackintosh, however, did not consistently keep the same principles he had always had. Much of his postrevolutionary writing contextually repudiated principles he had celebrated in *Vindiciae Gallicae*. This constituted a series of revisions of both his life and opinions, a subject to which I will also recur. For now, three examples will suffice. Throughout the *Vindiciae*, Mackintosh stresses the return to first principles and the mathematical simplicity of rules and laws that make government fundamentally uncomplicated and simple. In the *Discourse on the Law of Nature and Nations* (1799), replete with Burkean sentiments and sentences, some directly inspired by the *Reflections*,[26] Mackintosh wants "to avoid that which appears to me to have been the constant source of political error: I mean the attempt to give an air of system, of simplicity, and of rigorous demonstration, to subjects which do not admit it" (*Works*, 40; cf. 41). In the *Vindiciae*, Mackintosh had severely criticized the reactionary deficiencies of the English constitution (*Works*, 444, 454–56), but in the *Discourse*, he criticizes the "imperfect representations" of some "celebrated writers" who have written about it, while he intends to show, instead, how it had helped make England a "fortunate island" (*Works*, 39). Since he was, in effect, abjuring positions he had previously maintained, his revisions are yet another contextual confession of "political error."

This is even clearer in his "Speech in Defense of Jean Peltier" (21 February 1803), in which Mackintosh scorns the "leaders" of the French Revolution who "twelve years ago" scorned the British constitution and maintained that the English were not free. These leaders are now "compelled to pay a reluctant homage to the justice of English principles" (*Works*, 494). "Twelve years ago" was, of course, the year 1791—the year the *Vindiciae* was published and in which Mackintosh scorned the British constitution and also suggested that the English were not free. His subsequent revisions are also a contextual homage to principles he once repudiated.

The remainder of Mackintosh's life can be dealt with briefly. He returned from India to England in 1812 and became a member of the House of Commons. He spent most of the winter of 1814 in Paris and subsequently published "On the State of France in 1815," arguing that the Revolution had destroyed aristocratic abuses and improved French agriculture but that it had produced other abuses. Its support was made possible by a complicitous incorporation of the French people into revolutionary crimes, as when "the division of the confiscated lands among the peasantry" provided "that body an interest and a pride in the maintenance of the order or disorder which that Revolution had produced." Because so many people had a vested interest in the Revolution, even after the Terror, it was necessary to have a "government established on Revolutionary foundations," and Napoleon provided this, appealing again to the French people's national pride and material interests. The militarization of society intensified, and the Revolution continued producing "diametrically opposite effects" (*Works*, 466–72). This was Mackintosh's last public assessment of the Revolution's legacy. Seamus Deane, however, has provided a new private assessment by Mackintosh, based on the Mackintosh Papers in the British Library.

Reading a series of French memoirs dealing with the old regime, Mackintosh had concluded that sexual libertinism during the Regency of the duke of Orléans (1715–23) had "so sapped the French character that it became vulnerable to the infection of dangerous ideas."[27] This was also, mutatis mutandis, a standard interpretation of the Revolution's supporters: degenerate Bourbon concupiscence and the corrupt orgiastic court as a cause of the Old Order's collapse. Mackintosh, however, "was convinced that sexual purity was a necessary condition for the attainment of liberty. This was the reason for the French failure after 1789. Lasciviousness denied liberty; French society had become decadent, and the Revolution was the culmination of that decay, not a recuperation from it."[28]

In Parliament, Mackintosh vigorously opposed the government's repressive legislation ("Seditious Meetings Bill," the "Alien Bill," and the "Six Acts") and worked for penal reform and the abolition of capital punishment. He also labored for electoral reform, supporting the second reading of the Reform Bill in 1831. He was a moderate Whig, primarily interested in expanding the middle-class franchise.[29] Mackintosh's other writings (historical and philosophical surveys and sketches) have elicited little interest, although some, especially *Review of the Causes of the Revolution of 1688*, bear on his rewriting of the French Revolution and *Vindiciae Gallicae*.

After accidentally swallowing a chicken bone (February 1832), Mackintosh declined in health and died on 30 May 1832—at the conclusion of the last great political change in England. Primarily remembered for *Vindiciae Gallicae*, which "lives parasitically off the great name of Burke,"[30] Mackintosh elicited an intellectual admiration and interest in the 1790s, the substance of which we now need to recover. I begin this recovery by considering the principal themes of Mackintosh's *Vindiciae*: the Glorious Revolution, landed property, and revolutionary representation. Since Mackintosh confronts Burke on his own intellectual and cultural grounds, he claims a superior understanding and reading of the histories energizing Burke's *Reflections*, specifically as they impinge on the history of the French Revolution. Just as Burke orchestrates a variety of texts and contexts, which he positions and reads against the Revolution, Mackintosh marshals a variety of histories and "backgrounds" that he reads contratextually against Burke's *Reflections*. The intersecting lines of this intertextual war constitute the backgrounds and histories with which both Burke and Mackintosh frame their respective histories.

8

Mackintosh, Burke,
and the Glorious Revolution

In the 1790s, the Glorious Revolution was another context incorporated into the revolutionary debate, illustrating that issues of the 1640s, 80s, and 90s were being refought and reread into the war over the French Revolution's meaning. For almost a hundred years, in England, there had been a fictional consensus about the Glorious Revolution's significance: James II had conspired to install forcibly the Catholic religion and absolute monarchy ("popery" and "slavery") but was providentially defeated by William III, the great Protestant "deliverer," who rallied the country, including Whigs and Tories, and helped reinstate the ancient liberties and rights of free Englishmen. [1]

The principal exceptions to the consensual celebration of 1688 were those Jacobites who connected the Revolution with the English Civil War and the deposition of a legitimate king.[2] By the 1770s, however, Dissenters who no longer feared the restoration of a Stuart, Catholic monarchy began to suggest gingerly that perhaps the Revolution had not gone far enough. The French Revolution subsequently provided England's dissidents the opportunity to attack the terms of the Revolution Settlement, specifically the reaffirmation of the Test and Corporation Acts that deprived them of rights and freedom.

By the 1790s, the attack on the Revolution Settlement was simultaneously an attack on the British constitution and English electoral representation—all three dismissed as "fictions" in dissident discourse. To orthodox Whigs and Tories, on the other hand, the Dissenters' subversive identification with the French Revolution meant that church and state were again in danger and that Dissenters were trying to repeat the regicidal republican revolution of the 1640s—this time with success.[3]

Likewise, some, not all, English dissidents envisioned the French Revolution as the Good Old Cause triumphant. To many English the astonishing revolution in France seemed to resemble either the Puritan or Glorious Revolutions, and hence they translated the French Revolution into English discourse. The French Revolution was defined in context of its similarities or differences with the two English revolutions. Referring to the Glorious Revolution, J. G. A. Pocock notes that, to English disputants such as Burke and Price, "the news of the French Revolution necessitated a renewed discussion of the English Revolution a century before":

> They debated whether the revolution in France was legitimated by the revolution which had occurred in England, and whether the revolution in England should be interpreted in such a way as would render it a precursor of the revolution in France. These theses and anti-theses for interpreting what had happened in 1688 were well in place by the time of the events of 1789, and even when it was agreed—as it was on all sides—that the revolution in France was an event of a different order of magnitude from any which had occurred in modern history, these arguments furnished the norms, the parameters and the contexts in and by which such a statement could be made.[4]

In *A Discourse on the Love of our Country* (4 November 1789), Richard Price, in a sermon supposedly praising the Glorious Revolution, criticized it for not going far enough, suggesting that the ongoing French Revolution was bringing to fruition what the Glorious Revolution had inadequately completed—a democratic monarchy, true religious freedom, and real electoral representation. That Price and others were hyping the Revolution as a universal event was not missed by Burke who protested that radicals were deliberately blurring England's bloodless revolution with France's sanguinary rebellion.

Burke, in the *Reflections*, rearticulated the conventional reading of the Revolution as one that had crucially preserved English freedoms and the legitimacy of English succession: the "deviation" into the Hanoverian line was necessary and just. Rejecting Price's contention that the Revolution had established the right of the English people to choose their own governors, to cashier them for misconduct, and to frame their own government, Burke quoted the controversial binding declaration in which the 1689 Parliament submitted themselves, "their heirs and posterities forever" to defend a limited monarchy and to renounce any notion of monarchical election (104). Although Burke overstated his case and was compelled to clarify his reading of the Revolution in *Appeal from the New to the Old Whigs* (1791), he was, in the *Reflections*, providing the orthodox reading of 1688:

Most Whigs evaded any description of 1688 as an act of rebellion and deposition, justified by violations of the Original Contract by James II and justifying
the making of a new contract with William; equally unwilling to describe
1688 as a conquest, they labored instead, though uneasily, to give credibility
to the implausible idea of James II's abdication . . . to disguise *de facto*
power."[5]

Burke proceeded to connect Price and other of the French Revolution's
admirers with the republican regicides of the 1640s, ironically reinscribing the Jacobitical critique of the Glorious Revolution a century before.

Burke's respondents, in turn, replied with a radical revision of the
1688 Revolution. In *The Rights of Men*, Wollstonecraft reaffirmed the
resemblance between the English and French Revolutions that Burke
denied—affixing the adjective "glorious" with reference to French
revolutionary events (*WMW*, 5:46, 48, 114). In contrast, Paine, in *Rights
of Man*, responded to Burke's glorification of the Revolution by
representing it as one more tragic event in England's oppressive history:
the English Parliament had brought a foreign king and line to the English
throne and had tried to "bind" posterity forever. The Revolution was
infected with the language of the Norman Conquest—explaining the
sycophantic addresses to the king from a servile Parliament (*CW*, 1:296,
321). Paine noted that he "happened to be in England at the celebration
of the centenary of the Revolution of 1688" and that the "characters of
William and Mary have always appeared to [him] detestable; the one
seeking to destroy his uncle, and the other her father, to get possession of
power themselves" (*CW*, 1:419 n. 37). The *Bill of Rights* (the statutory
form of the *Declaration of Rights* extolled by Burke as one of the
Revolution's achievements) was "a bill of wrongs, and of insult" (*CW*,
1:383; cf. 2:495). "With the Revolution of 1688 . . . came the destructive
system of continental intrigues," foreign wars, and taxes. The English
Revolution had already been "eclipsed" by the "luminous revolutions of
America and France" (*CW*, 1:417, 296; see also 253 and 349). Thus there
were three principal ways radical discourse represented the revolutions of
1688 and 1789: the French Revolution establishing a British-style
constitution and bill of rights—a familiar and recognizable revolution
resembling the English one; a revolution fulfilling what had been
tragically unconsummated in the English Revolution; and a true
revolution in no way resembling the reactionary revolution of 1688. In
contrast to other advocates of the French Revolution, Mackintosh
incorporated all three representations into his critique of the Glorious
Revolution and, in contesting Burke's reading, was able to sustain a
radical critique of the world Burke defended.

I

Burke had, of course, made the Glorious Revolution a central issue by contrasting it with the barbaric revolution in France. Mackintosh, in turn, responded by comparing both revolutions and hence linking them subversively together. In the *Reflections,* Burke contended that the members of the French Estates General, particularly the Third Estate, had neither the legitimate right nor the constitutional authority to transform themselves into a National Assembly and to change the French constitution (230–31, 275–76). Since they had no pertinent instructions from the voters to do these things, their actions were illegal and the National Assembly was illegitimate. In response, Mackintosh drew a striking parallel between the English Convention of 1689 and the National Assembly of 1789. The Convention had been called by William III after James II had fled to France, and was hence technically illegal, since only the English king was empowered to issue writs and to convoke Parliament. The Convention was, in fact, an extra-legal body with no legal or constitutional authority. On 23 February 1689 the Convention, in an effort to enhance its legal status, transformed itself by statute into the Convention Parliament.[6] Quoting Burke against himself (in *Reflections*, 276), Mackintosh refers to Burke's beloved Glorious Revolution and the English Convention:

> [The deputies to the English Convention, like members of the French National Assembly,] "did not hold the authority they exercised under any constitutional law of the state." They were not even legally elected, as, it must be confessed, was the case of the French Assembly. . . . Had the people of England given instructions to the members of that Convention, its ultimate measures would probably have departed as much from those instructions as the French Assembly have deviated from those of their constituents, and the public acquiescence in the deviation would, in all likelihood, have been the same.

Conceding that the people of England would not have initially instructed their deputies to depose James II, Mackintosh argues that this, nevertheless, happened subsequently because, as the Revolution progressed, the people sanctioned the Convention's enlightened deposition of the king: "The formality of instructions was indeed wanting in England [and France], but the change of popular sentiment" ratified what both assemblies had done (*Works*, 414). Indeed, Mackintosh specifically connects the 1689 Convention with the 1789 National Assembly by noting that, in 1789, the Estates General was "transformed by . . . events into a National Convention, and vested with powers to organize a government" (*Works*, 414).

The Convention of 1689 had been self-conscious about its legal status, especially since its members had deposed a legal king, strengthened Parliament, and made succession legally impossible for a future Catholic heir. They were thus extraordinarily anxious to underplay the radicalness of their actions, sanctifying them with a language of traditional "custom" and the English constitution.

Mackintosh, in contrast, repeatedly fleshes out the radicalness of the Convention, connecting its "deviation" (the thematic word Burke uses to refer to the Convention's constitutional erasure of strict Stuart succession) with France's "deviation." By stressing the resemblance between both revolutions, Mackintosh emphasizes that Burke cannot criticize the French Revolution without criticizing the Glorious Revolution for effecting similar radical, unauthorized changes. He turns Burke's distinction between both revolutions into a striking similarity. He also subverts Burke's criterion of constitutional legality by arguing that, in a national crisis, the people ultimately legitimize de facto revolutions by subsequently supporting the changes of their representatives. Mackintosh thus opposes de facto revolutionary reality to Burke's de jure fiction. Moreover, by insisting that the "people" ultimately sanctioned the legitimacy of both revolutions, Mackintosh smuggles in a democratic point to subvert Burke's authoritative, aristocratic Parliament, which, in the name of the people, decided constitutional issues "forever" (*Works*, 414, 417, 422, 448, 453).

Since there is a resemblance between both revolutionary Conventions, and since the events of 1789 can be read into 1689 and vice versa, Mackintosh hypothetically suggests that a "general Convention of the British empire" might assemble the great lawyers of the empire, just as the National Assembly had gathered France's great lawyers into one body: France's revolutionary body is implicitly a model for a future revolutionary body in the United Kingdom (*Works*, 425).

In the last section of the *Vindiciae*, he focuses again on the English Convention to vindicate the National Assembly. In the *Reflections*, Burke had argued that the deputies elected to the 1688 Convention "acted by the ancient organized states in the shape of their old organization"—the constitutional corporate bodies of Lords and Commons, the traditional English Parliament (106). Mackintosh replies by truncating Burke's words and then adding an effective clincher:

"They acted," says Mr. Burke, "by their ancient states"—they did not. Were the Peers, and the Members of a dissolved House of Commons, with the Lord Mayor of London, & convoked by a summons of the Prince of Orange, the Parliament of England?—no: they were neither lawfully elected, nor lawfully assembled. But they affected a semblance of a Parliament in their Convention, and a semblance of hereditary right in their election. The subsequent Act of Parliament is nugatory [i.e., the statute by which the Convention turned itself into a Parliament]; for as the Legislature derived its whole existence and authority from the Convention, it could not return more than it received, and could not, therefore, legalise the acts of the body which created it. If they were not previously legal, the Parliament itself was without legal authority, and could therefore give no legal sanction. (*Works*, 453)

Because Burke had skirted the strict legality of the Convention, arguing instead that the deputies acted constitutionally by organizing and acting in their traditional corporate bodies (*Reflections*, 106), Mackintosh emphasizes the illegality of their acts and hence seems to win the argument. In eighteenth-century England, however, constitutional authority was more important than legal authority with reference to parliamentary representation.[7] The former stressed the balanced British constitution and the restraints on government power. Hence, Burke, in the *Reflections*, emphasizes the constitutional reformation, i.e., the transformation of an absolute monarchy into a constitutional monarchy, a regeneration effected through the two houses of Parliament—the unimpaired, balanced parts of the constitution (106).

Since the 1770s and the American Revolution, however, legal discourse was slowly replacing constitutional discourse, even though both, as in Burke's and Mackintosh's arguments, are about legitimacy. Although Mackintosh's point seems more familiar to us, Burke's constitutional argument would seem even more familiar to most eighteenth-century readers. Mackintosh had, however, previously contended that de jure arguments are senseless, since de facto revolutionary acts ultimately legitimize what is initially and technically illegal, an argument similar to one Burke has also made (with qualifications) in the *Reflections* (276). Mackintosh, as we will see, employs different and often contradictory arguments to win his war with Burke. He appropriates the various, available languages of eighteenth-century discourse, and, like Burke, he occasionally becomes entangled in discordant resemblances. Mackintosh's legal brief against the illegal 1688 Convention, for instance, reinscribes and hence resembles the discredited Jacobite argument against the same "illegal" Convention. But by arguing legality instead of constitutionality, he changes the sense of Burke's argument, contextualizing it with this fundamental contradiction: if the Convention Parliament was not legal, then Burke has no legal or moral grounds for criticizing the illegal National Assembly; if, however, the Convention was legal, then Richard Price and others were correct in concluding "that abused power is revocable, and that corrupt governments ought to be reformed" (*Works*, 453). If the latter is the case, Burke is confronted with a repetitive resemblance that he strenuously denied—the radical correspondence between both revolutions.

In the *Reflections,* Burke, like the members of the English Convention, prefers to emphasize instead the constitutional argument. Like the Convention's members, he openly places a "veil" over some of its actions, underplaying any suggestion of radical alteration, arguing that the change from strict succession to the Hanoverian line was a temporary "deviation," a grave necessity justified by the attempt of James II to subvert the constitution by changing the state religion and installing an absolute monarchy.[8] This slight and temporary "deviation," a word (in its various forms) Burke uses repeatedly (*Reflections*, 101, 105–7, 166, 203, 285), is mocked and parodied by Mackintosh: had the electors of England given instructions to the members of the Convention, the latter's "ultimate measures would probably have departed as much from those instructions as the French Assembly have deviated from those of their constituents" (*Works*, 414). Although English representatives to the Convention had not received instructions from the voters while French electors to the Estates General had, Mackintosh equates a hypothetical English deviation with the French fact: the French representatives had deviated from their instructions, just as the English would have if they had had instructions from which to deviate. Both the English deviation from strict succession and the French deviation from strict instructions resulted in revolutions subsequently ratified by both peoples. Mackintosh underscores again the similarities he believes Burke hides: Burke's conservative Glorious Revolution resembles the "radical" French Revolution; both revolutions deviated into correspondent freedom. The English Convention "deviated from the succession to destroy the prejudice of its sanctity," just as the National Assembly abolished titles, providing "a mortal blow to the slavish prejudices which unfitted their country for freedom" (*Works*, 417).

Contrasting both revolutions, Burke had argued that the French had broken the constitutional links uniting France with England: the similarity of constitutional corporate orders and constitutional custom. France had consequently deviated from both its own history and the available example of English history—England's Revolution and balanced constitution. Mackintosh, in contrast, turns Burke's emphasis on digressive difference into a correspondent swerve into truth and freedom. Instead of rupturing history, the French had reproduced the

English example: their revolution had also created a constitutional monarchy, a bill of rights, and a democratically elected assembly (*Works*, 417, 438–39). In addition, both revolutions produced the same ideological, class divisions: an enlightened "monied interest" and a reactionary landed aristocracy. Thus, Tories had said the same horrible things about the Glorious Revolution that counterrevolutionaries were saying about the French Revolution (*Works*, 426).

Earlier, however, Mackintosh had argued that the French had surpassed the English by perfecting enlightened principles, since "all improvements of human life have been *deviations* from experience": human improvement ensues from the discovery and perfection of new principles rather than from the repetitive imitation of old principles (*Works*, 422). In deviating from customary experience (e.g., England's and France's ancient constitutions), the French create a better Constitution, consequently improving the life of the French people. By discussing "principles," Mackintosh allusively refers to "Revolution principles" that had been established by the Revolution of 1688, albeit contradicted by the Convention Parliament. Mackintosh's allusive argument is that the French perfected revolution principles by historically realizing them: they put into practice and perfected theoretical principles that the Whig oligarchy had suppressed in England. Since he underscores *deviations* ("all improvements of human life have been *deviations* from experience"), evoking Burke and 1689, it is also possible that he evokes the very principles that Burke denied but that Price, in the *Discourse*, maintained the Glorious Revolution had established: "the right to chuse our own governors, to cashier them for misconduct, and to frame a government for ourselves."[9] Mackintosh subsequently re-evokes Price ("The Revolution of 1688 is confessed to have established principles . . . the right of the people to revoke abused power, to frame the government, and bestow the crown" [*Works*, 448]), so that if Price's principles are allusively in Mackintosh's previous subtext (*Works*, 422), as I believe they are, Mackintosh is suggesting that the French have indeed improved and "perfect[ed]" English Revolution "principles" (*Works*, 422).[10]

Since Mackintosh argues that the British Parliament had deviated from the principles of the Glorious Revolution (*Works*, 449 ff.) and that the Glorious Revolution was restrictively admirable only for establishing principles that were tragically not put into practice—that the Convention's timid Whigs did not complete the nation's regeneration and that the Revolution did not go far enough (*Works*, 448, 450, 454–56)— his real target is the Revolution he deceptively praises.

II

Mackintosh hence begins a subversive turn, for his comparisons of both revolutions are ultimately outstanding differences: the distinction between a defective English Revolution that had deviated from its principles and the French Revolution that had consummated Revolution principles. He does this by directly contesting Burke's allusions to the 1689 Convention Parliament. In the *Reflections*, Burke had contended that appeals to fictional natural rights are absurd, since real concrete rights are realized only in real historical societies. For Burke, these rights are settled by "convention" and if "civil society be the offspring of convention, that convention must be its law. That convention must limit and modify all the descriptions of constitution which are formed under it." If this is true, then "how can any man claim, under the conventions of civil society, rights which do not so much as suppose its existence? Rights which are absolutely repugnant to it?" (150). In contrast to a fictional state of nature and fictional natural rights, Burke allusively refers to real rights "settled by convention"—the celebrated *Declaration of Rights* established by a committee of the Convention Parliament and given statute form in the 1689 *Bill of Rights*, the *Declaration,* Burke has previously referred to as forever settling the constitution's "fundamental principles": "It is called 'An act for declaring the rights and liberties of the subject, and for *settling* the *succession* of the crown.' You will observe that these rights and the succession are declared in one body, and bound indissolubly together" (*Reflections*, 100). Burke refers his English audience to "real" rights settled by the "real" Revolution, and his repetition of *convention* (150) also plays on its meaning as a contract (see Samuel Johnson, 1755 *Dictionary, convention,* def. 3)—a charter of traditional rights concretely reaffirmed by the Convention that historically reasserted them in their statutory form. Likewise, the verb "settled" evokes the debates in the Convention Parliament and declarations to "settle forever" English rights and liberties,[11] as well as the Act of Settlement (1701), limiting the crown to Protestant members of the house of Hanover and establishing the independence of the law courts. As modern readers, we often miss these allusions to the Glorious Revolution as they are played out in the competitive discourses of the 1790s.

Two more examples from the *Reflections* are illustrative. Referring to Price's contention that the 1688 Revolution had established the right of the people to choose and cashier their governors and frame their own government, Burke disdainfully dismisses "this new, and hitherto unheard-of bill of rights," allusively conjuring up the "real" Bill of Rights—where, of course, Price's erroneous rights cannot be found. Similarly, the Glorious Revolution was "a parent of settlement" (i.e., the 1701 Act of Settlement) and not, like the French Revolution, "a nursery of future revolutions" (112).[12] The imagery intensifies Burke's distinction, for the allusion to the Revolution "*settlement*" of 1701, a word having a legal significance, as Samuel Johnson notes, "the act of giving possession by legal sanction" (1755 *Dictionary*, def. 2), makes the English Revolution the legitimate "parent" of a legal settlement and the French Revolution a "nursery" for illegitimate revolutions. The shift from the stable, singular "settlement" to the plural "revolutions" emphasizes the contrast between the former's legitimate stability and the latter's promiscuous proliferation of bastard revolutions.

Mackintosh, in the *Vindiciae*, recognizes all of Burke's puns and allusions to 1689 in the language of *convention* and *settlement*. He thus employs two strategies: having established a resemblance between both revolutions, a resemblance Burke would vigorously reject, he then subverts Burke's Glorious Revolution by allusively suggesting that it was really a reactionary revolution and not a true (French) revolution. After citing and referring to Burke's arguments against natural rights and his references to "convention" (*Works*, 436–37), Mackintosh observes that, contra Burke, all men have an equal political right "to a share in their own government" and that the "slightest deviation" from [this right] legitimizes every tyranny":

> If the only criterion of governments be the supposed convention which forms them, all are equally legitimate; for the only interpreter of the convention is the usage of the government, which is thus preposterously made its own standard. (*Works*, 437)

Mackintosh subverts the language by which Burke defends and celebrates the English Revolution ("slightest deviation," "convention") by suggesting that both Burke and the Convention renounced forever the right of people to share equally in their government and that this was the euphemistic "deviation" that legitimized governmental "tyranny." Mackintosh, in effect, delegitimizes Burke's legitimate Revolution with Burke's "illegitimate" language. Recognizing that Burke's allusive language evokes, for the English, the traditional meaning of 1689 and that the contested meaning of 1789 centers on Burke's conventional reading, Mackintosh responds in the same code but reverses its significance. Thus, if the "only criterion of governments be the supposed convention that forms them" (read the spurious Convention Parliament,

Burke's supposititious "parent" of legitimate English government), then all "governments" (like Burke's pejorative, plural French "revolutions") "formed" by (such a false convention and parent) are "equally legitimate," since "the only interpreter of the convention is the usage of the government, which is thus preposterously made its own standard" (*Works*, 437). Mackintosh subversively rereads Burke's reading of the Glorious Revolution with Burke's incriminatory language.

Since this language is, Mackintosh suggests, illegitimately self-conceiving—a conventional language based on the Convention of 1688—its usage and its Burkean interpreters reductively make it the promiscuous parent of all reactionary governments claiming the same convention and criterion. Rebelling against the commonplace language of 1689 and the Revolution's traditional meaning, Mackintosh's subversive response illustrates again the priority of linguistic revolution to those engaged in positively representing the French Revolution. The revolutionaries were waging a war against traditional historical readings and the traditional languages that sustained them.

Mackintosh also alludes to 1689 by arguing that natural rights are politically essential to protect the majority of the people from the privileged few: "the moment that the slightest infraction of these rights is permitted through motives of *convenience* [the reference is to *Reflections*, 150], the bulwark of all upright politics is lost. If a small convenience will justify a little infraction, a greater will expiate a bolder violation: the Rubicon is passed" (*Works*, 438). Specifically, the "small convenience" that constitutes "the slightest infraction" of natural rights, a "little infraction" producing "a bolder violation" alludes to Burke's "small and temporary deviation" from succession as well as his sarcastic reference to Richard Price's "little deviation from prudence" (*Reflections*, 101, 166), which Mackintosh reapplies to "the deviations of the magistrate"—deviations "checked" in France by the 1789 *Declaration of the Rights of Man and Citizen* (*Works*, 438). Since England is implicitly the oppressive government he alludes to, his reference to the French *Declaration of Rights* evokes the English *Declaration of Rights* (and its statuary complement), suggesting the systematic deviation from established rights and principles into aberrant, oppressive government—England's fatal inheritance. Mackintosh thus revises Burke's "deviations" to signify all the egregious deviations from natural truth and justice—all the deviations characterizing both the counterrevolutionary world and the oxymoronic "Glorious Revolution."

Mackintosh, in essence, reinscribes paradoxical ways of reading the Glorious Revolution: the Glorious Revolution as a revolution manquée, a tragically suppressed (French) revolution that had created those radical, albeit aborted, rights that Richard Price insisted on (ironically evoking Burke's a "revolution not made but prevented"), or a reactionary revolution, the parent of successive illegitimate, oppressive governments. Mackintosh, as we will see, ultimately distinguishes the real (suppressed) revolution from Burke's pretender revolution: a revolution sabotaged by Old (Burkean) Whigs who had betrayed revolution principles. Mackintosh additionally conjures up radical specters that Burke had tried to exorcise, oscillating between different readings to win his public, intertextual war. Consider, for instance, Burke's rearticulation of the Convention's representation of the Revolution in the *Reflections*: its members had emphatically insisted that the deviation from succession was in no way meant by the Parliament and the English people to establish a precedent making the English throne elective. "They knew that a doubtful title of succession would but too much resemble an election" and that an election would destroy the nation (*Reflections*, 103). But it is precisely this resemblance that Mackintosh emphasizes. In Mackintosh's reading, William of Orange could only have been made king in three ways: as a conqueror, as a successor in strict line of succession, or as an elected monarch. Since the first conjures up William the Conqueror and the illegitimate Norman Yoke and the second is palpably false, this leaves only election as the legitimate source of William's kingship.[13]

The English should thus exult that its monarchy is not one of conquest and that, since "the supreme magistracy of England" is "a direct emanation from the sovereignty of the people, it is as legitimate in its origin as in its administration" (*Works*, 448). Mackintosh cleverly makes the monarch the effective "emanation" of the people and election the criterion of the monarch's legitimacy (reformulating a point that Price had made in the *Discourse* and that Burke had attacked in the *Reflections*, 96–99); otherwise, "the whole history of our Revolution must be a legend" (*Works*, 449):

> The fact was shortly, that the Prince of Orange was elected King of England, in contempt of claims; not only of the exiled monarch and his son, but of the Princesses Mary and Anne, the undisputed progeny of James [cf. Burke, the English king "holds" his crown "in contempt of the choice of the Revolution Society.... His Majesty's heirs and successors ... will come to the crown with the same contempt of their choice with which his Majesty has succeeded to that he wears" (98–99)]. The title of William III was then clearly not by succession.... There remains only election.... It is futile to urge, that the Convention deviated only slightly from the order of succession. The deviation was slight, but the principle was destroyed.[14] (Ibid.)

Mackintosh blurs virtual representation with direct democracy ("the supreme magistracy of England" is "a direct emanation from the sovereignty of the people"), for the English people did not choose or elect William III—this was done by members of the Convention Parliament, who anxiously insisted that they had only ratified the succession the former king himself had legitimized by violating the constitution and leaving the throne vacant. Mackintosh, in contrast, suggests that members of the Convention ratified the original will of the people and, in doing *this*, rather than what they said they did, the Convention was a representative body directly representing the people's will. Since a contemporary English reader would realize that the monarchy was not elective and that all the people were not represented in Parliament, Mackintosh's argument also suggests that the Convention Parliament and all subsequent Parliaments had deviated from both revolution principles and the people's "sovereignty" (*Works*, 448).

In the *Reflections,* Burke had recognized that the strategy of Price and other dissidents was to base the legitimacy of the Revolution Settlement on the principle of popular choice in order to delegitimize it:

> The Revolution which is resorted to for a title, on their system, wants a title itself. The Revolution is built, according to their theory, upon a basis not more solid than our present formalities, as it was made by an [H]ouse of [L]ords not representing any one but themselves; and by an [H]ouse of [C]ommons exactly such as the present, that is, as they term it, by a mere 'shadow and mockery' of representation. (147)

Mackintosh reemploys this strategy by pretending that *only* the popular choice of the people legitimized the Revolution, while subverting this pretense by continually suggesting the obvious: the Revolution was not directly sanctioned by the people. Either the 1688 Revolution and England's settled constitution were and are the result of popular choice or the entire structure and settlement was and is illegitimate—this is the false dilemma by which Mackintosh and other dissidents were attempting to reradicalize English discourse. Mackintosh's discussion of the Revolution is really about democratic representation and the antithetical meanings of the English and French Revolutions. Rebelling against Burke's canonical reading of the former and what that implies for the latter, he continues to attack Burke's "reactionary" reading of history by linking Burke to reactionary members of the Convention Parliament.

III

In the *Vindiciae*, Mackintosh quotes the second earl of Clarendon, a royalist member of the 1689 Convention, who had opposed the phrase "breaking the original contract," with reference to James II, a phrase eventually appearing in the "Abdication" and "Vacancy" resolution passed by the House of Commons on 28 January 1689: "I may say thus much in general, that this breaking the original contract is a language that has not long been used in this place; nor known in any of our law books, or Public Records. It is sprung up but as taken from some late authors, and those none the best received!" Mackintosh then supplies the identifying clincher: "This language one might have supposed to be that of Mr. Burke. It is not his; it is that of a Jacobite Lord of the 17th century" (*Works*, 452). In the *Reflections*, Burke had quoted Hugh Peter, chaplain to the New Model Army, executed in 1660 for abetting the murder of Charles I, to underscore a linguistic, ideological resemblance between Peter and Richard Price (157–58), and Mackintosh employs a similar strategy. The quoted language does sound like Burke complaining about "unheard-of" language, and the association of Burke with the Jacobite Clarendon (who remained a nonjuror all his life) is perhaps meant to recall the latter's (and Burke's) ideological pedigree— Clarendon's father, Edward Hyde, first earl of Clarendon, advisor to Charles I and author of the anti-Puritan *History of the Rebellion* (a canonical classic in the eighteenth century) and associated (unfairly) with the infamous Clarendon Code (1661–65)—the four legislative acts directed against Dissenters—acts attacked by Mackintosh in the *Vindiciae* (*Works*, 455). That Clarendon had to spend the latter part of his life in exile and that his son was imprisoned, for a while, by Queen Mary for supposedly plotting against the king may also play in Mackintosh's allusive, ironic scenario.

But while Clarendon's language sounds like Burke, Burke (unlike Clarendon) subscribed to the Convention's assertion that James II had broken "the original contract": in the *Reflections* (113) and particularly in *An Appeal from the New to the Old Whigs* (1791), Burke embraced the language that the Convention had adopted but Clarendon had rejected. Aside, however, from Burke sounding like Clarendon, Mackintosh, I believe, is making another point. In the 1689 Convention, conservative Whigs and Tories initially objected to the Lockean phrase "original contract" (pushed by the radical Whigs), but they were overruled by the majority.[15] The Tories' subsequent acceptance was a part of a compromise that resulted in the consensual fiction of constitutional problems "forever settled"—the dominant representation of the Revolution that Mackintosh attacks. Whigs and Tories finally agreed that the language of an original contract referred to the traditional coronation oath by which the monarch pledged to retain the rights of the people.

Mackintosh was a student of the Glorious Revolution and later wrote extensively about it. He undoubtedly knew much of the above; in the *Vindiciae*, he shows his familiarity with the issues by quoting from the Convention debates. His citation from Clarendon suggests that Burke was secretly uncomfortable with the Revolution's real history and language, for "original contract" would certainly conjure up Locke and radical writers who were employing "natural rights" and contract theories in the seventeenth and eighteenth centuries.[16] Mackintosh, in effect, employs a new-historicist critique of Burke's Revolution to focus on the real significance of the Convention's and Burke's anxious language, rewriting both within the context of the French Revolution.

He hence emphasizes what he sees as the central contradiction in the Revolution Settlement: the Convention's language simultaneously disguised and belied the eventful significance of 1689. Citing Burke's citations from the Convention to prove that its members employed a disingenuous language—"'a politic, well wrought veil'" (*Works*, 449; *Reflections*, 103), Mackintosh notes the consequential clash "between the conduct and the language of the [1689] Revolutionists"—a language that "Mr. Burke has availed himself." The "conduct" of the Convention's members was "manly and systematic," but "their language was conciliating and equivocal" (cf. *Reflections,* 200: men's "conduct" is "the only language that rarely lies"). The Convention made the crown elective and responsive to Parliament but disguised the fact in the conservative language that contradicted and belied it. The Convention's fictional language deviated from revolutionary reality.

Similarly, Mackintosh attacks the Act of Settlement (1701), the Act limiting the crown to Protestant members of the House of Hanover, and formulates this hypothetical Jacobite response:

> Had a Jacobite been permitted freedom of speech in the Parliaments of William III he might thus have arraigned the Act of Settlement: "Is the language of your statutes to be at eternal war with truth? Not long ago you profaned the forms of devotion by a thanksgiving, which either means nothing, or insinuates a lie: you thank Heaven for the preservation of a King and Queen [William and Mary] on the throne of their ancestors—an expression which either alluded only to their descent, which was frivolous [i.e., slight, of no legitimate significance], or insinuated their hereditary right, which was false. With the same contempt for consistency and truth, we are this day called to settle the crown of England on a princess of Germany

[Sophia, Dowager Electress of Hanover], 'because' [the conjunction Burke used in quoting the Act of Settlement: "because, says the act, 'the most excellent Princess Sophia . . . *Reflections*, 109] she is the granddaughter of James the First. If that be, as the phraseology insinuates, the true sole reason of the choice, consistency demands that the words after 'excellent' should be omitted, and in their place be inserted 'Victor Amadeus, Duke of Savoy, married to the daughter of the most excellent Princess Henrietta, late Duchess of Orleans, daughter of our late Sovereign Lord Charles I of glorious memory [cf. *Reflections*, 109 and Burke's quotation of Parliament]. Do homage to royalty in your actions, or abjure it in your words: avow the grounds of your conduct, and your manliness will be respected by those who detest your rebellion." (*Works*, 449)

The Act of Settlement had declared that if Anne, Mary's sister, died without direct heirs, the throne would pass to the Electress Sophia of Hanover and her issue. Sophia died in 1714, two months before the death of Anne, and so the throne went to her son, George I, and the Hanover line. By formulating a Jacobite critique of the Revolution Settlement and its language, Mackintosh again questions the legitimacy of the entire Revolution, forcing Burke to concede either that the fiction of successive Stuart legitimacy was a lie (Sophia to be made queen because "she is the granddaughter of James the First") or to admit that the Hanoverian Germans were *elected* over the more legitimate Stuarts—the posterity of Henrietta of Orleans (1644–70), the youngest daughter of Charles I. Mackintosh's Jacobite point is that the granddaughter of Charles I (Anna d' Orleans, wife of Victor Amadeus II) is more legitimate than Sophia, granddaughter of James I, because she is closer in the Stuart line of succession. Since many British contemporaries accepted the claim that William was not made king but coregent with Mary and hence the legitimacy of their title did not lie in election but in her relationship to her father, Mackintosh emphasizes "Victor Amadeus," whose name should follow "excellent," stressing that it was William of Orange, rather than the strictly legitimate Mary, who actually ruled—contradicting again the fiction of strict Stuart succession. He revises Burke's quotation of the Act of Settlement (*Reflections*, 109), ignoring Burke's point that the Revolution and the Act constituted a slight deviation into the Stuart Protestant line: Henrietta and her daughter, Anna, were Catholics. By referring to Victor Amadeus, the "Jacobitical" Mackintosh suggests a legitimate William-and-Mary monarchical arrangement superior to the actual illegitimate settlement and the deviant Hanover line. By arguing for a strict Stuart succession, he exposes Burke and the Parliament's language to be a diversionary lie: the deviation actually constituted the election of a foreign, Protestant line. The real deviation, he suggests, was the deviation from truth: Parliament's election of the monarchy and the correspondent discrepancy between language and reality.

Likewise, Mackintosh imagines a response that John Somers (an important member of the 1689 Convention, chairman of the committee drafting the Declaration of Rights) would have made to Burke had he been alive in 1791: "You deny us the only praise we can claim [i.e., the "principles" Price insisted the Revolution established]; and the only merit you allow us is in the sacrifices we were compelled to make to prejudice and ignorance. Your glory is our shame" (*Works*, 454). Again having it both ways (Burke contradicted by a reactionary Jacobite and the "progressive" Whig, who was one of his heroes: in the *Reflections*, Burke "never desire[d] to be thought a better Whig than Lord Somers" [104]), Mackintosh speaks through the imaginary Somers who, if he had been alive, supposedly would have rebuked Burke in light of the progressive eighteenth century and the glorious French Revolution. What Burke glories in (the deceptive language disguising true principles) was actually Whig shame—a belated Whig confession of the fiction foisted on the English people. This real Whig confession is also Mackintosh's original prosopopoeial fiction.

He had earlier noted that, in the Convention debates, the Whigs wanted the throne to be declared "vacant" and that the Tories nervously asked if *vacant* really meant "elective." He quotes Sir John Maynard, the plain-speaking Whig, who replied with republican frankness that whenever the throne is vacant, it is elective (*Works*, 452). Mackintosh emphasizes the radical language that reflected reality but was subsequently contradicted by the Convention's illusory language. By citing the Convention's "true" radical language, he reinscribes the suppressed radical tradition Burke ignores. Indeed, he replicates the criticism of the radicals, such as the Whig pamphleteer who, in 1693, referred specifically "to the 'wretched inventions' of words and the 'hypocrisy'" displayed in the resolution passed by the Convention Parliament, criticizing "the use of 'desertion and abdication, instead of plain English forfeiture, which the Scotch Parliament honestly called forefaulting.'"[17]

Mackintosh, likewise, refers to the "absurd debates in the Convention about the palliative phrases of 'abdicate,' 'desert' . . . which were better cut short by the Parliament of Scotland, when they used the correct and manly expression, that James II had 'forfeited the throne'" (*Works*, 451). The contrast is again between a real revolutionary language corresponding to what really happened (the people's right to choose their king) and the timid revolutionaries who "perpetually" belied "their political conduct by their legal phraseology" (*Works*, 451). Mackintosh contextually places Burke in the tradition of the Convention Whigs whose language contradicts reality, while retextualizing himself within the tradition of the Convention radicals, whose language reflects reality.

Mackintosh's critique of the dominant canonical representation of the Revolution was thus a critique of the conservative Whig canon: the Convention's lawyers who "appealed to usage, precedents, authorities, and statutes" and whose language re-echoes in the derivative language of "the Cokes, the Blackstones, and the Burkes" (*Works*, 450)—all comprise a reactionary, linguistic pedigree and canon. These canonical Whigs fabricate a fiction of genealogical freedom, freedoms prescriptively possessed by English ancestors and passed down to posterity. Opposing natural rights to prescriptive precedent, Mackintosh insists that "it is not because we *have been* free, but because we *have a right* to be free, that we ought to demand freedom" (*Works*, 450). As Gary Wills reminds us, "Freedom, for Whigs in the eighteenth century, always had a pedigree. It was a child of paper, a *chartered* liberty."[18] Mackintosh sees the Whiggish words of Burke, Blackstone, and Coke as a pedigree of mystification; he wants to "hear no more of this ignoble and ignominious pedigree of freedom" (*Works*, 450). He provides, in its place, his own pedigree of freedom, a "Democratic Canon"—the republican writers (Buchanan, Harrington, Milton, Locke, Fletcher, and Sidney) who "contributed to the diffusion of political light" (see *Works*, 450–52).

In the *Reflections,* Burke had referred to Coke "and the great men who follow[ed] him to Blackstone"—great lawyers "industrious to prove the pedigree of our liberties"—and he had cited Parliament's statutory pledge (a pledge taken from a "preceding act of Queen Elizabeth") to "submit [in the name of the people] themselves, *their heirs, and posterities for ever,*" faithfully promising to defend the English monarchy and "the *limitation* of the crown" (103–4). Mackintosh cites Burke's citation up to "for ever" and concludes on this triumphant note:

Here is the triumph of Mr. Burke—a solemn abdication and renunciation of [the] right to change the monarch or the constitution! His triumph is increased by this statutory abolition of the rights of men being copied from a similar profession of eternal allegiance made by the Parliament of Elizabeth. It is difficult to conceive anything more preposterous. In the very act of exercising a right which their ancestors had abdicated in their name, they abdicate the same right in the name of their posterity. To increase the ridicule of this legislative farce, they impose an irrevocable law on their posterity, in the precise words of that law irrevocably imposed on them by their ancestors, at the moment when they are violating it. The Parliament of Elizabeth submit themselves and their posterity for ever: the Convention of 1688 spurn the submission for themselves, but re-enact it for their posterity. And after such a glaring inconsistency, this language of statutory adulation is seriously and triumphantly brought forward as "the unerring oracles of Revolution policy." (*Works*, 452–53; see *Reflections*, 101)

Mackintosh himself, however, engages in some linguistic mystification. To make Burke's citation seem especially absurd, he does not cite "the *limitation* of the crown" that Burke underscores, but he is, nevertheless, rhetorically triumphant, recreating his own angry version of Burke's rebuke of Price's "triumph" in the *Discourse*, as well as Burke's critique of revolutionary imitators. [19] His allusion to the Convention's language of "abdication" coheres with its supposed attempt to speak for the people and renounce their rights forever. His sarcastic reference to the Convention's statute "copied" from a previous Parliament of Elizabeth is in context of repetitive, reactionary imitation and hence in sham Whig words copied by Coke, Blackstone, Burke, and other canonical Whigs who impose the fiction of a paper pedigree actually signifying parliamentary (i.e., "conventional") slavery. Mackintosh again stresses the contradiction between language and reality: the Elizabethan Parliament linguistically binds posterity forever, a pact that "posterity" (the 1689 Convention) breaks in "the very act" (cf. *Reflections*, 102) of binding future posterity with the same words. The Convention repeats the *convention* of the Elizabethan Parliament, copying its words, recopied by Burke and others, in repetitive, contradictory citations of fictional, canonical contradiction. Mackintosh's sarcastic references to (sham) Whig appeals "to usage" and "reverence for usage" (*Works*, 450, 452) register his revolt against the prescriptive semantics of the old Whig order. For Mackintosh, these conventional words have no force because they do not correspond to reality. His linguistic critique, like Paine's, is simultaneously an endeavor to reconstitute the real rights and language of man.

Since the Convention's obfuscatory language suppressed the real facts of the Revolution, becoming the dominant canonical discourse of Burke and other Whig pretenders, Mackintosh, echoing Price, ultimately contends that the Revolution did not go far enough. The 1688 "ancestors" punished the Jacobite "usurper without ameliorating the government; and they proscribed usurpations without correcting their source"—the corrupt English government (*Works*, 454). By arguing that the government needed to be reformed, Mackintosh is really arguing that the constitution needed to be changed (à la the French)—precisely what English radicals had expected to happen in 1689. In 1689–90, there were "all kinds of 'constitutional' grievances and propositions—changes in the suffrage, adoption of the secret ballot, abolition of a standing army, creation of an independent judiciary"—in short, the old radical agenda.[20] The seventeenth-century Commonwealth men believed that the Convention should have become a constituent parliament and should have radically changed the constitution. They were bitterly disappointed and felt betrayed when this did not happen.[21]

Likewise, Mackintosh promotes the old radical agenda and attacks the English constitution as well as the Revolution's sanction of "pretended toleration" for Dissenters (*Works*, 422, 423, 431, 441, 443, 445, 446). But he also ironically reinscribes his own redounding critique of Burke and the 1689 Convention's language—language that disguised the radicalness of the Revolution. He re-presents the radical agenda in the disguised language of reform:

> We desire to avert revolution by reform; subversion by correction.[22] We admonish our governors to reform, while they retain the force to reform with dignity and security; and we conjure them not to await the moment, which will infallibly arrive, when they shall be obliged to supplicate the people, whom they oppress and despise, for the slenderest pittance of their present powers" (*Works*, 456).

Reform or face (a French) revolution, Mackintosh tells England's governors, but Mackintosh's reforms are a French revolution: complete religious and press freedom, the abolition of "oppressive" taxes, reform of the judiciary and the corrupt English constitution, because "no branch of the legislature represents the people" (*Works*, 456)—all the reforms, in short, that British radicals believed the French were instituting. His warning to English governors to reform or face the people's wrath evokes Price on the people's right to choose and cashier their governors: Revolution principles that had been suppressed in England but reasserted in the revolution of 1789—the true revolution of the *Vindiciae*.

Mackintosh's critique of the canonical English Revolution reveals a conspiratorial consensus, a fictional imposture imposed by Whigs and Tories: a prescriptive monosemantic revolution that had forever settled constitutional issues, a supposititious revolution that had been substituted for the real revolution, suggestively just as the Old Pretender had been supposedly smuggled into Saint James Palace in a warming pan. His contention that England's revolutionary ancestors disguised the Revolution's radicalness in a language of tradition and prescriptive rights (a critique originating in the 1690s) additionally coincides with that of many modern scholars, most notably Lois G. Schwoerer.[23] In repeating the "suppressed" radical agenda, Mackintosh was challenging the convention of the Revolution expressed by Burke and the Whig forefathers, who, in his view, had betrayed the true revolution. For Mackintosh, the sham Whig Revolution of 1689 was metaphorically the Jacobite pretender contradicted and exposed by the legitimate Revolution of 1789. His representation of the Revolution as a reactionary, "pretender" revolution prefigured the revisionist readings of the Revolution by some twentieth-century historians[24]—a re-vision of the Revolution that had begun with Paine, Price, and other of Mackintosh's canonical contemporaries.

In the *Reflections*, Burke had openly quoted how the Convention underplayed any suggestion of the Revolution's radicalness by covering the latter with a linguistic veil (103). Burke's reading of the Revolution was one of original intent: English ancestors really intended that the Revolution be understood as it really was—a restoration of a legitimate monarchy and ancient rights. They went out of their way to (author)ize the original, canonical reading; they actually did do what they said. Their (and Burke's) anxiety that the Revolution would be misrepresented by radicals had a resounding context in the 1790s, when the French Revolution reenergized the old radical agenda with an original sense of newness.

Mackintosh subsequently revised his revision of the Revolution, reinscribing Burke's reading into his defense of the English constitution and the Revolution Settlement. He continually revised himself in an effort to rewrite what he had written in the *Vindiciae*. In his letter to George Moore (6 January 1800), he announced his intention "to profess publicly and unequivocally, that I abhor, abjure and forever renounce the French Revolution, with all its sanguinary history, its abominable principles, and for ever execrable leaders."[25] Perhaps Moore recognized that Mackintosh was repeating the language of the oath included in the *Declaration of Rights*, an oath by which the English subject swore to "'Abhour, Detest, and Abjure, as Impious an Heretical [the] Damnable Doctrine and Position" of regicidal, Popish authority.[26] In this context Mackintosh was also abjuring the "abominable principles" of the *Vindiciae* and embracing the Glorious Revolution he had formerly renounced.

His recantation was in the traditional language of abjuration. In Britain there were various Oaths of Abjuration by which the British subject (including members of Parliament) renounced or abjured the doctrine of papal supremacy. The *OED* cites the following from the 1552 *Book of Common Prayers, Ordering of Deacons*: "I from hence forth shall utterly renounce, refuse, relinquish, & forsake the bishop of Rome" (*renounce*, def. 3). More pertinently, the informed eighteenth-century British reader would have recognized that Mackintosh's language was that of the standard Abjuration Oath, included in a series of parliamentary acts taken by the subjects and MPs in England, Wales, Ireland, and Scotland, dating back to the sixteenth century. The Abjuration Oath reappears, as we have seen, in the *Declaration of Rights* and is reincorporated in subsequent acts of Parliament in the eighteenth century, including George I.c.13 (1714). In addition, there were standard Abjuration Oaths renouncing the authority and legitimacy of the Stuart Pretenders. In 13 William III.c.6 (1701), everyone having office or receiving "Pay, Salary, Fee or Wages, by Reason of any Patent or Grant from his Majesty" is required "to renounce, refuse, and abjure any Allegiance" to James II, the pretender. Likewise, in 6 George III.c.53 (1766), every person in Scotland is required to "renounce, refuse, and abjure, any Allegiance or Obedience" to any of the Stuart Pretenders. Mackintosh renounces his political heresy and false faith (the French Revolution) in the statutory language that simultaneously reaffirms his allegiance to the church and state of England—the Revolutionary Settlement that he had rejected in the *Vindiciae.*

His *Review of the Causes of the Revolution of 1688* (posthumously published in 1834) dealt with the causes leading up to the Revolution, causes that made the Revolution "necessary," just as Burke and the Whig forefathers had said it was. [27] His "Memoir of the Affairs of Holland" glorified William III and demonized James II (*Works*, 384–97). With regard to the French Revolution, he had, in his letter to Richard Sharp (9 December 1804), explained his *deviation* from the Revolution, using the key thematic word from the *Reflections* with which he had mocked Burke in the *Vindiciae* to explain his consistency. In the end, he revised his deviation into a Burkean reading of both revolutions—the English Revolution necessary and legitimate, the French Revolution tragic and illegitimate.

In the *Vindiciae* he had also attacked the Septennial Act (*Works*, 445, 451), passed by Parliament in 1716. Since the principle of short parliaments had been declared by the 1689 Convention and enshrined in the Triennial Bill (1694), the notorious Septennial Act had, since its inception, been attacked by dissident Whigs and Tories, as an example of the Revolution's betrayal and the inadequacy of parliamentary representation: long parliaments negated the principle of frequent elections and hence the people's representation. In the last public endeavor of his life, his "Speech on the Second Reading of the Bill to Amend the Representation" (4 July 1831), Mackintosh affixed an appendix to the printed version, in which he justified the Septennial Act. In the appendix, Mackintosh returned to an original-intent reading: fearing a Jacobite resurgence and the imminent election of a Tory and

Jacobite majority in the Parliament, George I and the anti-Jacobite Parliament had passed the Septennial Act to protect the Revolution Settlement against a new Jacobite attempt to reintroduce popery and slavery:

> In these circumstances the Septennial Act was passed, because it was necessary to secure liberty. ... It was a deviation from the course of the constitution too extensive in its effects ... to be warranted by motives of political expediency: it could be justified only by the necessity of preserving liberty. The Revolution itself was a breach of the laws; and it was as great a deviation from the principles of monarchy, as the Septennial Act could be from the constitution of the House of Commons—and the latter can only be justified by the same ground of necessity, with that glorious Revolution of which it probably contributed to preserve—would to God we could say perpetuate—the inestimable blessings. (*Works*, 595)

Burke's spirit still radiates in Mackintosh's last lines, in which he returns to the glorious tradition that he had repudiated in the *Vindiciae*. The transformation of Mackintosh's intertextual wars into a series of intertextual recantations was, however, an event in the future that would color his revisions of both revolutions in a continuous civil war with himself.

For a brief period preceding the Terror (1793–94), the French Revolution provided British radicals with a variety of pre-texts by which they could reopen and revise the events of 1689 and issues supposedly settled forever—reconceiving them in the language of old radical tradition, a language that absorbed relevant, new energy from the French Revolution. In this context, Mackintosh and others did not invent a new historical paradigm; rather, they recreated an old one, reinvigorating it with a new significance—an English revolution that received its definitive meaning from the revolution in France—the historical culmination of what the (suppressed) English revolution might have become. In presenting this formulation, they used the French Revolution to legitimize the old radical agenda. Refighting old ideological wars in a new battle of texts and books, they wrote their rebellion against "history" on the palimpsest of the past. Mackintosh's reinscription of the Glorious Revolution into the text of the French Revolution made it possible to translate the latter into British discourse and to read the present forward and back. In a mutual exchange of comparisons and contrasts, the historical meaning of the French Revolution impinged on the real significance of England and vice versa. Mackintosh ultimately reread the "real" Glorious Revolution as a modern recovery, a recuperation of its suppressed significance through the texts that had been distorted by the dominant writers and readers of English history. For him, the revisionist war over the English Revolution reinforced other rebellious readings of history, including the debate over property that, as we will now see, he grounds in the recovered texts of a radical tradition reestablishing the true ownership of both England and France.

9

Revolution in Property

In *Vindiciae Gallicae*, Mackintosh's discussion of property emanates from a series of historical contexts that his eighteenth-century audience would find meaningfully familiar. The immediate, contemporary context was the National Assembly's controversial decision to confiscate church lands (2 November 1789) for security on *assignats* to pay off the national debt and raise revenue. In the *Reflections*, Burke had vigorously criticized both the confiscation and the *assignats*, and Mackintosh felt compelled to counterrespond in the *Vindiciae*. For the English, the confiscation of the church lands recalled confiscations that had taken place in England, and opponents of the Revolution stressed the resemblance.

I

In English history, church lands had been confiscated twice. In the sixteenth century, the Catholic Church had been a great corporation when Henry VIII forcibly confiscated its lands and the Reformation Parliament sanctioned the confiscations, annexing the church to the state. In 1536, the Parliament passed legislation dissolving small monasteries and granting the property to the king. In 1539, the Six Articles Act dissolved the larger monasteries; consequently, as much as one-sixth of all the land in England became the king's. Henry VIII subsequently sold or gave away the majority of the monastic lands, and the "propertied classes who shared in the plunder from the church" became firmly bound to the house of Tudor. Later, in the 1550s, the Protestant oligarchy proceeded with further confiscations of church property, and priceless treasures of medieval art were plundered or destroyed by Protestant mobs—a "desecration" that shocked many people.[1]

Even those who had supported or participated in the confiscations often felt as if they had desecrated sacred ground. Keith Thomas refers to "the widely disseminated tradition that the monastic estates confiscated by Henry VIII carried with them a divine curse upon their new owners for appropriating to secular uses property once dedicated to God." This belief became full blown in the seventeenth century and accounted "for the unprecedented mobility of land during the sixteenth and seventeenth centuries, and the remarkable number of noblemen who had come to an untimely end on the scaffold."[2] The "unprecedented mobility of land" is also one of Burke's antirevolutionary themes in the *Reflections*, and he critically discusses Henry VIII's confiscations and quotes Sir John Denham's condemnatory lines in "Cooper's Hill" (217–19, 247). In the *Vindiciae*, Mackintosh still remembers the belief in sacrilege, even as he mocks it: "When the British Islands . . . reformed their ecclesiastical establishments, the howl of sacrilege was the only armour by which the Church attempted to protect its pretended property. . . . The religious horror which the priesthood had attached to spoliation of Church property has long been dispelled; and it was reserved for Mr. Burke to renew that cry of sacrilege, which, in the darkness of the sixteenth century, had resounded in vain" (*Works*, 419).[3]

Throughout the seventeenth century, the English had an obsessional anxiety about the precariousness of their landed property (strongly identified with their lives and liberties and also associated with their money and goods)—an anxious preoccupation confronting all the Stuart monarchs and contributing to the constitutional crisis facing Charles I. It was thus another irony of history when church and crown lands were confiscated by the Puritan Parliament during the English Civil War, and royalists who wanted to recover their own confiscated lands were compelled to "compound," i.e., to buy them back at a fixed rate.

Another major confiscation occurred during Cromwell's rule. Faced with a series of foreign wars and the ensuing economic problems, the Rump Parliament "resorted to the renewed sale of [Anglican] church and Crown lands" and seized the property of Royalists as well.[4] Subsequently, radical "Levellers" were associated in the popular imagination with confiscated, "common" property. For many eighteenth-century English men and women, the similarity between what had happened in England and what was happening in France was striking. The radical 1640s again provided an orientative context for the revolutionary 1790s.

After the Restoration, the 1660 Convention Parliament returned crown and church lands to their original owners, but though Charles II was initially generous with those who had fought against his father and who had acquired confiscated property, the Act of Explanation (1665) "allowed one-third of the lands of the soldiers and adventurers to be confiscated to help meet the claims of royalists and others who had had their properties confiscated during and after the Civil War."[5] During the Exclusion Crisis (1678–81)—the parliamentary endeavor to pass bills excluding the duke of York (later James II) from the throne because he was a Catholic—Protestants feared that if the duke became king, he would reappropriate the lands confiscated from the Catholic Church. The propaganda campaign compelled him, once he became king, to issue a tract, reassuring his subjects "that their property rights would be respected."[6] Both models of confiscation served conservatives and radicals throughout the eighteenth century: conservatives evoked regicidal levelers, and radicals conjured up Catholic and Tory Jacobites who would repossess the land if they ever gained power.

Because of the confiscations in the sixteenth and seventeenth centuries, the concept of landed property possessed the English imagination. Landed property was, in many ways, deeply intertwined with English identity. Property provided "the foundation of political personality."[7] William Blackstone, in *Commentaries on the Laws of England* (1766), noted that English "courts now regard a man's personality in a light nearly, if not quite, equal to his realty."[8] The belief that only those who were economically independent had the time and freedom to devote to the common good—that only those who had a vested interest in a stable society could vote and represent that society— permeated Anglo-European discourse. The belief that the "landed interest" predominated in the English Parliament underscored that the country was firmly based on stable agrarian values—a belief shared by both the Left and Right. Land made a man independent; it made him a "freeholder" and hence a "freeman," providing him the right of franchise and the expression of his private and corporate identities. Land signified stability and continuity; in families and in nations, primogeniture ensured the perpetuation of lines, estates, and dynasties. In Anglo-European discourse, "landed" imagery grounds discussions of crowns, constitutions, and rights passed down immemorially. In the second volume of his *Commentaries on the Laws of England* (1766), William Blackstone had discussed the old common-law basis of English property, elaborating on the ancient distinction between moveable property and fixed landed property—between "personal" and "real property."[9] For the

English, real estate was solid and secure, representing a true and real value. In a profound sense, realty reflected reality.

In the *Reflections,* Burke had thrown the entire weight of this tradition against the revolutionaries in France and their admirers in England. He argued that, in England, in order for the church to be independent, the English people had "incorporated and identified the estate of the church with the mass of *private property*, of which the state is not the proprietor, either for use or dominion, but the guardian only and the regulator" (200). Thus, for Burke, the confiscations of church lands in France established a precedent for the robbery of private property, a robbery corresponding to the robbery of identity, since a person's private and political self (not mutually exclusive) was based on ownership and possession. The transmutations of land into paper, by which French speculators disrupted the land's stable value, represented, for Burke, the violent fluctuations of the unnatural revolutionary world. The result was a "revolution in property" (216, 270; cf. Blackstone, *Commentaries,* 2:49) and the creation of a new "speculative" interest, deracinated from the "real" world. For Burke, the sale of the confiscated church lands to speculators—the new "monied interest"—meant that property was no longer stable and that value (in all its senses) no longer corresponded to reality. In addition, Burke's attack on France's monied interest reinscribed traditional Tory and (Burkean) old Whig identifications of Protestant dissent with stock jobbing and speculation, with a revolution in land and values by rootless parvenus. Burke repeated the language of Queen Anne Tories who had criticized the new Whig oligarchy that had come into being following the Glorious Revolution and the attendant financial revolution that had created a national bank and a system of credit run by men who had no land and who had substituted paper for property.[10]

J. G. A. Pocock explains Burke's usage of the "monied interest" and its eighteenth-century significance:

It was a Tory term, developed in the reigns of William III and Anne ... to denote those who had invested capital in the systems of public credit set up after 1688 to stabilize the English Revolution and prosecute the wars against France in Europe. It denoted the investment of capital in the state rather than in commerce or industry, and though investors of this kind were obviously merchants and tradesmen for the most part, "the monied interest" was verbally as well as functionally distinct from "the trading interest" no less from "the landed." Burke uses the term of France as it had been used in England, to denote the creditors of the state: the proprietors of the public debt.[11]

Attacks on the monied interest came from both the Tories and the eighteenth-century Commonwealthmen (both of whom associated landed property with "virtue" and the monied interest with "corruption"), providing another example of how both the Left and Right appropriated and absorbed each other's discourse.

The central preoccupation of both was "corruption"—the corruption of voters and their representatives by the Crown's "influence"—power to sway by offering bribes of money or pensions as well as positions in government. Corruption subverted the free man's independence, his psychological and political integrity. Although many historians have dismissed the notion that the landed interest was threatened by the new monied interest, especially since the ministers of the Crown and both houses of Parliament were "dominated by territorial magnates in the eighteenth-century," W. A. Speck notes that it was the state itself that competed with the landed interest: "After 1689 . . . the state positively encouraged the development of other interests literally at the expense of the landed interest. Above all the creation of a public credit benefited the monied interest and hit landowners where it hurt, in the pocket."[12]

II

In the *Vindiciae*, Mackintosh confronts this history and Burke's correspondent critique by connecting the landed interest in England with a reactionary Tory "interest." Alluding to the confiscations of the 1640s and the financial revolution of the 1690s (both resembling property changes in revolutionary France), Mackintosh refers to "the great transfer of property to an upstart commercial interest, which drove the ancient gentry of England, for protection against its inroads, behind the throne [and which may be called] the 'Toryism of the landed aristocracy'" (*Works*, 451). In addition, Mackintosh knew that there were precedents for confiscated land in French history as well: the French monarchy had confiscated the property of the Huguenots after 1685, the Jansenists after 1709, and the Jesuits after 1764, and Mackintosh notes the latter (*Works*, 419). There was also a historical precedent for the confiscation of church land in Europe. During the Middle Ages, after the death of Charlemagne, church lands and offices had fallen "under the control of lay lords," compelling "pious churchmen throughout Europe" to turn "to their kings for leadership and protection."[13] According to Jules Michelet, proposals for the sale or confiscation of church lands were advanced but never enacted by John Law, the French minister of finances in 1720, and later, privately, by Madame Pompadour.[14] Michelet, of course, was interested in establishing a precedent for the confiscations of 1789. In general, however, property was considered sacrosanct, in France as well as in England.

At the beginning of the French Revolution, article 17 of *The Declaration of the Rights of Man and Citizen* (27 August 1789) stated that "since property is a sacred and inviolable right, no one may be deprived thereof unless a legally established public necessity obviously requires it, and upon condition of a just and previous indemnity."[15] Within seven weeks, however, the financial crisis led to Talleyrand's proposal (10 October 1789) that church property be "used as collateral against a new loan or even sold off to meet the pressing needs of the state."[16] This proposal, despite vigorous opposition in the National Assembly, became law on 2 November 1789. Mackintosh's problem in the *Vindiciae* was to justify the confiscations in light of the tradition of property that Burke had thrown against the Revolution. He responded by reproducing (unattributed) arguments for confiscation in the National Assembly, providing a subversive "translation" of radical French discourse into an English context.

In the National Assembly, proponents for confiscation had provided a series of supportive arguments: by reducing ecclesiastical property, the Church would be returned to its primitive purity; by having the state pay the salary of the clergy, the inequitable incomes between its higher and lower members would finally be addressed. More pertinently, for Mackintosh, Talleyrand had argued that the clergy was not the "proprietor" of church property as are owners of private land, because "'the property of which they have the use cannot be freely alienated and was given to them not for their personal benefit but for the exercise of an office or function.'"[17] By distinguishing between private and public property, Talleyrand and others endeavored "to alleviate fears that what happened to the Church's property might one day happen to the property of ordinary private citizens as well"—a fear Mackintosh also attempts to quell.[18]

For Mackintosh, the other key argument was most likely the one made by Jacques-Alexis Thouret (whom he mentions favorably in *Vindiciae* [*Works*, 425])—a lawyer and deputy of the Third Estate, who distinguished "'between real persons, actual living persons, and corporations (corps) that . . . constitute moral and fictive persons. . . . Individuals exist independent of the law. . . . By contrast, corporations exist only by virtue of the law, [which] has unlimited authority over all that pertains to them, indeed over their very existence. . . . Thus the law, having created corporations, can also abolish them.'" Another deputy, Le Chapelier,

"emphasized the need to rout out 'all these ideas of corporations and orders that are constantly springing up.'"[19] Mackintosh, I believe, appropriates this French discourse, stressing that the clergy is not the lands'
"proprietor" and distinguishing between private and public property,
between real estate (and "real" persons) and the "fictional" corporations
and people that can be created or destroyed by "the nation." There are
obvious parallels between the arguments and language of those who justified the confiscations in the National Assembly and the arguments and
language used by Mackintosh. Mackintosh reproduces the available
French discourse, a discourse replicated by the Revolution's English
advocates, but which was, as far as I know, nonexistent or tenuous in
England before 1789. Mackintosh translates this discourse into an
English context that he fleshes out with British examples (in England and
Scotland) that resemble and correspond to the French experience. The
French translation is contextualized and made familiar for the English
reader.

   In the *Vindiciae*, he contends that corporations are not real, that "the
three great corporations of the Nobility, the Church, and the Parliaments"
were legal fictions dissolved by the National Assembly. Private property,
however, is different. Although it often produces economic "fortune" and
hence "inequality," it is nevertheless necessary, "because property alone
can stimulate to labour," and labor is necessary for both existence and
happiness (*Works*, 415). Mackintosh, like the National Assembly,
endeavors to alleviate fears that private property could also be
confiscated; hence, he keeps focusing on the difference between private
property and public corporations. The wealthy classes "combine" into
corporate bodies and conspire to accumulate even more power and
wealth, "the perpetual source of oppression and neglect to the mass of
mankind" (*Works*, 415). His class critique of "*corporation spirit*"
(*Works*, 415, 444) centers on the "preference of partial to general
interests" (*Works*, 415), i.e., the classic republican critique of selfish
private interests over general, public interests—a critique repopularized
by civic humanists as well as Enlightenment and revolutionary writers.[20]
Because the three corporations (Nobility, Church, and *Parlements*) are
conspiratorial "combinations" of the wealthy class, one cannot argue that
they comprise competitive balances (an "English" view), since they have
a vested interest in maintaining power and oppressing the poor. The
wealthy members comprise one corporate class: "all bodies and
institutions" of the Old French Order were assimilated by the absolute
monarchy—"They were tainted by the despotism of which they had been
either members or instruments" (*Works*, 415). France had no balanced

constitution; every corporate body depended on the monarchy; the body politic was infected by corporations embodying a single "corporation spirit."

In 1789, the dissolution of the corporations restored the body politic; the "dissolution of the Church as a body," the "dissolution of the Church as a corporation," for instance, resulted in "religious liberty" and the "diffusion of knowledge" (*Works*, 417, 427). Although English kings and queens had the right to "dissolve" Parliament, *dissolution*, in the eighteenth century, also had radical resonances. Henry VIII had, for instance, resided over the dissolution of the monasteries (cf. *OED*, def. 7); in the 1689 Convention Parliament, radical Whigs had argued that, with the "forfeiture" of the throne by James II, the government and constitution were "dissolved" and power was returned to the people to reconstitute a new government. Radical pamphleteers made the same point in a language reminiscent of the Levellers. They defended "the 1689 revolution as the outcome of the dissolution of government, a return to the state of nature, and political power reverting into the hands of the people."[21] Likewise, John Locke titles the last chapter of his *Second Treatise* "Of the Dissolution of Government," arguing that when a government is "dissolved," the people are returned to a state of nature and may reconstitute a new government (pars. 218–20). Mackintosh uses the word precisely in this sense when he discusses the "dissolution of society" at the time of the Glorious Revolution: when "there are no remedies to be found within the pale of society . . . we are to seek them in nature. . . . No man can deduce a precedence of law from the Revolution, for law cannot exist in the dissolution of government" (*Works*, 449–50).[22] Mackintosh's usage of *dissolution* again revives the radical language of the 1690s, suggesting that the correspondent dissolution of the old French corporations and government resulted in the return of power to the people and the creation of a new, popular government (see *Vindiciae* in *Works*, 409, 411, 420, 439, 457). For Burke, the Revolution is a radical "revolution" in property; for Mackintosh, it is a traditional *revolution*: a return to an original source (the people) and the restoration of the true nation's property and rights.

Discussing the confiscated church property, Mackintosh cites a passage in the *Reflections*, where Burke sarcastically refers to the new legal fiction, "found out in the academies of the *Palais Royale*, and the *Jacobins*, that certain men have no right to the possessions which they held under law, usage . . . and the accumulated prescription of a thousand years" (*Reflections*, 206). Mackintosh responds with the discovery of a legitimate source and origin justifying the confiscations:

That the Church lands were national property was not first asserted among the Jacobins, or in the Palais Royal. The author of that opinion . . . was . . . Turgot! a name now too high to be exalted by eulogy, or depressed by invective. That benevolent and philosophical statesman delivered it, in the article "Foundation" of the *Encyclopédie*, as the calm and disinterested opinion of a scholar, at a moment when he could have no object in palliating rapacity, or prompting irreligion [what Burke accused the revolutionaries of doing]. . . . [I]t was a principle discovered in pure and harmless speculation, by one of the best and wisest of men. . . . If [Burke] insinuates the flagitiousness of these opinions by the supposed vileness of their origin, it cannot be unfit to pave the way for their reception, by assigning to them a more illustrious pedigree. (*Works*, 418)

Jacques Anne-Robert Turgot had been Louis XVI's controller-general (1774–76) and had tried to institute financial reforms, promoting physiocratic ideas and attacking the guilds and corporations that he believed were stifling France's economy. Although he called out troops, instituted summary tribunals and exemplary hangings, and issued *lettres de cachet*—landing his opponents in the Bastille—his promotion of free-market policies and the abolition of the corvée earned him the reputation of an enlightened liberal. When he additionally urged a property tax to replace the corvée, to be paid by all sections of the population, the entrenched aristocracy forced his dismissal.

By bringing forth Turgot as the pristine originator of the idea that "church lands were national property," Mackintosh suggests that Burke knowingly ascribes a "vile origin" (the Jacobins, the Palais Royal), when, in fact, Turgot provides the idea an "illustrious pedigree." Mackintosh, however, disingenuously changes Burke's point—the "seizure of [private church] property," the rationale of which is supplied by "the academies of the *Palais Royale* and the Jacobins" (*Reflections*, 206)—to the *origin* of the assertion that church lands are national property (*Works*, 418). In addition, the causal "assertion" did not originate in the National Assembly with Turgot's article in the *Encyclopédie*: it was made, as Mackintosh knew, by Talleyrand and Mirabeau in the National Assembly, and it is this vile origin that Mackintosh hides. He mentions neither because they are conspicuous targets for an antirevolutionary response. In the *Reflections*, Burke had attacked Talleyrand (308, 360–61), the cynical, worldly bishop of Autun, and he had quoted unfavorably Mirabeau (whom he does not name, 162), who had a reputation for being a corrupt opportunist. Mackintosh's comment that Turgot made his proposal when he "could have no object in palliating rapacity or promoting irreligion"—precisely what Mirabeau and Talleyrand were accused of doing—allusively acknowledges the origin he hides. He disingenuously cites an obscure article, keeping the proposal in the Assembly out of sight, accusing Burke of hiding the origin of what he himself hides.

Moreover, Mackintosh misrepresents the "origin" to which he refers. The unsigned article "Fondation," in the seventh volume of the *Encyclopédie*, has traditionally been assigned to Turgot. In the article, however, Turgot does not assert or suggest that, as Mackintosh says, "Church lands were national property" (*Works*, 418). Turgot criticizes foundations, "corps particuliers," that impede economic progress and individual talent. He contends that since "l'utilité publique est la loi suprème," the government (i.e., the king) has the right to modify or abolish existing civil foundations. This corresponds to Mackintosh's corporation argument and can, I suppose, be stretched anachronistically to apply to church lands—a proposal that Turgot would not have openly made in the 1750s. Turgot, in fact, is careful to say that, within the realm of religion, the right to dissolve ancient foundations and to redirect their funds to new objects is shared equally by both the government *and* the church: i.e., neither could dispose of religious foundations or funds without the other's consent.[23] Turgot's article was not, as far as I know, cited in the National Assembly debates.

Additionally, Mackintosh's reference to Turgot's "discovery" in "harmless speculation" makes a redounding, ironic Burkean connection between intellectual speculation and economic speculation in land and money. In its pejorative sense, economic *speculation* was associated with the endeavor to make a profit from conjectural fluctuations in price rather than from earnings of the ordinary profit of trade, involving risk and chance (cf. *OED*, def. 8), and, by extension, intellectual speculation signified ideological conjecture, like Swift's projectors—speculation based on an abstract "mental scheme not reduced to practice" (Samuel Johnson, 1755 *Dictionary*, def. 5; cf. *OED*, defs. II c., 5, 6, 6c, 6e). The word *speculator* had the same negative significance (see *OED*, defs. 1, 6). Since both words were essentially pejorative in the eighteenth century and were used disparagingly by Burke in the *Reflections*, where the insane speculations of philosophes and revolutionaries replace "reality," it is curious that Mackintosh uses the word with reference to Turgot—an economist whose "harmless speculation" prefigures or culminates in the confiscations forty years later. Perhaps Mackintosh ironically makes Burke's point: in the *Vindiciae,* the writings of the philosophes contribute to the French Revolution. Turgot's article in the *Encyclopédie* is hence an original cause of the restorative confiscations.

Mackintosh then argues, referring to the clergy, that "it has not hitherto been supposed that any class of Public Servants are proprietors.

They are salaried by the State for the performance of certain duties."[24]
Conscious of his English audience and individuals having a share in
corporate property, Mackintosh distinguishes between private
corporations formed by individuals—"corporate property," which is "as
sacred" as individual private property—and state corporations whose
property is public and national (*Works*, 418). Mackintosh's point is that
the clergy contains members of a public corporate body sustained by the
state: the clergy are public servants employed by the nation; hence, they
occupy but do not own state lands. He reiterates the contention of
Talleyrand (10 October 1789) that "'the clergy is not a proprietor in the
same sense that others are; since the property of which they have the use
cannot be freely alienated and was given to them not for their personal
benefit but for the exercise of an office or function.'"[25] Mackintosh bases
the claim that French Catholic priests are salaried, public servants on the
state's right "to regulate the salaries of those servants whom it pays,"
where "there is an established religion" (*Works*, 418). Mackintosh was,
again, allusively linking the Glorious and French Revolutions, for "the
Glorious Revolution's religious settlement [had] reduced the Church of
England from the *national* to merely the *established* church";[26] likewise,
the French Catholic Church had been similarly reduced. On 12 April
1790, the National Assembly had voted down a motion that Catholicism
be declared the official religion of France,[27] albeit its clergy would be
supported by the state, just like the Church of England.

By arguing that the established church is subordinate to the state,
Mackintosh makes a subversive, Erastian point, for it would also occur to
the English reader that the Anglican Church was the established church
of England and that it could be similarly reformed à la the French
Revolution. He uses the French example to establish a revolutionary
resemblance: he conspicuously does not discuss the ownership of church
land in England, but since the Anglican Church was also a corporation,
the English reader could infer that the English clergy were also state
servants and that Anglican land could be reappropriated by the real
proprietor—the nation. Mackintosh intended his translation of the French
Revolution to be read this way: the French example corresponds to
contemporary England; both contexts mirror each other.[28]

Likewise, he translates the French context into the legal language of
English discourse: eighteenth-century English property law and custom.
In England, a "proprietor" owned his land outright and could pass it on
without restrictions to his heirs (fee simple), whereas other kinds of
property were not owned outright (fee tail)—they carried restrictions,
usually in the form of rent paid out to the original owners, who still
possessed the legal title. Mackintosh's proprietorial argument, in the

Vindiciae, operates on this distinction. The "lands of the [Catholic] Church possess not the most simple [with the pun on fee simple] and indispensable requisites of property." The French clergy are salaried state functionaries occupying state land, which the state resumes, choosing to pay them with money instead of, as before, with land. Just as "great landed estates" were historically awarded by the monarch for military service, so the church historically acquired land for service to the sovereign, as "the early history of Europe" testifies (*Works*, 418). Mackintosh's reference to "the early history of Europe" is rather perverse, however, since he cites as a precedent the feudal, "gothic" history both he and other revolutionaries reject. Likewise, he cites the example of Scotland, "where lands are still held by feudal tenures" (*Works*, 419). Both examples, however, are English translations of the French text he reinscribes.[29] Since "no individual priest" was ever "a proprietor" of national lands, it is absurd to contend that the "priesthood" owns the land, because "the priesthood is a corporation, endowed by the country, and destined for the benefit of others: hence the members have no separate, nor the body any collective, right of property. They are only entrusted with the administration of the lands from which their salaries are paid" (*Works*, 418). Land, money, and positions conditionally granted to an established church subversively conjure up the state-supported Anglican church—an unspoken resemblance that Mackintosh wants his English reader to see in the fee-tail English nation: like a landholder who pays his steward for collecting his rents by allowing him to live on his farm gratis, the state, like the landholder, is the real owner of the land and can repossess it whenever it pleases (*Works*, 419). Since the French state is the nation, Mackintosh suggests that there was a glorious *revolution* in property: the lands were returned to the rightful owner.

Employing the (understood) distinction between private fee-simple ownership and restricted fee-tail rentals that he extends to fee-tail corporate ownership, Mackintosh then confronts Burke's contention that English church property is "identified" with stable private property and cannot be alienated by the state (*Reflections*, 200). Conceding that in "charters, bonds, and all other proceeding of law" the clergy's salaries (drawn from the administration of state lands) "are treated with the same formalities as real property" and that Burke's "language is correct" if "our view is limited to form," Mackintosh explains that the distinction between "these formalities" and "legal truth" rests on a legal fiction: in order to protect state land "vested in the clergy" in "contests of law," the state created "the fiction [of the clergy] being proprietors." The real right of ownership, however, resides in the state, and this is only one of many cases that, for purposes of practical convenience, "the spirit and the forms of law are at variance respecting property" (*Works*, 418–19). The legal language that contradicts "legal truth," the fiction that disguises real ownership, should remind us of Mackintosh's critique of the Revolution Settlement, which also linguistically disguised what happened (a king cashiered and another elected) in a fictional, legal language. Thus, there is another implicit distinction between Burke's fictional England (and language contradicting reality) and France's real Revolution, which reveals things as they really are: the clergy, a corporate fiction that may be dissolved by the state, and church real estate that may be repossessed by the rightful national owner.

Like other respondents of Burke, Mackintosh's cardinal theme is illusion and reality. Thus, Burke's argument (*Reflections*, 260) for prescription is irrelevant, since "prescription implies a certain period during which the rights of property have been exercised; but in the case before us they never were exercised, because they never could be supposed to exist" (*Works*, 419). Church property was always the state's; the Church never really owned the land, since the Church itself—and its embodied priesthood—was a corporate fiction created by the state. Unlike real proprietors who pass down real property to individual family members, the celibate, sterile clergy pass down nothing (*Works*, 420). Once the fiction of corporate church property was dissolved, Mackintosh suggests, property was restored and became "real" estate. The National Assembly's language restored reality: the land was the nation's, that is, the state that represents the people. Similarly, if the clergy (like the corporate land) is a legal fiction, it may also be dissolved, because it also is not real, and the same applies to the nobility and the *Parlements* and all of the other old corporate fictions (*Works*, 420–21).

In the *Reflections,* Burke, who had read the National Assembly debates, rearticulated the revolutionary argument:

> They say that ecclesiastics are fictitious persons, creatures of the state; whom at pleasure they may destroy, and of course limit and modify in every particular; that the goods they possess are not properly theirs, but belong to the state which created the fiction; and we are therefore not to trouble ourselves with what they may suffer in their natural feelings and natural persons, on account of what is done towards them in this their constructive [i.e., their corporate] character. (206)

Mackintosh, in effect, reaffirms Burke's representation of revolutionary discourse and says the latter is true. He responds to Burke's emphasis on individual suffering by acknowledging that the dissolution of a corporation often results in individual difficulty and that, in the case of the clergy, the state should make allowances for their maintenance

(*Works*, 420), which of course the National Assembly did, when it turned those who supported the Civil Constitution of the Clergy (12 July 1790) into state functionaries, providing them their new, corporate identity. Burke had confounded "sympathy with individual suffering" with the dissolution of an old, corporate fiction (*Works*, 419–20). It is as if Mackintosh believes that an individual who suffers in his corporate capacity is less real, since his corporate identity is not real.[30] Using a language of distance that cancels out temporary defects (cf. *Works*, 432), he predicts that the dissolution of corporations "will be justly applauded by a posterity too remote to be moved by comparatively minute afflictions." Since the Catholic Church is the refuge of superstition and fanaticism, there will be "no sorrow at the downfall of a great corporation . . . the rise, progress, decay, and down-fall of spiritual power in Christian Europe" (*Works*, 420). The allusion to Edward Gibbon reinforces his approval of the dissolution of the corporate priesthood, suggesting that he also is writing a classic historical treatise on the fall of the Old Order.

Mackintosh is, however, apprehensive that his propertied, English audience might think that the confiscation of corporate property establishes a precedent for the confiscation of private property as well. Burke, in fact, had made just this point (*Reflections*, 260–61, 264–65). In a long footnote, Mackintosh poses as a moderate who rejects the radical contention that "property, being the creature of civil society, may be resumed by the public will," that it is "on this principle" that the National Assembly had acted. This, as he knows, is a straw argument, for he then (mis)quotes article 17 of the *Declaration of the Rights of Man and Citizen* (27 August 1789) to prove that the National Assembly had acted to protect private property: "One of the first maxims of their Declaration of Rights [is] 'that the State cannot violate property, except in cases of urgent necessity, and on condition of previous indemnification'" (*Works*, 419). The relative clause actually reads, "Since property is a sacred and inviolable right, no one may be deprived [of their property] unless a legally established public necessity obviously requires it, and upon condition of a just and previous indemnity."[31] Mackintosh adds the words "that the State cannot violate property" and shortens the *Declaration of the Rights of Man and Citizen* to "Declaration of Rights," evoking the 1689 Declaration of Rights, allusively, and probably pejoratively. He then contends that private property "is one of those *fundamental* acts which constitute society" and that since property has always "existed," the "property of individuals is established on a *general principle*, which seems coeval with civil society itself." Corporations, in contrast, "are subsequent and subordinate; they are only *ordinary expedients* of legislation." Thus, corporate bodies created by legislation can be dissolved once they cease having a useful purpose—a point Thouret had made in the National Assembly.[32] Since individual property is coeval with civil society, and since, as Mackintosh later maintains, there is no "actual existence of any state antecedent to the social" (the "natural rights" of man were always protected by unions of "public force ... coeval and co-extensive with man"), Mackintosh dismisses "all theories" of a state of nature (*Works*, 436), and thus suggests that private property, natural rights, and society were all coevally present from the beginning.

His citation of article 17 in the French *Declaration of Rights* and his translation of "public necessity" into "urgent necessity" is, for him, the contextual financial crisis that justified the necessary return of land to its rightful owner—the corporate nation embodied in that other corporate body—the National Assembly. The "urgent necessity" alludes ironically to the urgent necessity by which the 1689 Convention justified its deviation, emphasized by Burke as an "act of *necessity*, in the strictest moral sense which necessity can be taken"—"a grave and overruling necessity" (*Reflections*, 102, 113). More pertinently, it alludes to Burke's criticism of the National Assembly, which takes its "examples for common cases, from the exceptions of the most urgent necessity" (*Reflections*, 316). Mackintosh allusively contrasts again the Convention with the Assembly, employing Burke's vocabulary to validate his counterreading of both revolutions.

His subsequent examples (from the "British islands, the Dutch Republic, and the German and Scandinavian States") of how the churches were "reformed" and "secularized" effectively illustrates that many modern states historically made de facto confiscations of church property. Mackintosh moves thematically from de jure appropriations, legally spelled out in the French *Declaration*, to de facto confiscations that become de jure, despite "the howl of sacrilege" (*Works*, 419). He contests Burke on two fronts, denying the identification of church and private property that Burke claims.

He also uses an argument of social utility, in which the clergy are "sterile" and unproductive and hence have no social value or use to society. In the *Reflections,* Burke argued that, since the surplus produce of the land constitutes income that will be circulated and spent, it does not matter whether that income is circulated by one landholder (who does no labor) or a society of idle monks, provided that "the capital taken in rent from the land, should be returned again to the industry from whence it came." Since "idleness" is paradoxically the "spring of labor," Burke means that profit taken from the land inspires the laborer's industry: the capital is returned to the worker (and also reinvested in the land) by the idle landholder who rewards the worker for his fruitful labor (*Reflections*, 270). Burke uses the language of "surplus," labor, rent, and capital popularized and made famous by Adam Smith in *The Wealth of Nations* (1776).[33] He makes a point that Smith repeatedly makes: the proprietor improves his land and "stock" by reinvesting his profit into land and labor.[34]

Mackintosh, in response, reformulates Burke's Smithean point (omitting Burke's reference to the "return" of "capital" to "industry") and then postulates that the "wealth of society is its stock of productive labour" and that, although there will always be unproductive consumers, the less there are, "the greater . . . must be the opulence of the state." He counterresponds in the language of *The Wealth of Nations* by employing Smith's distinction between "productive" and "unproductive" labor. Burke, in effect, employs Smith's example of the productive landowner, while Mackintosh uses Smith's example of the bad landowner to make his correspondent point. The pertinent passage that Mackintosh allusively evokes is book 2, chapter 3, where Smith discusses both kinds of landowners.[35] Mackintosh thus insists that forty monks are forty times less productive than a single landholder who owns the land but does not work it, and that "there is forty times the quantity of labour subtracted from the public stock, in the first case, than there is in the second." While a landowner's "domestics" are also "unproductive," they, unlike monastic "servants," often become "farmers and artisans" and besides they often marry (Mackintosh is responding to *Reflections*, 273, even though Burke's contrast is between the laborers who work church lands and the wealthy man's "useless domestics"). Mackintosh assumes that monastic lands lay fallow and that this coincides with the monk's chaste sterility: the monks are not producers of useful children who will contribute to the nation's future "stock" (*Works*, 429). But he also assumes that the conversion of dronish monks into salaried functionaries will make them useful members of society. In *The Spirit of the Laws* (1748), Montesquieu had referred favorably to Henry VIII, who reformed the English church by destroying the "lazy" monks.[36] Joseph II, the Austrian emperor, had, in the 1780s, tried to convert monks and nuns into "useful citizens"—probably a useful example for Talleyrand.[37]

Mackintosh's critique of unproductive landowners has an English context as well. During the exclusion elections (1679–80), Whigs had criticized the "useless" Tory aristocracy. Locke, in the *Second Treatise*, attacked "the idle, unproductive, and court-dominated property owners."[38] Mackintosh, in effect, reaffirms and reinscribes what Burke had warned against: the "innoxious indolence" of proprietors "may be argued into inutility; and inutility into an unfitness for their estates" (*Reflections*, 265). Against Burke, Mackintosh extols "the infinite utility which arises from changes of property in land," since the new purchasers "seldom adventure" without capital, and "the novelty of their acquisition inspires them with the ardour of improvement" (*Works*, 429). The metaphors make inherited, monastic lands static and sterile, whereas changes of property are dynamic and productive—energetic capitalists and investors replace the sterile class of monastic consumers.

Burke is hence incorrect in assuming that lands will be transferred to speculators and *stockjobbers*, always a pejorative word in the eighteenth century. But Mackintosh then inverts his argument by noting that, once the new owner has "tasted the indolence and authority of a landholder," he "will with difficulty return to the comparative servility and drudgery of a monied capitalist": the formerly energetic capitalist who expends money and labor will become "indolent," just like the unproductive monks. But Mackintosh again has it both ways, for if "the usurious habits of the immediate purchaser be inveterate"—if he remains a stockjobber, a speculator, his progeny will (like the useful offspring of the landholder's domestics) become productive improvers of the land: "His son will imbibe other sentiments from his birth. The heir of the stock-jobbing Alpheus may acquire as perfectly the habits of an active improver of his patrimonial estate, as the children of Cincinnatus or Cato" (*Works*, 430). In the *Reflections*, Burke had observed that the new possessors of church lands, speculators and "money-dealers," will soon become disenchanted with the real labor of country life and instead of investing capital and labor back into the land will end like "their great precursor and prototype," the moneylender Alpheus in Horace's Epode II (*Reflections*, 309). Having it both ways, Mackintosh appropriates Burke's Horatian text and rewrites it: the moneylender, Alpheus, who leaves the country and returns to the city with money made off the land which he lends out at interest (Epode II.11:67–70) is provided productive children, like the republican "children of Cincinnatus or Cato" (*Works*, 430).

Mackintosh posits a republican pedigree of landed inheritance. His central point, however, (and here he deviates from the traditional Country ideology) is that changes in land and the investment of new capital transforms inert, inutile property into productive, social stock. Likewise, he deviates from the traditional left-right critique of the new monied interest, for the monied interest infuses new life into sterile, static property: "The commercial or monied interest has in all nations of Europe (taken as a body) been less prejudiced, more liberal, and more intelligent than the landed gentry," producing all the world's useful reforms, both practical and philosophical (*Works*, 426). In identifying the "money interest" *as* the commercial interest, Mackintosh reproduces the Scottish School's solution to the Country critique: trade and commerce make civilization possible, "liberalizing the modern world" (*Works*, 426), introducing the useful changes that improve it.[39] Radical Whigs and Queen-Anne Tories had argued that the monied interest reintroduced Old Corruption. Mackintosh, by equating the monied interest with the commercial interest, contends that it abolishes Old Corruption by destroying the old world's decrepit values.

There is a final context for the proprietorial landscape of *Vindiciae Gallicae*: the book's title looks like another "Vindication" of Gaul or France, and Mackintosh plays on this resemblance. But *Vindiciae* would immediately evoke for his learned audience the radically republican *Vindiciae, Contra Tyrannos* (1579)—the famous Huguenot tract that maintained that all political power originates in the people, who may rebel against bad rulers. Mackintosh's complete title is also allusively brilliant. In Latin, *Vindiciae* means property, the ownership of which is in dispute, given into the custody of one of the claimants by a magistrate until the issue may be settled definitively. Mackintosh's Latin title equates Gaul (France) with such property: "Gaul as property possessed only temporarily and subject to final arbitration." In Latin the title might also mean properties of this sort in Gaul: since *Vindiciae* is almost always plural, there is no way to tell from the isolated phrase.[40] Mackintosh, I believe, uses the title in both ways, since the meaning of modern Gaul is being contested by both Mackintosh and Burke, and the judge is English public opinion, which has not yet made a definitive ruling. Properties in France are also being contested, specifically the church properties whose ownership Mackintosh and Burke, revolutionaries and counterrevolutionaries, ascribe to different entities— the Church, the nation. By titling his book *Vindiciae Gallicae*, Mackintosh suggests that the real *title* and meaning of France resides in his hands. The Latin title suggests that his representation, his "claim" is the original true, legal one. It is the kind of learned virtuosity by which Mackintosh contests Burke on his own ground: the classical property and heritage appreciated by the learned audience to whom they both appeal.[41] It also underscores his own appropriations of a variety of available discourses that he reinscribes into his proprietary text. In the *Vindiciae,* the thematic right to the land belongs to those whose title and representation are truer, and truer representation is, as we will now see, what Mackintosh claims.

10

Revolution in Representation: Electoral and Economic Paradigms in *Vindiciae Gallicae*

By the 1790s, electoral representation had been an issue in England for over a century, and the French Revolution accelerated dissident demands for reform. Traditionally, in England, there were two principal ways of acquiring the right of suffrage: by county or by borough. Since 1430 a man in the counties could vote if he possessed freehold property valued for the land tax at forty shillings per annum, which, at the rate of inflation, was a negligible amount in the eighteenth century. The forty counties traditionally were represented by the gentry or landed interest, while the boroughs were intended to represent the interests of towns and cities (the universities represented themselves). With regard to economic restrictions on the right to vote, there was no standardized value in the boroughs, since many were corporations and the qualifications and restrictions varied from place to place. There were, in the 1790s, seven types of boroughs, "each distinguished by a particular franchise."[1] In some boroughs, there was wide suffrage, while in a corporation borough only the members of the corporation, invariably a very small amount, could vote. The notorious "rotten boroughs" usually contained only a few eligible voters but retained the privilege of sending a member to Parliament. These boroughs had often received their charters decades or centuries in the past, had lost their importance, and were often controlled by an aristocrat who had the borough in his pocket and who could consequently influence the vote for the candidate of his choice. Critics of electoral representation highlighted the rotten boroughs but rarely stressed the property and economic restrictions except to criticize the lack of uniformity in the boroughs.

The English generally associated property and suffrage with independence and interest: economic independence to vote freely and a vested interest in the nation's prosperity. They envisioned a franchise restricted to those who had an economic stake in the country and the economic independence to vote for the candidate who would serve both the national interest and the local interest of the county or borough. Throughout the seventeenth century, this exclusionary paradigm had been criticized and challenged, most notably during the English Civil War, in the Putney Debates (October and November 1647) and in the exchanges between Thomas Rainborough, Henry Ireton, and Oliver Cromwell (especially 29 October 1647). Rainborough pushed a Leveller agenda, including an expanded franchise, extending, in part, to all males above the age of twenty-one, regardless of income or property, while Ireton and Cromwell favored a more restricted franchise.[2] Although Ireton and Cromwell prevailed, the English Civil War and the Putney Debates are hauntingly present in the political discourse of the 1790s.

In the seventeenth century, the counties had accounted for the largest constituencies, and the franchise was large compared to that of the eighteenth century.[3] Richard Ashcraft notes that "the turn toward oligarchy and an increasing dominance of large property owners within the electorate is a distinctive feature of the eighteenth century."[4] During that time, at least half the members of the Commons were not elected but nominated by a patron.[5] Opponents of the Whig oligarchy criticized the restricted franchise and the corporation boroughs, but they still valorized the traditional notion of independence in their critique of what they called "Old Corruption": the ability of the court to corrupt the Parliament by peddling "influence"—buying votes through bribes and pensions, the promises of places—coupled with the power of the aristocratic elite, who controlled many of the boroughs. According to the Country critique, finance corrupted the voter's independence, rendering him dependent. This Country ideology was a language shared by all critics of the Whig oligarchy, Left and Right. The Country agenda traditionally included frequent parliaments, free elections, and the banning of placemen from Parliament. Dissenters who had the franchise pushed the Country agenda, as did those eighteenth-century commonwealthmen who called themselves "Real," True," or "Honest" Whigs, and who identified with the Puritan commonwealthmen of the late 1640s.

The issue of representation resurfaced in the late eighteenth century with the annulment of the election of John Wilkes by the House of Commons (1769), the American Revolution, and the publication of James Burgh's *Political Disquisitions* (1774–75), a critique of English parliamentary corruption. In the 1780s, Dissenters supported electoral reform as a way of repealing anti-Puritan legislation, such as the Test and Corporation Acts, still technically in effect—rejecting the doctrine of "toleration" and hence the Revolution Settlement of the 1690s. The French Revolution revivified these issues with a new relevance, and its advocates presented revolutionary France as a contrastable example of what the English did not have—an extensive and comparatively free franchise, resulting in real representation.

Richard Price, in *Discourse on the Love of our Country* (1789), had referred to the "inequality in our representation," a "defect" in the British constitution, a representation that was only "partial," providing only the "semblance of liberty." The English representative was "corruptly chosen, and under corrupt influence after being chosen." The "inadequateness of our representation," he noted, "has been long a subject of complaint."[6] Indeed, in criticizing British representation and in calling for a purer representation that is "fair and equal," Price was consciously echoing Locke (*Second Treatise*, par. 157 and 158), who had been directly cited in this context earlier by John Wilkes, James Burgh, and others.[7] More significantly, Locke's usage of "equal" representation, i.e., manhood suffrage, was used by the Levellers in the 1640s and had been an issue in the Putney Debates.[8] Price's phrase thus reverberated with a radical tradition that Burke likely recognized.[9] While Old Corruption and the lack of a manhood franchise were behind Price's critique, he alluded to France's "pure and equal representation" (while the English "are mocked with the shadow"), and suggested that if England were not reformed, she might have her own French Revolution.[10] In an allusive contrast to France, Price contended in a footnote that England's "representation [is] chosen principally by the Treasury, and a few thousands of the dregs of the people, who are generally paid for their votes."[11]

Likewise, Wollstonecraft, in *The Rights of Men*, criticized corrupting "influence" and the wealthy son who obtained his rank "on account of . . . the prostituted vote of his father, whose interest in a borough, or voice of a senator, was acceptable to the minister. . . . [T]he majority in the House of Commons was often purchased by the crown. . . . [T]he people were oppressed by the influence of their own money, extorted by the venal voice of a packed representation." Many voters were corrupt and could be bought: "Sordid interest . . . is the spring of action of most elections," accounting for "the venality of [the people's] votes"; she had "animadverted" before "on our method of electing representatives, convinced that it debauches both the morals of the people and the candidates, without rendering the member really responsible, or attached to his constituents." Echoing Price, she wonders if French elections, unlike the English, will "be more than a shadow of representation" (*WMW*, 5:15, 21, 36, 59).

In *Rights of Man*, Paine criticized the English electoral system in toto: the House of Lords is, as Lafayette has said, "'a corporation of aristocracy,'" representing "nobody but themselves"; the House of Commons is largely "made up by elections" in "corporation towns"; England's chartered towns restrict the franchise, creating a minority monopoly of Parliament; the House of Commons "is elected but by a small part of the nation"; in England, "election . . . is separated from representation." The franchise is limited because "not one man in a hundred . . . is admitted to vote: capricious—because the lowest character that can be supposed to exist, and who has not so much as the visible means of an honest livelihood is an elector in some places," while, in other places, the tax-paying man of fortune and property "is not admitted to be an elector." The egregious example is the rotten borough of "old Sarum which contains not three houses [but] sends two members," while the industrial "town of Manchester, which contains upward of sixty thousand souls, is not admitted to send any" (*CW*, 1:280–82, 289, 330, 384, 447).[12] Price, Wollstonecraft, and Paine were reproducing the standard Country critique, the latter two using it in response to Burke's critique of Price in the *Reflections*.

Significantly, neither Wollstonecraft nor Paine responded to Burke's critique of electoral representation in France, choosing instead to emphasize the notorious elements of the English electoral system. Hanna Pitkin has argued that Burke himself believed in virtual representation by which interests (as in the constituencies comprising the "landed" or "trading" interests) rather than people are represented.[13] It is often forgotten that the view (that "interests" rather than people are represented) was the dominant paradigm in England[14]—a paradigm challenged (and eventually replaced) by the new paradigm of representation presented during the American Revolution and by similar examples of representation advocated by admirers of the Revolution in France. Mackintosh's contribution to the debate over representation was his recognition that the textual war over the Revolution included representation, in its manifold senses, and that the contested meaning of the Revolution was about the Revolution's representational superiority to England. This necessarily entailed French electoral representation, an issue Burke had raised in the *Reflections* and that Mackintosh, unlike Paine and Wollstonecraft, responded to in the *Vindiciae*.

In the *Reflections,* Burke had subversively accepted the criterion of democratic elections by which the people directly elect their representatives and applied the criterion to France. He appropriated the radical critique of English representation and correspondingly delegitimized the French Revolution with the same revolutionary standard. Burke proceeded by reiterating the radical critique, noting that English supporters of the Revolution contended that England was not free because there was no popular election of the House of Commons and therefore no "popular representation" of the people (*Reflections*, 147). Since neither the monarchy nor the House of Lords was elected to office, supporters of the Revolution stressed the inequality of representation, an inequality that rendered the English government illegitimate. As Burke points out, summarizing a revolutionary argument, "If popular representation, or choice, is necessary to the *legitimacy* of all government, the [H]ouse of [L]ords is, at one stroke, bastardized and corrupted in blood" (147). Burke then proceeds to delegitimize the Revolution by applying the same criterion of popular elections to revolutionary France. In effect, he uses the revolutionary criterion to contradict the Revolution's representation.

His critique of revolutionary representation consists of showing how the representative is systematically separated from the citizen, how "there must be many degrees, and some stages, before the representative can come in contact with his constituent" (*Reflections*, 287).[15] First, he contends that the Revolution's democratic elections are based on a policy of exclusion, specifically the distinction between active and passive citizens, which restricts the vote to those active citizens paying a direct tax amounting to thrice the daily wage for unskilled labor. Thus, as Burke notes, the man who has nothing but his "natural equality" is excluded by a restrictive money qualification. Burke stresses the discrepancy between how the revolutionaries represent the Revolution and how they practice it. The Revolutionary government resembles a "tyrannous aristocracy"—the demonized order it supposedly replaces (288).

Second, Burke notes that the active citizens in the cantons gather in assemblies to elect deputies to the commune. The result, he contends, is a barrier "between the primary elector and the representative legislator"; but this is just the beginning (*Reflections*, 288), since those elected to the commune must pay an annual direct tax ten times the amount of the local daily wage—yet another economic qualification effectively excluding the primary elector.

Third, this process of exclusion continues as the representatives of the commune elect deputies to the *department*, and these, in turn, elect deputies to the National Assembly—deputies who must pay an annual direct tax equivalent of a mark (244.5 grams) of silver, or approximately fifty-one livres, in addition to owning land (*Reflections*, 289). (Burke notes only the first qualification.) In effect, Burke highlights revolutionary hypocrisy by arguing that the vaunted "rights of man" are only rhetorical; he suggests that revolutionary representation is more vicious, since it is based on three economic qualifications and three successive elections of representatives removed from the original voter by three stages. The result is a series of exclusive barriers, a series of debased representations. Burke suggests that there is an ontological distance by which debased representations are more and more removed from a real source.

As Burke takes the reader through each cumbersome stage, there is a sense of both spatial and moral distance between the disenfranchised passive citizen and the revolutionary system contradicting those it supposedly represents. By illustrating these discrepancies, he exploits the contradictions of what to him is illusory representation: "There is little, or rather no, connection between the last representative and the first constituent. The member who goes to the national assembly is not chosen by the people, nor accountable to them"; he is "too far removed . . . [from the primary electors] in the chain of representation" (*Reflections*, 304–5). Burke underscores the distinction between a revolutionary world of fantasy and illusion and a traditional European world based on correspondence and reality. He depicts revolutionaries interested only in representing themselves, thus misrepresenting both themselves and all that the (sham) Revolution supposedly stands for.

II

In the *Vindiciae,* Mackintosh first broaches the theme of representation by noting that "the Third Estate demanded deputies equal to those of the other two Orders jointly." He relates how the Third Estate began subverting the concept of corporate representation (voting by Orders) by demanding that the "authenticity" of each representative be reconfirmed by a popular consensus to ensure "the purity of the national representative" (*Works*, 410). As the old paradigm of corporate representation was replaced by democratic representation, the Third Estate constituted itself into one body, a National Assembly, representing the entire nation, not separate orders or interests. Mackintosh contrasts this unified legislative body consisting of "one voice" with the fragmented and divisive "voices" representing the corporate aristocracies.[16] Since corporations and orders are legal fictions, the contrast is again between illusion and reality, diversity and unity, contradiction and correspondence. Mackintosh posits a corporate body, the National Assembly, that cannot contradict itself, a corporate fiction representing France's mythical unity. France is a "commonwealth, which is vitally one" (*Works*, 440).

In the *Reflections,* Burke had noted that the landed interest was not represented in the Third Estate, and Mackintosh agreed, observing that the Second Estate, the nobility, composed the landed interest—an interest that no longer existed because the Second Estate was a dissolved fiction and because, as he later notes, "the representation of *land or money* is a monstrous relic of ancient prejudice: *men only can be represented*" (*Works*, 425, 440; my emphasis). Today the assertion that only people, not interests or things, can be represented sounds quite commonsensical. The concept of represented interest (e.g., the land or monied interest), however, had been the predominate paradigm for most of the eighteenth century. Even such a writer as the earl of Abingdon, a critic of Burke from the Left, articulated the conventional view that property, rather than individuals, was represented in the House of Commons: "The Members of Counties being the Representatives of all the Land of England, for the interests of that Land, whilst the Members of the Cities and Boroughs are the Representatives of all the Money and Trade of England." John Phillip Reid emphasizes what Abingdon did not say: "He did not say that the members represented the owners of that land or the plyers of that trade. They represented the land and the trade, not the proprietors."[17] In attacking this representational model as a "monstrous relic" of the past, in a discussion ostensibly about the French Revolution, Mackintosh attacks the traditional English view of representation, for bogus English representation is his real target. Although his critique is in the context of his criticism of the National Assembly's directive that the number of representatives be in proportion to territory and taxation,[18] his English audience would understand the "representation of land or money" as an allusion to English representation. But Mackintosh also uses the traditional language of "interests" throughout the *Vindiciae*: he frequently uses contradictory language to cover all ideological bases. Linguistically, he has it all ways.

Mackintosh does, however, "cordially" agree with Burke in "reprobating" the economic distinction between active and passive citizens "by which the [National] Assembly has disenfranchised every citizen who does not pay a direct contribution equivalent to the price of three days' labour" (*Works*, 439). He ignores, however, two other economic distinctions stressed by Burke (*Reflections*, 288–89): the deputy who pays an annual direct tax ten times the amount of the local daily wage and the representative who pays an annual direct tax equivalent of a mark of silver amounting to the equivalent of fifty days' labor.[19] Focusing solely on the economic distinction between active and passive citizens, Mackintosh decides that this injustice and "inconsistency" was due to "the more timid and prejudiced members," who, in combination with the "aristocratic minority" in the National Assembly, "stained the infant Constitution with this absurd usurpation." These timid, "temporizing characters" (*Works*, 439) conjure up the language by which he also criticizes the 1689 Convention Parliament, which, in his reading, consisted of trimming Whigs and reactionary Tories (the aristocratic minority) who produced the defective constitutional settlement of 1689. The Convention Whigs were "the sincere though timid and partial friends of freedom," who, out of fear of "Jacobitism," compromised their principles and formed an "unnatural coalition" with the monarchy (*Works*, 451). Mackintosh thus suggests another allusive connection between the defective 1689 Convention Parliament and that which is defective in the 1789 National Assembly. Aberrant French revolutionary history resembles reactionary English history, and Burke's condemnation of the restricted French franchise reflects on the restricted English franchise as well.

Mackintosh himself would extend the franchise to domestic servants (denied the franchise in the National Assembly's Decree of 22 December 1789), since "they subsist . . . on the produce of their own labour" and are not dependent, as are paupers, "the unproductive poor" (*Works*, 439). He assumes, however, that the logic of progressive history will soon result in the enfranchisement of the productive poor, for "the man who is too poor to pay a direct contribution, still pays a tax in the increased price of his food and clothes"; besides, "life and liberty are more sacred than property" and can only be protected by "the right of suffrage." Rejecting Burke's comparison of France with ancient democracies (*Reflections*, 228), Mackintosh realizes that these democracies were classically associated with anarchic mob rule and, following Aristotle, the degeneration of the polity into the despotism of the poor. Revolutionary France, he insists, "does not resemble" these ancient "governments." He hence formulates what had become a standard eighteenth-century distinction between ancient and modern democracies: "In the ancient democracies there was neither representation nor division of powers: *the rabble legislated, judged and exercised every political authority*" (*Works*,

439).[20] France is not a *democracy* in the "historical sense," for a
"degenerate democracy" is correctly called an "ochlocracy"—the word
Polybius used in lieu of Aristotle's "democracy."[21]

Mackintosh assures the English reader that France's new Constitution
resembles the "balanced" English constitution: legislative authority
vested in "the representatives of the people, the executive in an
hereditary First Magistrate, and the judicial" in elected, independent
judges (*Works*, 439). But this reassuring resemblance is deceptive, since
England's constitution is neither representative nor balanced.

For instance, Mackintosh reproduces the traditional dissident critique
of England's constitution: war debts, "persecuting statutes" against
Dissenters, the corrupting "venality" of the House of Commons, press
censorship, and taxation without real representation, since "no branch of
the Legislature represents the people" (*Works*, 455, 456). Alluding to
Burke's indignant query—"When did you hear in Great Britain of any
province suffering from the inequality of its representation?"
(*Reflections*, 303)—Mackintosh responds that "to be 'unequally
represented'" is absurd, since "unequal freedom is a contradiction in
terms. The law is the deliberate reason of all, guiding [the people's]
occasional will. Representation is an expedient for peacefully,
systematically, and unequivocally collecting this universal voice."
Equating the franchise with inviolable freedom, Mackintosh contrasts
unrepresented England with the French nation, a unified "general will":
in England there is no real "popular representative body," no true House
of Commons (*Works*, 455).

This is because, in Mackintosh's view, there is a class conspiracy.
Burke, in the *Reflections*, had contended that the Revolution was a conspiracy of atheistic *philosophes* and economic speculators. Throughout
the *Vindiciae*, Mackintosh rejects any notion of conspiracy (*Works*, 407,
413, 426, 433–34), except conspiracies against the Revolution (412).
Conspiracy theories abound in the revolutionary era because they ratio-
nalize history, making events understandable in terms of the designing
agents behind them. For Mackintosh, the conspiracy of the English upper
class against the people explains why there is no real representation in
England. Since the wealthy combine and unite through their vested class
interests—interests more important than minor differences—both Houses
of Parliament are "ruled by the same class of men." To disguise their oppressive power, they fabricate the fiction that there is a balanced constitution—a series of competitive interests that balance and equalize each
other, making it possible for the people to be virtually represented. But
all this is "imaginary," since the wealthy actually conspire to keep the
people powerless, and there "never was, and never will be, in civilized

society, but two grand interests—that of the rich and that of the poor" (*Works*, 415, 444–45). Even the "differences of interest among the several classes of the rich will be ever too slender to preclude their conspiracy against mankind"—a sentence in the first edition (*Vindiciae Gallicae*, 269) that was deleted in the third (*Works*, 445).

The unbalanced English constitution is, in essence, a conspiracy of the wealthy, a "conspiracy which can only be repressed by the energy of popular opinion" (*Works*, 456). Popular opinion is "public opinion," which referred "to the unrepresented but active sector of the population . . . not because the unrepresented lacked opinions . . . but because the unrepresented had nothing else by which to make their presence felt."[22] For Mackintosh, virtual "English" representation is a fiction, since the people who vote either elect representatives of their own (upper) class or are misrepresented by their upper-class representatives. Since the House of Lords represents only the upper class and the House of Commons is a middle-class fiction, "no branch of the Legislature represents the people" (*Works*, 456). Who can hear without "indignation," he asks, "the House of Commons of England called a popular representative body? A more insolent and preposterous abuse of language is not to be found in the vocabulary of tyrants" (*Works*, 455). Responding to Burke's challenge to show that there is not adequate representation in Britain (*Reflections*, 146), he employs a proto-Marxist explanation of British representation. His initial contradictory message that France's balanced constitution resembles England's but that England's constitution is fictional resolves itself in his subsequent, subversive reading of English history. What in England is a shadowy theory (i.e., "true" representation), an illusive fiction, is reality in France.[23] England's constitution is a debased copy of a "theory"; French revolutionary history is an original model for contemporary England. He thus suggests that a correspondent revolution in England would allow the fictional England to be finally realized.

Having argued that there is no real representation in England, Mackintosh contests Burke's contention that there is no real representation in France: Burke was incorrect to maintain that three elections separate the original active citizen from the representative to the National Assembly. The background is as follows: On 22 December 1789, the National Assembly had passed the *Decree Establishing Electoral and Administrative Assemblies*, abrogating the election in the districts, so that, as article 21 explained, between "the primary assemblies [in the cantons] and the National Assembly there shall be only one degree of intermediate election."[24] In a footnote, Burke, who had based his critique of the three separate elections on a preliminary proposal in the National Assembly, acknowledged that the "assembly, in executing the plan of their committee, made some alterations," striking "out one stage in these gradations; this removes a part of the objection: but the main objection, namely, that in their scheme the first constituent voter has no connexion with the representative legislator, remains in all its force" (*Reflections*, 288). In the Decree of 22 December, the elections within the primary assemblies are ignored, so that the elections within the departments constitute "one degree of intermediate election." Mackintosh cites the decree to suggest that, since Burke was incorrect about one stage of French election, his entire argument is erroneous. But Mackintosh is also sensitive to Burke's claim that the primary active citizen has no direct electoral connection with the representative.

Ignoring Burke's footnote and observing that Burke based his critique on the original proposal of "the Constitutional Committee" and had hence incorrectly produced another "medium" (the district, or what Burke had called the commune), Mackintosh notes that the active citizens in the primary Assemblies "send representatives . . . to the Assembly of the *Department* directly" (*Works*, 440). Burke, in the *Reflections*, had emphasized the fiction by which "every [French] man would vote directly for the person who was to represent him in the legislature" and the contradiction embodied in the actual, exclusive elections (287). The adverb *directly* apparently disturbed Mackintosh, who, in the first edition, underscored it to emphasize the correspondence between the primary voter and his representative. In both editions (first and third), he ignores Burke's point that there was still an intermediate stage, since the elected deputies to the departments subsequently elected the representatives to the National Assembly. Whether there were one or two intermediate elections is, of course, irrelevant, since any intermediate election contradicts the criterion of direct, democratic elections. Preoccupied with Burke's critique, Mackintosh continues to insist that Burke was in error to maintain that there were "three interposed elections" when, in fact, "the Electoral Assemblies in the Departments, who are the immediate constituents of the Legislature, are directly chosen by the Primary Assemblies" (*Works*, 442). The repetition of the adverb *directly* again suggests a direct correspondence between the active citizens who elect the deputies to the departments and who, in turn, reflect the choice of these voters in electing representatives to the National Assembly. But just as Burke, Mackintosh suggests, hides the removal of one stage of the elections, Mackintosh hides Burke's modest, concessionary footnote (blunted by Burke's discussion of the three electoral stages) in a polemical diversion by which he focuses attention on the last election: he hence retains the fiction of a direct correspondence between the primary elector and the last representative—

connected by the department deputy who perfectly reflects the first elector's choice.

But Mackintosh begs the question by suggesting that the representatives to the National Assembly are always the ones elected by the deputies in the departments representing the active citizens in the primary assemblies, and that there is thus a direct connection between the original active citizen and the representative. He suggests that the department deputy votes for the representative for whom the primary active citizen would have voted if he himself had been elected. Thus, in voting for the representative, the deputy reproduces the active citizen's delegated choice—the active citizen is perfectly represented by the deputy, who elects the representative, who, in turn, mirrors both the deputy and the active citizen. The deputies in both the primary assemblies and the departments were, however, elected by a majority, so those voting for another deputy could not be directly represented. Mackintosh was responding to Burke's criticism that "of all the powers unfit to be delegated . . . that most peculiarly unfit is what relates to *personal* choice. In case of abuse, that body of primary electors never can call the representative to an account for his conduct. He is too far removed from them in the chain of representation" (*Reflections*, 305). Mackintosh, in effect, turns Burke's criticism into an electoral paradox: personal choice can be perfectly delegated. By crystallizing a fiction of direct, "delegated" democratic representation, Mackintosh suggests that the intermediate French election paradoxically reproduces a true resemblance—an authentic representation of the people. The brunt of both Burke's and Mackintosh's electoral minutia pertains to the fiction of a direct correspondence between signifier and signified—an episteme that still influenced eighteenth-century thought. Mackintosh confronts Burke's critique by arguing that the French Revolution replaced chaos and division with unity and correspondence.

Mackintosh, however, employs contradictory arguments because there were contradictory paradigms pertinent to English thought: the paradigm of a direct correspondence between the elector and the representative and an antagonistic paradigm of the representative's independence. In order to have it all ways—perhaps suggesting that the Revolution paradoxically reconciles all apparent contradictions—Mackintosh selectively argues on one side and then moves to the other, without acknowledging either contradiction. He is compelled by Burke's criticism to provide elaborate explanations for contradictions that he insists are paradoxes. In the *Reflections*, Burke had stressed the absence of accountability in French elections: since representatives serve only two years and then are ineligible the two following years for reelection, the representative who "acts improperly at the end of his two years lease" is not responsive to any constituency.[25] Moreover, since the electoral departments are dissolved after each election, "all the members of this elective constitution are equally fugitive, and exist only for the election, [and] may no longer be the same persons who had chosen [the representative] to whom he is to be responsible" (*Reflections*, 306). For Burke, the *fugitive* nature of the entire electoral process means that electoral responsibility "cannot exist." In arguing for accountability, Burke insists that the electors must "retain some hold" on the representative "by personal obligation of dependence"—something impossible in a bogus electoral process in which the "primary electors" do not personally know the representative chosen by the department electors (305). For his English audience, Burke evokes the direct, "democratic" elections of the members of the House of Commons that he allusively contrasts to the antidemocratic French farce.

Without mentioning Burke's criticism, Mackintosh also responds allusively by arguing against the electoral dependence of the representative, contending that the fugitive French elections actually guarantee the *independence* of the representative. He undercuts Burke's democratic criterion (considerably extended since his celebrated speech to the electors of Bristol) with an aristocratic argument that would appeal to the upper-class audience of both the *Reflections* and the *Vindiciae*. Thus he argues that the members of the National Assembly were independent from the constituencies that elected them, because the latter (the assemblies, administrative and elected) are "biennially renewed," as was the National Assembly. The National Assembly could not be instructed, since its members would have no inclination to obey "the mandates of those who held as fugitive and precarious a power as their own," and who might not be able to vote in the next election, since they could also be turned out by the voters who had elected them (*Works*, 441). In other words, frequent elections would make influence and corruption impossible, and Mackintosh's English audience would understand the formulation in context of the traditional radical critique of infrequent English elections and the Septennial Act. English dissidents, however, had traditionally promoted frequent elections as a way of making the representative more responsive to the voters, whereas Mackintosh extols them as a way to make the representative more independent. English dissidents had also maintained that frequent elections would make the MPs independent of court influence, so Mackintosh may have been revising the standard dissident argument to fit French circumstances. He does, nevertheless, try to have it both ways: the French representative is independent of the voters who elected him, yet French elections are democratically representative of the people's will.

After stressing the independence of the representative but recognizing that he sounds too traditional, he adds that he does not mean to suggest that the elector's "voice" would not be "respected," for "that would be to suppose the Legislature as insolently corrupt as that of a neighboring nation" (*Works*, 441; in the first edition, the neighboring nation is "a neighboring Government of pretended freedom," *Vindiciae Gallicae*, 239). He only means "to assert" that the electors do not have the power "to dictate instructions to their representatives as authoritatively as sovereigns do their ambassadors." This apparently alludes to article 34 of the Decree of 22 December 1789: "The liberty of the [representatives'] votes may not be restricted [by the electors] by any special mandate; the primary and electoral assemblies shall address directly to the legislative body whatever petitions and instructions they wish to send thereto."[26] Members of the National Assembly were preoccupied with their independence, especially since many of them had been criticized for exceeding their original instructions, when the Third Estate declared itself to be the National Assembly on 17 June 1789.

In England, the right of the electors to issue binding instructions to their representatives had long been part of the dissident agenda and had been more or less accepted in America.[27] Writing in 1791, Thomas Christie noted that, in England, the controversial issue of binding instructions was still undecided: "There are differences of opinion amongst us."[28] Conscious of his upper-class audience, Mackintosh conspicuously ignores the issue and emphasizes instead an electoral position resembling Burke's: an independent representative who represents the nation but not specific individuals. Because Burke had confronted the Revolution's British supporters with the most radical, democratic criteria (direct popular elections and the mythical mirroring of the elector and representative), contesting the way revolutionary representation really worked (restrictive and repressive), Mackintosh had to explain why French "delegation" was actually more practical and representative in the real world: "I profess I see no reason why the right of election is not as susceptible of delegation as any other civil function,—why a citizen may not as well delegate the right of choosing lawgivers, as that of making laws" (*Works*, 442).

Acknowledging that "representation itself must be confessed to be an infringement on the most perfect liberty," since "even the best organized system cannot preclude the possibility of a variance between the popular and the representative will," Mackintosh contends, nevertheless, that the different "gradation of elections" (primary and departmental) actually approximates the popular will—unlike messy English elections where the "intoxication of an election mob" results in tumult and venality (*Works*, 442). Suddenly the direct correspondence between signifier and signified, the voter and representative, is an illusion, as Mackintosh explains that, in the real world, the representative's "sincerity" can never be transparent, "for the secrets of political fraud are so impenetrable, and the line which separates corrupt decision from erroneous judgement so indiscernably minute," that it is simply impossible to ascertain an individual's true intentions. Suggesting that the "radical" Burke labors under the delusion that there must be direct popular elections, Mackintosh contends that holding frequent elections and the possibility of the representative's "dismissal" are the best and only "probability of [the] unison between the constituent and his deputy" (*Works*, 442).

Since the deputies to the departments ("numerous" and "popularly elected") must themselves face biannual elections, they will be responsible to those who, in the primary assemblies, elected them: "They have too many points of contact with the general mass to have an insulated opinion, and too fugitive an existence to have a separate interest" (*Works*, 442). This is implicitly the case of the representatives in the National Assembly, who must also face biannual elections and who must also be accountable to the electors in the departments or face dismissal in the next election. The biannual elections ensure that each deputy will be responsive and responsible to the constituency that elected him. But Mackintosh had previously maintained that the frequent biannual elections of the primary and departmental assemblies ensured the independence of the representatives in the National Assembly, since the assemblies' "fugitive nature" guaranteed that members of the National Assembly could not be pressured or intimidated (*Works*, 441). He then contends that the assemblies' "fugitive" existence ensures that they will be responsible to their constituencies (*Works*, 442). It makes no sense, however, to argue that frequent elections make the primary and department deputies responsive to their constituencies yet ensure the National Assembly's independence from its constituency. Mackintosh ignores the unresolved contradiction: the direct, dependent link between the electors in the assemblies and their deputies versus the independent National Assembly, pristinely removed from the democratic "chain."

Mackintosh, in effect, argues that the French electoral system guarantees the representative's independence yet is more democratic than the English system by which the voter directly elects his representative. The French system is simultaneously aristocratically restrictive and democratically popular. Mackintosh's democratic diction asserts the latter: the deputies to the departments are "popularly elected"; they have "too many points of contact with the general mass to have an insulated opinion." At the same time, however, the French system is not degraded by the "polluted medium of a popular canvass" (as in England), since the "direct right of electing legislators" involves that "tumult, venality, and intoxication of an election mob"—the messy corruption by which English voters are pandered to and bought. If the French primary elector were "mocked" with "the direct right of electing legislators," he would, like his implicit English counterpart, "give his suffrage without any possible knowledge of the situation, character, and conduct of the candidates" (*Works*, 442). Fortunately, the French are not *"mocked"* with such a dubious right—the verb Price had used in the *Discourse* referring to illusory English representation ("We are mocked with the shadow," *Political Writings*, 192) and that Burke had angrily quoted in the *Reflections* and reapplied to the primary electors who do not know their representatives and are consequently "mocked" with the bogus, French elections (146, 305).

By contrast, the French medium of indirect elections guarantees that the "peasant or artisan" in the primary assemblies will know "intimately among his equals, or immediate superiors, many men who have information and honesty enough to choose a good representative, but few who have genius, leisure, and ambition for the situation themselves" (*Works*, 442; cf. first edition [246–47] where the class dimension is more pronounced). Through a politics of deference, the peasant or artisan will rely on the judgment of "equals" and (again having it both ways) "immediate superiors" who will decide who can best represent the primary assemblies in the departments. These elected deputies will then decide who can best represent the nation in the National Assembly, since "few have genius, leisure, and ambition"—i.e., the economic independence—"for the situation themselves" (*Works*, 442).[29] Having it both ways, Mackintosh understandably does not mention the two additional economic qualifications for each subsequent election.

For Mackintosh, the "hierarchy of electors" in France (*Works*, 442) ensures continuity and order as well as the proper expression of popular democracy. The restrictive, indirect elections paradoxically produce true, representative democracy. The barriers that Burke insists separate the original active citizen from the twice-removed representative become, in Mackintosh's representation, the medium through which participatory democracy actually works. Burke had contended that "there is little, or rather no, connection between the last representative and the first constituent. The member who goes to the national assembly is not chosen by the people, nor accountable to them"; he "is too far removed . . . [from the primary electors] in the chain of representation" (*Reflections*, 304–5). Mackintosh inverts Burke's critique by making the chain of representation connect the last representative with the first constituent. He himself holds the contradictory links together by connecting a democratic diction with disdainful aristocratic imagery: without this "hierarchy of electors," the elections would have degenerated into a tumultuous democratic farce—the "intoxication of an election mob," resulting in the election of deputies "so numerous as to have made the national assembly a mob" (*Works*, 442).[30]

If the gradations and mediums paradoxically guarantee a stable representative order, Mackintosh returns to a paradigm of mythical unity by arguing that the old French constitution could not, as Burke suggested, have been reformed along the lines of the "balanced" British constitution: two Houses of Parliament and the monarchy (*Works*, 443–44). The background of his discussion is the decision of the National Assembly to remain unicameral, unlike the bicameral British and American "Houses" proposed by its advocates. Burke and others had criticized the decision, contending that one house dominated by the Third Estate meant that the other interests, e.g., the landed, were not represented and hence that the new French constitution was packed and unbalanced (*Reflections*, 129–32, 316). Mackintosh responds by again mixing French and English discourses.

His French argument is that the clergy and nobility constituted fictional corporate classes at odds with the very essence of the Revolution. Since the Revolution had destroyed the corporate spirit, it would have contradictorily reintroduced it if different representative bodies, like different orders and estates, were allowed to exist (*Works*, 415, 420–21). Since the French nation is one and indivisible, different representative "voices" would have fragmented the mythical unity of the indivisible French people represented in the univocal National Assembly (443–44). But in arguing against corporate spirits and fictions, Mackintosh reasserts his own French fiction—the idea of one indivisible people whose general will is transparently represented in one mystical body. Mackintosh reinscribes what the French themselves were asserting: the National Assembly represents the collective national "will" but not individual Frenchmen possessing private, selfish interests at odds with the nation's will.

The English side of his French fiction concerns pejorative dependency, a familiar theme to his English audience. Since the French clergy and nobility constitute corporate "castes," they could be influenced by the monarchy, which would acquire both of their "voices" through perks and privileges. The poorer children of the nobility, for instance, would seek service in the military and be servilely dependent on the monarchy for any promotions or advancements. The combination of the nobility and clergy in one or two Houses would have united them against the "monied and commercial interest": "The aristocracy could have been strong only against the people, impotent against the Crown" (*Works*, 443). The people, the nation's true voice, would be overpowered by the two voices granted the aristocracy or, if the latter were combined in one House, their collective voice would cancel the popular voice, and their permanence (like the House of Lords' nonelective life tenure) would have overpowered a transient "Commons." The result would be the reintroduction of "corporation spirit"—France's national voice would be again divided against itself. In discussing why the National Assembly had to be a univocal body, Mackintosh repeats what he had said about the Estates General: it was necessary that all three Orders be composed in one body—otherwise, the "possession of two equal and independent voices must have rendered the exertions of the Commons impotent and nugatory" (*Works*, 411). In arguing against a bicameral National Assembly (*Works*, 443–44), Mackintosh reasserts the same points made by the Abbé Sieyès against a bicameral Estates General, as well as Sieyès's criticisms of the English House of Lords and Commons.[31] Mackintosh concludingly returns to his French fiction:

> It will not be controverted, that the object of establishing a representative legislature is to collect the general will. That will is one: it cannot, therefore, without a solecism, be *doubly* represented. Any absolute negative opposed to the national will, decisively spoken by its representatives, is null, as an usurpation of the popular sovereignty. (*Works*, 444)

For Mackintosh, national unity literally signifies *one* representation—the mythical "unanimous voice of the nation" (*Works*, 413; cf. Paine, *CW*, 1:372, 390).

The regnant point of Mackintosh's fiction is, of course, the balanced constitution of England (*triply* represented), for if a balanced constitution of different interests is a contradiction in terms, a fragmentation of the indivisible national will, the reader must also conclude that England's vaunted constitution is an egregious "solecism." Mackintosh had initially suggested that the (un)balanced French constitution was not comparable to England's constitution, since, in England, both the commercial and landed interests were represented in the House of Commons, and the House of Lords were "united to the mass," just as the deputies to the French departments were united to the "mass" by "innumerable points of contact" (*Works*, 443, 442). Besides, in England, the House of Lords

"only preserves its dignity by a wise disuse of its power" (*Works*, 444).
But all this is disingenuous and contradictory, since he proceeds to argue
that the balanced English constitution is a fiction foisted on the English
people by the conspiratorial upper classes:

> It is perhaps susceptible of proof, that these governments of balance and
> control have never existed but in the vision of theorists. The fairest example
> will be that of England. If the two branches of the Legislature, which it is
> pretended control each other, are ruled by the same class of men, the control
> must be granted to be imaginary. The great proprietors, titled and untitled,
> possess the whole force of both Houses of Parliament that is not immediately
> dependent on the Crown. The Peers have a great influence in the House of
> Commons. All political parties are formed by a confederacy of the members
> of both Houses [cf. Paine, *CW*, 1:411]. The Court party, acting equally in
> both, is supported by a part of the independent aristocracy—the Opposition
> by the remainder of the aristocracy, whether peers or commoners. Here is
> every symptom of collusion,—no vestige of control. (*Works*, 444)

The initial distinction (*Works*, 443–44) between the traditional English
and French constitutions disappears as the former now resembles what
Mackintosh insisted the latter would become if the French had foolishly
tried to imitate the English example. The distinction disguises a
complicit, circular argument ending with the inference that the English
should reform their fictionally balanced constitution by imitating the
French example. Inverting and reversing Burke (who now resembles the
visionary "theorists" criticized in the *Reflections*) and his representation
of the English example, Mackintosh subversively translates the French
Revolution into English discourse, for only a comparable revolution
would create the French example he promotes.

Mixing his French and English discourses, Mackintosh presents a
representational myth of French unity versus English division. His
divided discourse asserts the paradox of unity out of division, e pluribus
unum. He responds to Burke's critique of active and passive citizens and
the distinctions and barriers that separate and exclude both kinds of
citizens by arguing that the initial divisions and gradations paradoxically
produce the mythic unity of the "general will," perfectly represented in
the univocal National Assembly. The other discourse that allusively
informs Mackintosh's discussion is Rousseau's *Social Contract*, specifically Rousseau's contention that electoral representation contradicts
transparency—that it is impossible to represent another person.[32]
Mackintosh had previously referred to the "general will," allusively
invoking Rousseau's *Social Contract* (*Works*, 440; cf. 455), noting that if
"Rousseau has had any influence in promoting the Revolution, it is by his

Social Contract" (*Works*, 426). Although he quotes Rousseau approvingly in spite of Burke, citing the *Social Contract* (*Works*, 436, 447), he says nothing about Rousseau's antirepresentational stricture, since it contradicts his French fiction. Rousseau's presence is, however, behind Mackintosh's acknowledgment that the intentions of the representative cannot be transparently known, that "representation itself must be confessed to be an infringement on the most perfect liberty," since there is always the "possibility of a variance between the popular and the representative will" (*Works*, 442). But, in the end, the elaborate electoral gradations (connecting the representative with the primary active voters and the "passive" people) produce the transparent, Rousseauan "general will." In spite of Rousseau, he reinscribes what Rousseau insists is impossible, devising his discourse to fit his argument.

Throughout the *Vindiciae*, Mackintosh selectively applies a variety of contradictory solutions to particular problems. Lionel McKenzie has noted that Mackintosh used the available languages of progressive discourse (Commonwealth or "real Whig," natural rights, and utilitarianism) but that each of these languages often contradicted the others. By locking himself into a particular language, during a particular argument, Mackintosh exposed himself to forthcoming embarrassments—the discrepancies between discordant French events and his prior representations.[33] A different way to put this is that Mackintosh employs different arguments and languages to reconcile the various revolutionary contradictions that Burke exposes in the *Reflections*. Mackintosh counterresponds by marshaling a variety of languages and discourses to account for those apparent contradictions, and his discussion of the French *assignats* is, as we shall now see, another case in point.[34]

III

The controversy over the *assignats*, the paper currency created after the confiscation of the church lands to liquidate the national debt and to stabilize the economy, complements the theme of representation in the *Vindiciae*. Because the *assignats* were theoretically tied to the confiscated land and were supposedly backed up by real property value, there were various discourses available to Mackintosh, both English and French.

In England, after the Glorious Revolution, there had been a financial revolution, culminating in the mid-1690s with the establishment of institutions of public credit. The Bank of England and the financing of the national debt enabled the English government to wage wars in Europe and expand its empire in the Atlantic, the Mediterranean, and India.[35] Consequently, a new class of investors surfaced, the speculators, who made their living by financing the public debt. Referred to as stockjobbers, they often manipulated the rise and fall of market values, basing their speculations on people's financial fears and expectations. To many people, this new economic episteme seemed frighteningly unnatural, and it was common to contrast the new fluctuation of prices based on future projections with the old episteme, in which land and money supposedly represented a true fixed value. The two epistemes hence constituted two antithetical models: illusory artificial paper versus real money or land containing, or backed up by, an intrinsic, stable value.

The disaster of the English South Sea Company (1720) accelerated the anxiety over debt financing, speculation, and a paper currency that did not correspond to any "real" value. Theoretically, the company was supposed to have taken "over a portion of the National Debt," but inflated speculation in its stock resulted in its financial collapse and the ensuing crisis in England.[36] Throughout the eighteenth century, Commonwealth and Country writers contended that the new economic order created sources of wealth by which the monarchy and court could corrupt Parliament with bribes and patronage—affecting the Parliament's independence and destroying the constitution's "balance." For these writers, "personal independence . . . could only belong to men whose property was their own and did not consist in expectations from the men in government; and the moral quality which only propertied independence could confer, and which became almost indistinguishable from property itself, was known as 'virtue.'"[37] The contrast of independent virtue with dependent "corruption" was commonly used by both Tories and opposition Whigs. Queen Anne Tories "had thundered against Whig rule as that of a monied interest, made up of men" who utilized "the paper tokens of a fluctuating public confidence, in which the determinants of the rate at which money could be had, and the value of all property created, had themselves become a species of commodity." Burke, in the *Reflections*, was using the language of Queen Anne Toryism—"a language," as Pocock notes, first created "to attack the foundations of the Whig order [Burke] is concerned to defend," although Burke believed the latter to be more stable than the French ancien régime.[38]

Writers on both the Left and Right often associated paper money with fantasy and illusion, connecting economic speculation with theoretic or political "speculation." Economic speculators were also associated with theoretical projectors; a *projector*, according to Samuel Johnson, is "one who forms wild impracticable schemes" (1755 *Dictionary*, def. 2), like those in Swift's *Gulliver's Travels*. The promoters of joint stock companies formed in England, Holland, and Italy were also called "projectors."[39] A *projector* was, as the *OED* notes, "In invidious use: A schemer; one who lives by his wits; a promoter of bubble companies; a speculator, a cheat" (def. 1b; cf. Adam Smith, *Wealth of Nations*, 1:131, 304, 307, 310–12, 315–16, 374).

There was a correspondent French context, for the classical episteme in which signifier and signified, the representative and represented directly reflected each other, still preoccupied French writers in the seventeenth and eighteenth centuries, even as it was being displaced by a new episteme that acknowledged fluctuant discrepancy, in place of correspondent unity.[40] In France, the disaster of the Mississippi Company had coincided in time (1720) with the disastrous collapse of the South Sea Company in England.[41] In *The Wealth of Nations*, Adam Smith had criticized both stock-jobbing projects, and Burke, in the *Reflections*, referred to both in connection with egregious economic "speculation" in revolutionary France (310). In both countries, there were long memories of the financial crises caused by exorbitant economic speculation. All the above impinged on the debates over the *assignats* in the National Assembly in 1789–90. Opponents of the *assignats* referred to the Mississippi Company, arguing that the *assignats* would force gold and silver out of circulation, resulting in hoarding and the creation of fictitious paper money.[42] Talleyrand, for instance, argued that, although the *assignat* supposedly represented gold and silver, it did not have the intrinsic value of its model and would depreciate because people would doubt its correspondence with the value of the land theoretically backing it up. The Chamber of Commerce of Lyons agreed: "Effective numéraire [specie] is representative of all other values only because it has a value independent of this representation; paper money can never fulfill this function adequately." Others feared that the *assignats* would depreciate and precipitate inflation.[43]

The proponents of the *assignats*, however, saw them as a way of solving France's financial crisis. To pay off the national debt, the government would issue *assignats* on the security of the confiscated church lands. In theory, the *assignats* would be backed up by the land's real, presumably stable value, constituting a true correspondence of represented value. The sale of land would correspond to the controlled release of *assignats* valued at the land's worth: the *assignats* would be issued to creditors who would use them to purchase the land and then be burned at the time of purchase, canceling a portion of the national debt.

Through a system of strict control, the *assignats* would not depreciate nor would they cause inflation. Although many of the French people were suspicious of the expediency of paper money, the correspondence between the *assignats* and the land was a key selling point of its advocates.[44] In "The Third Address of the National Assembly to the People of France" (3 May 1790), the National Assembly, nervous over the confiscation of church lands, the conversion of the *assignats* into common currency, and memories of the Mississippi Company fiasco, endeavored to convince the French people that the *assignats* had a real, fixed value backed up by the land: "The effects [i.e., the lands], of which the *assignats* represent the produce, form their intrinsic value; and that value is as evident as that of the metal contained in our common coin. . . . [P]aper money, without an effective value (which it cannot have, unless it represents special property), is inadmissible, in commerce, to stand in competition with the metals which have a real value, and independent of all convention. . . . [This is why, when] the National Assembly . . . gave the Assignats an obligatory value of convention, they had first assured to them a real and immoveable value."[45]

The troubled history of the *assignats* is well known. They were used for things other than what they were originally intended: instead of being spent for national property and burned, they were allowed to circulate and become legal tender; carrying five percent interest (later lowered to three), the *assignats* could also be redeemed in lieu of the purchase of land; speculators consequently bought them, creating a cycle of inflation—the *assignats* lost their face value, causing specie to be hoarded. Even when they were used as intended, the government issued too many and exceeded the value of the land; in addition, the land on which the *assignats* were based was frequently encumbered with debt and heavily mortgaged.

For Burke, the *assignats* illustrated the dangers of illusory paper money and the correspondent collapse of France's new representational order. His critique of electoral representation complements his critique of economic representation. In the *Reflections*, he asks his English audience if they should imitate the economy of revolutionary France and substitute a "compulsory paper currency" for the "legal coin of this kingdom" (145).[46] He suggests that the revolutionaries are forcing their illegitimate values, their bastard currency, on the French people. Hence, the French *assignat* becomes the illustrative example of fictitious representations of revolutionary reality. By tracing the circular cycle of the *assignat*— church and crown lands are confiscated and auctioned off as plunder purchased in the form of *assignats* used to pay off France's creditors, which the latter use to buy the confiscated lands—Burke documents a series of representations that contradict rather than complement each other. The rationalization for the confiscation of the lands and the creation of the *assignats* is that they will pay off the national debt, yet the result is the enforced bankruptcy of France. The "madness of the project of confiscation" depreciates the value of the land, and revolutionary financiers exacerbate the financial crisis as inflationary *assignats* become the basis of "fictitious wealth" (223, 224). The new paper money creates inflation, not stability, because its true value does not correspond to what it supposedly represents.[47]

Burke's economic critique of revolutionary representation indicts revolutionary "managers" for violating what he believes are natural moral laws and a normative order of reality. What emerges is a kind of Burkean law suggesting that, in a revolutionary crisis, false representations replace true representations just as, in Gresham's law, bad money drives out good money. France's bankrupt economy "swells" with "fictitious representation" (*Reflections*, 357). Since the depreciated lands and the inflated *assignats* do not reflect an intrinsic value, the French people are forced to accept a paper fantasy similar to all the proclamations and pamphlets Burke sees inundating France. The depiction of revolutionary robbers establishing illusory values and attempting "to reverse the very nature of things" (359) suggests an inverted world of uncontrolled madness. By making "their paper circulation compulsory in all payments" (225), the revolutionaries force their false values on the French people—they force the people to accept their fictitious representation of economic reality. They attempt to sanction the illegitimate confiscations by binding "the nation in one guilty interest" (225): the enforced acceptance of the *assignats* suggests a de facto acquiescence legitimizing revolutionary values.

The enforcement of these values is especially illustrative in the plight of the clergy, who have been reduced to state functionaries and com pelled to receive their state allowance in *assignats*, "the depreciated paper . . . stamped with . . . the symbols of their own ruin" (*Reflections*, 226). Burke is outraged that the Revolution's victims are forced to accept the very values that destroy them: "So violent an outrage upon credit, property, and liberty, as this compulsory paper currency, has seldom been exhibited by the alliance of bankruptcy and tyranny, at any time, or in any nation" (226). Because real credit has been systematically discredited, the Revolution has no real money, no real credit, and there can be no correspondent faith, trust, or belief in it. He stresses this again when he refers to revolutionary managers: "For credit, properly speaking, they have none" (359). The corollary is that, despite the enforcement of these fictitious representations, the French people do not believe them, because the discrepancy between illusion and reality cannot be papered over. The upshot is also obvious: when the revolutionaries "force a currency of their own fiction in the place of that which is real," they end by "establishing an unheard of despotism" (261).

English currency, however, is soundly based on either deposited wealth (*Reflections*, 357) or gold or silver specie; even when Burke is referring to British paper currency, which is not valuable in itself, he assumes that it corresponds to a real value because it is based on real wealth (357–58), rather like American Silver Certificates before the switch to Federal Reserve Notes. This representative order (money) consequently, for Burke, reflects the correspondent economic reality on which it is based.

During the French Revolution, this fundamental understanding of representation tinctured Burke's thinking about almost everything, whether it was a stable semantic vocabulary expressing linguistic continuity or traditional European values reflecting a genuine ontological order. While Burke recognized the discrepancies between reality and representation, he reaffirmed what to many seemed a beleaguered world view, because he believed that these discrepancies were deviations from a natural order of reality. It followed that the Revolution and all that it represented was not based on anything real. Burke delights in documenting all the chaotic contradictions that he contends are destroying the revolutionary world. His emphasis on the need to contain this world within France was an effort to turn the Revolution against itself—to implode it on its own inflationary contradictions.

Burke's opponents responded differently to the issue of *assignats*. Early in her *Letters from France* (1790), for instance, Helen Maria Williams mentions the *assignats* once, noting that some people have profited from the new paper money while the loss that others have incurred has inspired them to "extraordinary industry and activity. Commerce has benefited in both cases." If French aristocrats have left France carrying with them France's gold, it is a profitable trade-off, since they "have also carried away" an "immense load of prejudices. . . . If the French money" has disappeared so have "the corvée, the gabelle," and other old injustices. She ends with this optimistic prediction: "Paper money, when the crisis of the revolution is past, will, by a process only known to free states, be transformed into pure gold."[48]

Wollstonecraft, several years later, in *An Historical and Moral View of the French Revolution* (1794), had a necessarily different perspective. The *assignats* might have worked if they had been strictly secured to the land, but the issue of paper notes to finance the accumulating debt actually increased it. She then contrasts the stable value of gold and silver with the arbitrary value of paper: "Gold and silver have a specific value, because it is not easy to accumulate them beyond a certain quantity," but paper "is a dangerous expedient, except under a well established government: and even then the business ought to be conducted with great moderation and sagacity" (*WMW*, 6:181–82).

Paine had long been preoccupied with the dangers of paper money— his experience with worthless continentals in the American Revolution was instructive—and he continually predicted the collapse of England's "paper" economy. In *Rights of Man*, however, he avoids any direct mention of the *assignats*. Distinguishing between the old government and the new French nation, he contends that the French people rendered the government insolvent by refusing to pay taxes for extravagant expenses, thus assuming control of the government and making France's creditors more secure. The new revolutionary government discharged the debt by actually paying it off in two ways: by reducing government expenditures and "by the sale of the monastic and ecclesiastical landed estates" (*CW*, 1:336–37). This is, however, rather disingenuous, since Paine tacitly assumes a strict correspondence between the lands and the *assignats*, the latter of which he keeps out of sight and which had been functioning as currency since April 1790. He proceeds to argue that France actually possesses more gold and silver than England and hence possesses more real wealth, that ever since the Hanoverian succession, England had compounded its proliferating debt by issuing more paper currency and trying to pay off the debt through an absurd sinking fund—the government tax that theoretically created a surplus over current expenditures—a surplus placed in a fund used to liquidate the national debt. But the debt, Paine notes, only proliferates. As the government borrows to pay off interest, the fund requires "an amount of taxes at least equal to the whole landed rental of the nation in acres, to defray the annual expenditure": "The funding system is not money; neither is it, properly speaking, credit. It in effect creates upon paper the sum which it appears to borrow, and lays on a tax to keep the imaginary capital alive by the payment of interest, and sends the annuity to market, to be sold for paper already in circulation" (1:332). English finances are based on a paper fantasy: Paine, in effect, throws Burke's representation back at him, making the same point about English "paper" that Burke makes about the *assignats*. Like Wollstonecraft, Paine notably does not contest Burke's critique of the *assignats,* and, like other radicals and conservatives as well, he shares common assumptions about true representation and the direct correspondence between signifier and signified in language, politics, and economics that are supposedly properly correct and hence real. Likewise, he insists, as they do, that contradiction and misrepresentation characterize the opposition's language, politics, and economics.[49]

Mackintosh also shares these assumptions, but he also meets head-on Burke's criticisms of the *assignats*. In the *Vindiciae,* Mackintosh begins by using Burke's language of "credit" to discredit the old regime. Like Burke, he uses *credit* in its various senses: a reputation for solvency and integrity, entitling a person to be trusted in buying or borrowing; the confidence in a buyer's ability to fulfill financial obligations at some future time; the positive balance in a person's account; the faith, trust, and confidence that a promise or obligation will be effectively carried out—the influence or power of a person who is credited and believed. The concept of credit is based on correspondence: different things will be balanced; understandings will be mutually fulfilled.

Using this language, Mackintosh contends that the old regime was not reformable, that it had no credit, neither economic capital nor the required confidence of the French people. The history of the old regime's "profligate expedients" resulted in the loss of its "power" and "credit"; the immense deficit was the cause of the calling of the Estates General "to guarantee the ruined credit of bankrupt despotism by the sanction of the national voice" (*Works*, 407, 408). He argues that the economic crisis inflated the political crisis: despotism was financially and politically bankrupt; the economic crisis led to political change. While Necker's "personal reputation" for "probity," momentarily "reanimated the credit of France," the financial disaster was irresoluble. The Estates General was consequently convoked (*Works*, 409–10). Necker's own "credit" in the royalist "Court declined every day"; in contrast, the "authority of the [National] Assembly was ... first conferred on it by public confidence"—the genuine source of its credit. Likewise, the Church "languished in the discredit of miracles," while new revolutionary nations like America had "affluence and credit" (*Works*, 411, 414, 429, 431). Mackintosh reverses Burke's representation, crediting the new revolutionary order that Burke denounces.

His major challenge is to credit the *assignats* that Burke had discredited: "The only financial operation which may be regarded as complete is [the National Assembly's] emission of *assignats*—the paper representative of the national property; which, while it facilitated the sale of that property, should supply the absence of specie in ordinary circulation" (*Works*, 428). Confronting Burke's characterization of the fluctuating, transient nature of the *assignats*, Mackintosh regards the establishment of the *assignats* to be based on and backed up by the lands it represents: the *assignats* are "the paper representative of the national property."

His reference to the "absence of specie" (*Works*, 428) tacitly concedes that specie was, in fact, being hoarded and that the *assignats* had been converted to legal tender to replace it. But this does not apparently matter, since, according to him, the French people have faith and credit in the miraculous *assignats*. Indeed, the predictions of the Revolution's enemies had proven wrong: they erroneously predicted that there would not be sufficient purchasers of the lands who trusted "their property on the tenure of a new and insecure establishment," that the estimate of the lands' value would be exaggerated, and that the depreciation of the *assignats* would increase "the price of the necessities of life," hurting the poor. The "most unanswerable reply" to those who have criticized the *assignats* is the fact that millions of *assignats* have already been "committed to the flames": i.e., there is a strict correspondence between the sale of the land and the burning of the *assignats*, so that paper money would not proliferate, as Burke and others predicted, but would disappear from circulation once the correspondent land was sold (*Works*, 428). In retrospect, the discredited predictions of the Revolution's enemies were fulfilled, especially once the issue of *assignats* exceeded the estimated value of the lands (2.5 billion *livres*): by January 1793, the total amount of *assignats* in circulation was 3.2 billion, exceeding "the entire value of the originally confiscated national properties."[50] This was not unforeseeable, and Mackintosh's criticism of Burke's paper fantasy was itself a paper fantasy based on revolutionary projections.

For Mackintosh, the *assignats* had two principal advantages: "The first was to attach a great body of proprietors to the Revolution, on the stability of which must depend the security of their fortunes. This is what Mr. Burke terms, making them accomplices in confiscation [see *Reflections*, 225]; though it was precisely the policy adopted by the English Revolutionists, when they favoured the growth of a national debt, to interest a body of creditors in the permanence of their new establishment" (*Works*, 428). Mackintosh refers to the creation of the English National Bank and the expansion of the empire through "a body of creditors" who financed the debt that made this possible. He again throws 1688 and the Revolution Settlement back at Burke, who cannot consistently criticize the French for doing precisely what the English had done. But in articulating this revolutionary repetition, Mackintosh disingenuously suggests that the 1688 English revolutionaries had also made proprietors and creditors "accomplices in confiscation," just as the French had subsequently done, when, in fact, confiscations took place in Ireland, not England, and the land was given again to the Protestant Ascendancy, not to creditors.[51] There is, however, enough resemblance to make the English reader see the 1690s in the 1790s. There is also a possible French context, since

Mirabeau and others had also argued that the extended use of the *assignats* would attach the people to the Revolution, providing them a vested interest in the lands as well as the Revolution's values.[52]

The second principal advantage of the *assignats* is the "liquidation of the public debt," something very probable, since the value of the national property is, "according to the best calculations," more than four *milliards*, even though the counterrevolutionary Calonne had misrepresented it as worth "only two *milliards* (about eighty-three millions sterling)." The "best calculations" discredit "so gross a representation" (*Works*, 428). Mackintosh does not, however, cite his source for "the best calculations" and if Calonne underestimates, he himself overestimates, since all participants in the debates over the *assignats* in the National Assembly agreed that the national properties were worth somewhere between 2 and 3 billion *livres*, i.e., 2 or 3 *milliards*. The Assembly's finance committee put the value of the properties at 2.5 billion *livres*.[53] Mackintosh, like Calonne, also engages in "so gross a misrepresentation" and predicts that France will soon liquidate the majority of her debt, removing taxes impeding her "industry," and opening the nation to its destined "prosperity" (*Works*, 428).

He does concede that the *assignats* "have promoted, in some degree, a spirit of gambling" (*Works*, 428), i.e., the spirit of "gaming" and "speculation" that Burke had predicted (*Reflections*, 310), perhaps giving "an undue ascendant . . . to the agents of the paper circulation." These are fugitive evils, however, since the *assignats* will disappear once all the national lands are sold. This is, as we have seen, based on the strict correspondence between the sale of the lands and the burning of the *assignats*—a relationship that had been violated before Mackintosh had started writing the *Vindiciae*. Thus, Mackintosh keeps out of sight a series of inconvenient facts contradicting his own representations: the *assignats* were not always tied to the lands—they could be redeemed for interest and could be used to purchase "anything else as well";[54] to deal with hoarding and the exportation of specie, French authorities had also permitted the *assignats* to be issued in smaller denominations, so that they could become legal tender, in April 1790.

Although Mackintosh alludes to the latter, he contends that the only fundamental question is whether or not the *assignats* retain their value. If their value remains stable, then all pessimistic prognostications are without credit. If the *assignats* are, however, "discredited," the ensuing depreciation and inflation would discredit them with the public as well, motivating people to exchange them for land, since "no man would retain depreciated paper who could acquire solid property" (*Works*, 428; cf.

Reflections, 132, 11.8–10). Since the fall in value would cause people to exchange the *assignats* for land, the *assignats'* value would actually increase because there would be fewer in circulation: "The failure as a medium of circulation, must have improved them as an instrument of sale; and their success as an instrument of sale must in return have restored their utility as a medium of circulation." This, for Mackintosh, is the central paradox of revolutionary economics: the failure of the *assignats* "as a medium of circulation" guarantees their success as an "instrument of sale," which in turn guarantees "their utility as a medium of circulation" (*Works*, 428). This protean solution by which he turns a seemingly Burkean contradiction into a revolutionary paradox results, in his reading, in the inevitable absence of contradiction and the mythic unity of signifier and signified. As legal tender, the *assignats* will continue to diminish in circulation as they are exchanged for the land that backs them up. Mackintosh assumes that the new paper value will eventually be replaced by the solid, intrinsic value of the land: just as frequent elections result in the canceling out of old discredited representatives, so frequent exchanges of *assignats* for land result in extinguishing both the old debt and old values. In the end, there is a mythic unity of the nation represented in the National Assembly and the Revolution backed up by the new class of landholders, just like the Old Order that Burke extols. The logic of Mackintosh's representation assumes the restoration of real value and stability—a restoration of real specie and the creation of a new representational order.

Thus the confiscation of lands is actually a restoration of what was originally the nation's, and the nation's property guarantees the liquidation of the old debt—the old discredited values of the ci-devant representational order—the discredited past that is finally dissolved and replaced by new values and a new order.

Flux and change underwrite the new order's permanence; a variety of representations dissolve into unity. Primary assemblies send deputies to the departments that send representatives to the National Assembly—representatives either retained or replaced, through subsequent elections, by the collective people signifying the general will. Just as the *assignats* are replaced by a stable land and currency, revolutionary representation culminates in the liquidation of conflict: the Assembly is the Nation; money and land have intrinsic reflective value. In the end, the revolutionary dialectic replaces contradiction with unified correspondence.

The antithetical themes that Mackintosh explores are themes explored by both Burke and his respondents: illusion and reality, contradiction and correspondence, misrepresentation and truth. Backed up by historical "facts," both sides write the Revolution into their reflective texts. For Burke, especially after 1790, the Revolution creates the contradictions that can be contained or destroyed only when the Revolution is annihilated; for his respondents, counterrevolutionary contradiction must be erased or canceled before the Revolution fulfills its apocalyptic destiny. Both sides thus rewrite the facts to fit their teleologic histories. Mackintosh illustrates this tendency in the prorevolutionary historiography of eighteenth-century Britain: employing assorted contradictory discourses, he nevertheless insists on a higher representation that is, like the mythic French republic, ultimately one and indivisible.

Conclusion

In the early 1790s, the French Revolution was classically represented in terms of opposition and contrast by its fervid supporters—freedom/slavery, equality/hierarchy, fraternity/fragmentation, enlightenment/superstition, rebels/reactionaries, and a host of other differences that could be extended ad infinitum. Likewise, the Revolution was counterread by Burke and his supporters as a war between religion and atheism, civilization and savagery, hierarchy and anarchy, and a series of correspondent oppositions that could be mutually extended. In a fundamental sense, these were traditional terms that were and are repeatedly read into other "revolutions"—terms that can be traced back to the Reformation and Enlightenment and that reappear in their respective historical contexts in the English Civil War, the Glorious Revolution, and (in another book) the American Revolution. With regard to the French Revolution, there were real and intrinsic differences, but there was also another side to the conventional contrasts. By emphasizing similarities and resemblances, I have focused on the traces and secret signatures of a series of complicitous texts telling the same disguised story—texts that are written out in the same system of representation, in which the repression of the "other" inevitably elicits a mutually denied resemblance. This focus recognizes oxymoronic links, as when both sides reinscribe Tory and Jacobite arguments into the text of the French Revolution. Historically, until the 1760s, what has been retrospectively and conventionally read as a "reactionary" critique constituted the principal ideological resistance to the new Whig order established by the Glorious Revolution, representing the principal "radical" opposition to the status quo.[1] When Burke and his respondents repeated the Tory critique of paper credit and speculation, it illustrated again how the Left and Right repeatedly absorbed each other, writing in and out of the same representational system.

In my readings of these antagonistic texts, I have additionally attempted to recrystallize the intertextual confrontations that take place within and between the lines—to rehistoricize the contexts of the revolutionary debate. In doing so, I have offered interpretations constituted by my own historical perspective: I see in some of these texts what we recognize today as psychological projection, but this may be just a resemblance and not the entire story. I do think it is some of the story, but others may see a different one, with different implications. I have also read two other contemporary contexts into my interpretations of the Revolution's first readers.

In the 1790s, radical writers were engaged in recognizable deconstructions of the Old Order's tradition, but not in order to reveal the arbitrariness of language—they intended to reveal the real, covert, sinister meaning of "oppression" disguised and mystified by the language of tradition. In their rebellious readings, they deconstructed traditional distinction, revealing a privileged term and the suppression of the "other." But their readings of opposition mirrored and provided the very terms for reading them in turn: in a world of binary polarities, they also privilege some and suppress or keep out of sight "others." Only Wollstonecraft, briefly, attempted to unite warring polarities. In *The Rights of Men*, she deconstructively read Burke's polarities in the *Enquiry* (sublime and beautiful, male and female) attempting to reunite them, initiating a double reading or, what Jeffrey Nealon characterizes as Derrida's final deconstructive move: "the wholesale displacement of the systematics of binary opposition and the reinscription of the opposition within a larger field—a 'textual' field that can account for nonpresence as other than lack of presence." Nealon quotes Rodolphe Gasché, who explains that "'[for Derrida], since concepts are produced within a discursive network of differences, they not only are what they are by virtue of other concepts, *but they also, in a fundamental way, inscribe the Otherness within themselves.*'"[2] Wollstonecraft begins this second move but then deconstructs her deconstructive reading, returning to the privileged term of sublime, masculine judgment. In the end her reading resembles the first reading or the initial move of deconstruction, which, as Derrida notes, is incompletely defective: "'To remain content with *reversal* [the first deconstructive move] is of course to operate within the immanence of the system to be destroyed.'"[3] The "first" reading is also the definitive or primary reading of the oppositional readers of the 1790s, who nevertheless betrayingly reveal the "other" in their antagonistic representations. For the bellicose readers of the early 1790s, the Revolution was more variegated and complex than the reductive binary oppositions they emphasized, but the controversy and crisis compelled them to represent the Revolution in stark and strident contrasts of truth and error, illusion and reality. It also compelled both sides to privilege a "truer" mythical reading of the Revolution.

Discussions of binary oppositions additionally complement another retrospective context that I have read into late eighteenth-century texts. In *The Order of Things*, Michel Foucault discusses two predominate epistemes in Western representation: a classical episteme of correspondence and identity, in which signifier and signified are one, and a modern episteme emphasizing discrepancy and difference—an episteme that displaces the earlier classical one. These two epistemes correspond, in my reading, to the ongoing myth of a fall from unity into fragmentation and the dream of reintegration in the future. This is the central myth of the French Revolution and the writers who revised and represented it. It is a myth as old as world history. The classic episteme is not, however, displaced but nostalgically reinvoked against a contradictory opposition or, later, ironically against itself, in the rewriting of fallen history. The tension between both epistemes creates mythic readings of paradise and a fall, apocalypse and redemption. The modern episteme does not ultimately cancel or suppress the other: it belatedly acknowledges it.

Supporters and opponents of the Revolution rejected each other's myths while they recreated their own. Burke, for instance, did not believe in a direct correspondence between signifier and signified in elections and language. He had been clear about this earlier, in his "Speech to the Electors of Bristol" (1774) and in section 5 of the *Enquiry* (1757). But the great pressures of the Revolution compelled Burke and his respondents to rearticulate myths of fragmentation and unity—to address what they saw as a crucial moment in Western civilization: restoration and regeneration or chaos and regression. For both sides the stakes were colossal, and they both used (in Leo Damrosch's phrase) similar fictions of reality.[4] Because the entire meaning of the world seemed in balance, because the cosmic consequences of revolution and counterrevolution seemed so imminent, both sides explained the apocalyptic importance of the events transforming the world in myths that challengingly resembled each other. Burke attacked the French fiction of direct, democratic elections while presenting a world picture of a homogeneous, filiopietistic Europe. Believing that God's natural order was under assault, he saw the Revolution sundering the links between God and man, Logos and language. In the last years of his life, the fixed and "settled" meaning of Europe seemed to him forever shattered. Similarly, Burke's respondents attacked the illusions, the mythology that underwrote the old, fallen world, counterpresenting a French fiction of unity and regeneration. Against the contradictions and the discrepancies of the "other," both sides hurled antagonistic myths that told similar stories. The Revolution was ultimately so complex and confusing that only myth—in its highest sense—could rearticulate its significance. Moreover, the revolutionary myth has been rewritten and repeated for two centuries. Even Marx's revision of the Revolution as a *révolution manquée*, a kind of Mackintoshian Glorious Revolution, plots the Revolution as a necessary stage in the progressive unfolding of history—the dissolution of contradiction.

The writers I have examined—Wollstonecraft, Paine, and Mackintosh—formulated their correspondent critiques of Burke during the Revolution's mythical moment (1790–91), a moment when there seemed to be a true correspondence between what they were writing and what was really happening. In the halcyon days of 1790, antirevolutionary opposition could be written off as counterrevolutionary contradiction, but the subsequent acceleration of the Revolution's own contradictions created a representational crisis for its admirers—a crisis confronting their previous writings. Burke and the Revolution had to be retrospectively rewritten and revised. Mackintosh, as we have seen, responded to this crisis by contextually rewriting Burke "in" and the *Vindiciae* "out" of his subsequent oeuvre, and in a concurrent book I follow the lines of the succedent revolutionary debate, focusing on how Wollstonecraft, Paine, and Helen Maria Williams responded to their previous representations.

Representations frequently resemble what they resist. The jacket illustration of the present book reproduces a detail from the frontispiece to the 1710 edition of Swift's *Battle of the Books*. In the library of St. James, antagonistic knights, emblematic of the hostile books affixed to their armor, wage a furious bibliomachy over the canon, in an intertextual war between Ancients and Moderns. Above the fray, a victorious knight soars among the bookcases, assaulting enemy texts with a sword that sends the vanquished pages falling into the melee below, while an angel trumpets the commencement (or climax) of this biblio-Armageddon. From one angle, the perspective is mock heroic: the warring knights seem archaic, medieval, quaintly dated—textual warriors of past battles. From another angle, the antique armor and the weapons carried by the combatants suggest that the battle is being refought in the timeless terms of Swift's beloved Ancients. Similarly, in the great book war of the 1790s, textual adversaries engage over competitive canons, refighting previous issues in the oppositional idioms and language of the past. While both sides surmised that the powerfully discordant revolution had released conflictive forces of modernity, they both wrote out the revolution—a revolution straining the bounds of the old paradigmatic language—in the familiar terms of the past. Sharing a series of assumptions dealing with contradiction and correspondence—illusion and reality—both sides demonized the "other" as writing outside the representational system they both validated, and hence they both appealed to a common standard they accused the other of violating. The Revolution was, in many ways, the culmination of the past(s) circulating through a system that paradoxically rejected yet reabsorbed its own blood. Writing within a mutual representational system, Burke's respondents struggled to rehistoricize the Revolution's original, rebellious history. Two centuries later, the issues and language of the 1790s continue to be reinscribed and fought out in the texts that comprise the ongoing writing of the French Revolution.

In this context, the controversy and debate over the Revolution continues across the centuries, for each time we reenter the great intertextual war through the language that is our principal historical repository of what Burke and his respondents "are," we tacitly acknowledge that the French Revolution is not over—two centuries later, it continues to color our world, even as it wars in our language.

Appendix:
Paine's Letter to Burke

In early 1790, when Paine, in Paris, learned that Burke intended to publish a pamphlet critical of the Revolution, he felt personally betrayed: he considered Burke an ideological ally and had sent him a glowing account of the Revolution's course in a letter dated 17 January 1790. On 9 February, in the House of Commons, Burke had declared that he would break with his closest friends over the issue of the French Revolution. Then, within a week, came the announcement of his intention to publish a public letter on the Revolution. Paine, however, was unaware that Burke had previously received a letter (4 November 1789) from a French correspondent requesting his views or that he had read Richard Price's *A Discourse on the Love of our Country* in mid-January, just about the time Paine was writing to him from Paris. Paine, consequently, assumed a causal relationship between Burke's attack on the Revolution and what he took to be Burke's rejection of his letter and hence himself.

In *Rights of Man*, he angrily refers to his correspondence with Burke, mentioning his January letter on three occasions. First, he notes that when Burke made his "violent speech" against the Revolution (9 February), Paine was in Paris "and had written to him but a short time before, to inform him how prosperously matters were going on. Soon after this, I saw his advertisement of the pamphlet he intended to publish" (*CW*, 1:244). The temporal proximity of the two events indicates that, for Paine, there is a causal connection between his January letter and Burke's betrayal of both the Revolution and himself.

Second, Paine refers to his January letter when he quotes Thomas Jefferson, "in a letter which I communicated to Mr. Burke," as his anonymous source for the characterization of "Count de Broglio" (Victor-François, duc de Broglie, commander of the king's troops in July 1789) as a "high-flying aristocrat, cool and capable of every mischief"

(*CW*, 1:261; cf. *Correspondence*, 6:70). Although Paine, in *Rights of Man*, does not identify Jefferson, he insists that the characterization comes "from an authority which Mr. Burke well knows was good" (*CW*, 1:261). Indeed, in his letter to Burke in January, Paine had quoted approvingly from a letter Jefferson had sent him on 11 July 1789, three days before the Bastille's fall.

Finally, he notes that he "used sometimes to correspond with Mr. Burke, believing him then to be a man of sounder principles than his book shows him to be," referring, for a third time, to his affirmative account of the Revolution in his January letter (*CW*, 1:297).

But Paine's January letter, as Thomas W. Copeland and others have noted, probably reconfirmed Burke's increasing mistrust of the Revolution (see Copeland, *Our Eminent Friend*, 146–82). For instance, Paine refers to the political use of the term *aristocrat* to stigmatize anyone hostile to the Revolution, and he quotes approvingly Jefferson's comment that the National Assembly intended "to set fire to the four Corners of the Kingdom and perish with it themselves, rather than relinquish an Iota of their Plan of a total Change of Government."

Paine proceeds to relate that, when Louis XVI entered Paris (17 July 1789), he was surrounded by a crowd armed with "Scythes, Sickles, Carpenters Chissels and Iron Spikes fixed with Sticks Blacksmith's with sledge Hammers and in short every thing and any thing that could be got." When the king arrived at the Hôtel de Ville, "he had to pass through an Alley of Men," who crossed their weapons "over his head under which he had to pass, impressed perhaps that some one was to fall upon his head." Amazingly, Paine mentions this "to show how natural it is, that [the king] should now feel himself tranquil.—The Revolution in France is certainly a forerunner to other Revolutions in Europe" (*Correspondence*, 6:70–71). Paine's letter undoubtedly did not make Burke feel tranquil, reconfirming ironically his worst suspicions.

Notes

Introduction

1. William Godwin, *Memoirs of Mary Wollstonecraft* (1798; rprt., New York: Haskel House Publishers, 1927), 51–52.

2. Thomas Christie, *Letters on the Revolution of France* (London: J. Johnson, 1791), 65–66.

3. Paine, letter to Burke (17 January 1790), in *Correspondence*, 6:70–71.

4. Hayden White, *Tropics of Discourse: Essays in Cultural Criticism* (Baltimore: The Johns Hopkins University Press, 1978), 63.

5. J. G. A. Pocock, *Virtue, Commerce, and History: Essays on Political Thought and History, Chiefly in the Eighteenth Century* (Cambridge: Cambridge University Press, 1985), 282–84.

6. In this regard, cf. Hannah Arendt:

For it is by no means irrelevant that our political vocabulary either dates back to classical, Roman and Greek, antiquity, or can be traced unequivocally to the revolutions of the eighteenth century. In other words, to the extent that our political terminology is modern at all, it is revolutionary in origin. And the chief characteristic of this modern, revolutionary vocabulary seems to be that it always talks in pairs of opposites—the right and left, reactionary and progressive, conservatism and liberalism, to mention a few at random. . . . To be sure, these opposites have their origin, and ultimately their justification, in the revolutionary experience as a whole, but the point of the matter is that in the act of foundation they were not mutually exclusive opposites but two sides of the same event, and it was only after the revolutions had come to their end, in success or defeat, that they parted company, solidified into ideologies, and began to oppose each other.

Terminologically speaking, the effort to recapture the lost spirit of revolution must, to a certain extent, consist in the attempt at thinking together and combining meaningfully what our present vocabulary presents to us in terms of opposition and contradiction. (*On Revolution* [Harmondsworth: Penguin Books, 1963], 223–24)

1. Hic mulier, Haec vir: Wollstonecraft's Feminization of Burke in *The Rights of Men*

1. Ronald Paulson, *Representations of Revolution, 1784–1820* (New Haven: Yale University Press, 1983), 81.

2. *The Collected Writings of Thomas De Quincey*, 14 vols., ed. David Masson (Edinburgh: Adam and Charles Black, 1890), 10:300–301. By the end of the eighteenth century, *female* and *feminine* were synonymous (Mary Poovey, *The Proper Lady and the Woman Writer: Ideology as Style in the Works of Mary Wollstonecraft, Mary Shelley, and Jane Austen* [Chicago: The University of Chicago Press, 1984], 6).

3. See Genevieve Lloyd, *The Man of Reason: "Male" and "Female" in Western Philosophy* (Minneapolis: University of Minnesota Press, 1984), 46–48, 50, 52; Katherine Rogers, *Feminism in Eighteenth-Century England* (Urbana: University of Illinois Press, 1982), 38.

4. Samuel Richardson, *Clarissa: or, The History of a Young Lady*, 4 vols. (1748; London: John Dent, 1932), 4:495.

5. John Locke, *An Essay Concerning Human Understanding*, ed. Alexander Campbell Fraser (1690; rprt., New York: Dover Publications, Inc., 1959), 2.11.2.

6. See ibid.

7. Ibid.; my emphasis.

8. Wollstonecraft, in *The Rights of Men*, refers directly to Locke's *Essay*, calling the House of Commons "a hot-bed for wit" and noting that "Mr. Locke would have added, who was ever of opinion that eloquence was oftener employed to make 'the worse appear the better part' [see *Paradise Lost* 2.113], than to support the dictates of cool judgement" (*WMW,* 5:43). In the *Essay*, Locke attacks "wit and fancy, . . . figurative speeches" that "mislead the judgement," concluding that as far as the world is concerned, "eloquence, like the fair sex, has too prevailing beauties in it to suffer itself ever to be spoken against" (Locke, *An Essay Concerning Human Understanding*, 3.10.34).

9. Hannah More, *Essays on Various Subjects Principally Designed for Young Ladies*, in *The Works of Hannah More*, 11 vols. (New York: Harper, 1847), 2:335–36.

10. Christopher Reid, "Burke's Tragic Muse: Sarah Siddons and the 'Feminization' of the *Reflections*," in *Burke and the French Revolution: Bicentennial Essays*, ed. Steven Blakemore (Athens: University Press of Georgia, 1992), 18.

11. Ralph M. Wardle, *Mary Wollstonecraft: A Critical Biography* (Lawrence: University of Kansas Press, 1951), 73.

12. Syndy McMillen Conger provides the best treatment of the subject in an analysis of Wollstonecraft's ambiguous, shifting relationship with a language of textual sensibility, which she at various points incorporates, rejects, or accommodates—a language that expressively confines her (*Mary Wollstonecraft and the Language of Sensibility* [Rutherford, N.J.: Fairleigh Dickinson University Press, 1994]).

13. See, G. J. Barker-Benfield, *The Culture of Sensibility: Sex and Society in Eighteenth-Century Britain* (Chicago: The University of Chicago Press, 1992), passim.

14. Ibid., 151 and chap. 3, passim; cf. Adam Potkay, *The Fate of Eloquence in the Age of Hume* (Ithaca: Cornell University Press, 1994), 204–6.

15. For the cultural context, see Lloyd, *The Man of Reason.*

16. See Michel Foucault, *Madness and Civilization: A History of Insanity in the Age of Reason*, trans. Richard Howard (New York: Vintage Books, 1988), 102, 122–23, 132, 140, 146, 152; Barker-Benfield, *The Culture of Sensibility*, 19.

17. Margaret Tims, *Mary Wollstonecraft: A Social Pioneer* (London: Millington Books Ltd., 1976), 107.

18. Cora Kaplan, *Sea Changes: Essays on Culture and Feminism* (London: Verso, 1986), 46. For Wollstonecraft's description of her own "lively imagination," see her letters to Gilbert Imlay in 1793 and 1795 (*Collected Letters*, 236, 291).

19. For Wollstonecraft's apprehension that she herself might be accused of "feminine hysteria," see Poovey, *The Proper Lady*, 67.

20. See Phillip R. Slavney, *Perspectives on "Hysteria"* (Baltimore: The Johns Hopkins University Press, 1990), 18, 20, 23; Foucault, *Madness and Civilization*, 143–51; Roy Porter, *Mind-Forg'd Manacles: A History of Madness in England from the Restoration to the Regency* (Cambridge: Harvard University Press, 1987), 48–49.

21. Barker-Benfield, *The Culture of Sensibility*, 28; see esp. chap. 1, "Sensibility and the Nervous System."

22. George Cheyne, *The English Malady* (1733; Delmar, N.Y.: Scholars' Facsimiles & Reprints, 1976), ii, 33, 69, 71–72, 136, 153, 180, 184–86.

23. See Porter, *Mind-Forg'd Manacles*, 57–60, 101.

24. Laetitia Matilda Hawkins, *Letters on the Female Mind, Its Powers and Pursuits*, 2 vols. (London: Hookham & Carpenter, 1793), 1:10.

25. For other references to her "nervous disorders," see *Collected Letters*, 117–18, 122, 126, 128, 143, 155, 221; cf. Porter, *Mind-Forg'd Manacles*, 244; Moira Ferguson and Janet Todd, *Mary Wollstonecraft* (Boston: Twayne Publishers, 1984), 8; Gary Kelly, *Revolutionary Feminism: The Mind and Career of Mary Wollstonecraft* (New York: St. Martin's Press, 1992), 24–25. In her private letters, Wollstonecraft's references to her gendered, nervous disorders underscore her *femininity*. In *The Rights of Woman*, however, she significantly rejects and repudiates such gendered responses. With reference to Burke in *The Rights of Men*, Virginia Sapiro is mistaken that "in no case ... did [Wollstonecraft] imply that the men she charged with unmanliness or effeminacy were acting or looking like women" (*A Vindication of Political Virtue: The Political Theory of Mary Wollstonecraft* [Chicago: The University of Chicago Press, 1992], 221).

26. There was a technical distinction between the National Constituent Assembly (28 June 1789–30 September 1791) that created the Constitution of 1791 and the Legislative Assembly (1 October 1791–20 September 1792) that succeeded it. Anglo-American writers usually referred to both as the National Assembly—a usage I follow unless the distinction is important.

27. Meena Alexander, *Women and Romanticism: Mary Wollstonecraft, Dorothy Wordsworth, and Mary Shelley* (Totowa, N.J.: Barnes and Noble Books, 1989), 49; Ferguson & Todd, *Mary Wollstonecraft*, 53; Sapiro, *A Vindication of Political Virtue*, 221–22.

28. Poovey, *The Proper Lady*, 79.

2. Intertextual War: Wollstonecraft and the Language of Burke's *Enquiry*

1. Frances Ferguson, "The Sublime of Edmund Burke, or the Bathos of Experience," *Glyph* 8 (1981), 76–77.

2. Locke, *An Essay Concerning Human Understanding*, 2.11.2.

3. For the historical context, see Barker-Benfield, *The Culture of Sensibility*, 362, 401.

4. Alan Craig Houston, *Algernon Sidney and the Republican Heritage in England and America* (Princeton: Princeton University Press, 1991), 163.

5. Alexander, *Women and Romanticism*, 49.

6. On Townshend, see Gerald W. Chapman, *Edmund Burke: The Practical Imagination* (Cambridge: Harvard University Press, 1967), 51; on Burke's effort to shame England, see Steven Blakemore, *Burke and the Fall of Language: The French Revolution as Linguistic Event* (Hanover, N.H.: University Press of New England, 1988), 50–51.

7. Isaac Kramnick, *The Rage of Edmund Burke: Portrait of an Ambivalent Conservative* (New York: Basic Books, 1977), 59.

8. Conger, *Mary Wollstonecraft*, 100.

9. Conger notes, however, that "Wollstonecraft frequently characterizes herself in her private correspondence in Burkean terms: physically and emotionally delicate, weak, and eager to please," accounting for some of her anger and the sullen "clarity with which sees the logical consequences of adhering to Burke's feminine ideal" (ibid., 101). This suggests that she again projects onto Burke her private feelings and terms and, retrospectively, Burke's own "feminine ideal."

10. Paulson, *Representations of Revolution*, 84.

11. In *The Female Reader*, Wollstonecraft's juxtaposed quotations favor Mary's femininity over Elizabeth's masculinity. She leaves out Hume's admiring comment that Elizabeth considered solely "as a rational being placed in authority" deserves our "applause and approbation." If Wollstonecraft rewrites Burke, she also rewrites earlier works of her own, which she no longer acknowledges.

12. Burke alludes to Locke's theory of "personal identity" in *An Essay Concerning Human Understanding* (2.27.7–29).

13. Poovey, *The Proper Lady*, 57; cf. Mary Jacobus, "The Difference of View," in *Women Writing and Writing about Women*, ed. Mary Jacobus (New York: Barnes and Noble, 1979), 14–15.

14. "Transgressing gender boundaries," in Kelly, *Revolutionary Feminism*, 101–2; sexual demonization, in Ferguson & Todd, *Mary Wollstonecraft*, 73; Wardle, *Mary Wollstonecraft*, 320, 322.

15. Godwin, *Memoirs of Mary Wollstonecraft*, 54–55; cf. Barker-Benfield, *The Culture of Sensibility*, 277–78.

16. Wardle, *Mary Wollstonecraft*, 141.

17. Ferguson, "The Sublime of Edmund Burke," 77.

18. She had previously informed Burke that, once she discovers that the opinions of her opponent are only "empty rhetorical flourishes," her "respect is soon changed into that pity which borders on contempt" (*WMW*, 5:30); this also prefigures the heading to chapter 5 in *The Rights of Woman*: "Animadversions On Some Of The Writers Who Have

Rendered Women Objects Of Pity, Bordering on Contempt" (*WMW*, 5:147; cf. 5:75, 3rd. par.). This suggests that Wollstonecraft is still thinking of Burke as a weak woman (or effeminate man) in *The Rights of Man* (*WMW*, 5:55), but it also suggestively makes her resemble, in retrospect, those patronizing male writers whom she "animadverts" against.

19. In chapter 24 of Wollstonecraft's autobiographical romance *Mary* (1788), the protagonist meets "a man, past the meridian of life, of political manners, and dazzling wit" (*WMW*, 1:59–60)—an erudite man who resembles Edmund Burke in *The Rights of Men*:

> He knew men, as well as books; his conversation was entertaining and improving. In Mary's company he doubted whether heaven was peopled with spirits masculine; and almost forgot that he had called the sex "the pretty play things that render life tolerable."

> He had been the slave of beauty, the captive of sense. . . . He was humane . . . but was vain of his abilities, and by no means a useful member of society. He talked often of the beauty of virtue; but not having any solid foundation to build the practice on, he was only a shining, or rather a sparkling character: and though his fortune enabled him to hunt down pleasure, he was discontented. (*WMW*, 1:60)

The references to the unnamed gentleman's age ("past the meridian of life"), his "polished manners and dazzling wit," his "shining or rather sparkling character," and his condescending reference to women as "the pretty play things that render life tolerable," rendering him "the slave of beauty," suggest that Wollstonecraft was either basing Burke, in *The Rights of Man*, on the unnamed gentleman in *Mary* or was thinking of Burke in her description of this gentleman.

3. Reflected Resemblances: Wollstonecraft's Representation of Burke in *The Rights of Men*

1. Godwin, *Memoirs of Mary Wollstonecraft*, 51; Eleanor Flexner, *Mary Wollstonecraft: A Biography* (New York: Coward, McCann & Geoghegan, Inc., 1972), 125.

2. Flexner, *Mary Wollstonecraft*, 127

3. Ferguson & Todd, *Mary Wollstonecraft*, 55; Poovey, *The Proper Lady*, 66.

4. Here is the entire passage quoted by Todd and Butler:

> Did they recollect they were talking of a sick King, of a monarch smitten by the hand of Omnipotence, and that the Almighty had hurled him from his throne, and plunged him into a condition which drew upon him the pity of the meanest peasant in his Kingdom. Ought they to make a mockery of him, to put a crown of thorns on his head, a reed in his hand, and dressing him in a raiment of purple, to cry, "Hail, King of the Britons." (*WMW*, 5:27 n. c)

Burke's contrastable comparison of George III to Christ suggests that he would be mocked and crucified by those who would maliciously emphasize that he was not really a "sane" king. In Wollstonecraft's account of this passage, Burke supposedly contended "that it was the most insulting mockery to recollect that he had been king, or to treat him with any particular respect on account of his former dignity" (*WMW*, 5:27). She had previously quoted Burke's comparison of the king and Christ and turned Burke into the cruel mocker (crucifier) of the king: "Where was your sensibility when you could utter this cruel mockery, equally insulting to God and man?" (*WMW*, 5:26). Perhaps Burke's comparison is behind her outrageous claim that, had he lived at the time, he would have "joined in the cry" to crucify Christ (*WMW*, 5:14). Wollstonecraft's Christ is, not surprisingly, a revolutionary, the "promulgator of a new doctrine, and the violator of old laws and customs," not unlike the Christly Richard Price whom Burke had already "crucified" in *Reflections*: a Price whose "political opinions are Utopian reveries," in a reactionary world "not sufficiently civilized to adopt such a sublime system of morality"—a Price whom Burke had mocked and branded "with so many opprobrious epithets" (*WMW*, 5:18–19).

5. Christopher Reid, "Burke, the Regency Crisis, and the 'Antagonistic World of Madness,'" *Eighteenth-Century Life* 16 (May 1992), 69.

6. *The Speeches of the Right Honourable Edmund Burke*, 4 vols. (London: Longman and Hurst Rees, 1816), 3:391–402.

7. See Stanley Ayling, *Edmund Burke: His Life and Opinions* (New York: St. Martin's Press, 1988), 191; *WMW*, 5:28.

8. In this context, Wollstonecraft understood that Burke further qualifies the beautiful in the *Enquiry* by suggesting that its impingement into the sublime or its excessive predominance destroys that sublime alertness and exertion necessary for survival and sanity. In the *Enquiry*, the sublime is the reality principle. For other ways in which Wollstonecraft suggests Burke is insane, see Kelly, *Revolutionary Feminism*, 90, 99.

9. Foucault, *Madness and Civilization*, 87–88, 93; cf. Porter, *Mind-Forg'd Manacles*, 47, 51–52; George S. Rousseau, "Nerves, Spirits, and Fibers: Towards Defining the Organs of Sensibility—with a Postscript 1976," *The Blue Guitar* 2 (1976), 125–53.

10. Foucault, *Madness and Civilization*, 126–27.

11. Ibid., 132; cf. Porter, *Mind-Forg'd Manacles*, 46–47.

12. Hawkins, *Letters on the Female Mind*, 1:36–37.

13. Sapiro, *A Vindication of Political Virtue*, 60.

14. Porter, *Mind-Forg'd Manacles*, 107.

15. Richard Price, *A Discourse on the Love of our Country*, 4th ed. (London: T. Cadell, 1790), vii. The preface to the fourth edition of Price's *Discourse on the Love of our Country* appeared six days before Wollstonecraft's *The Rights of Men*. In the preface, Price alters the controversial phrases of the *Discourse*, placing them in quotation marks so that they accord with his interpretation of what he really meant rather than with Burke's. He then accuses Burke of disingenuous misrepresentation (vi–vii). See Steven Blakemore, "Misrepresenting the Text: Price, Burke, and the October Days of 1789," *The Friend: Comment on Romanticism* 1 (October 1992): 1–9.

16. Kelly, *Revolutionary Feminism*, 100.

17. Cf. Wollstonecraft's posthumous "Hints," where this passage is, with a few changes, reproduced, *WMW*, 5:276.

18. Cf. *The Rights of Women*: when we see a "folly . . . burst suddenly in our sight, fear and disgust" render "us more severe than man ought to be," perhaps leading "us with blind zeal to usurp God's will and denounce damnation on our fellow mortals, forgetting

that we cannot read the heart, and that we have seeds of the same vices lurking in our own" (*WMW,* 5:177).

19. See Steven Blakemore, "Repression and Resemblance: Burke's Critique of the Revolution," *Consortium on Revolutionary Europe* 1 (1989): 33–42.

20. Frances Ferguson, "Wollstonecraft Our Contemporary," in *Gender and Theory: Dialogues on Feminist Criticism,* ed. Linda Kauffman (Oxford: Basil Blackwell, 1989), 58, 61.

4. Paine and the Myth of Burke's Secret Pension

1. William St Claire, *The Godwins and the Shelleys: A Biography of a Family* (New York: W. W. Norton, 1989), 50.

2. Alfred Owen Aldridge, *Man of Reason: The Life of Thomas Paine* (Philadelphia: J. B. Lippincott, 1959), 132.

3. Sir Gilbert Elliot, *Life and Letters of Sir Gilbert Elliot,* ed. Countess of Minto, 3 vols. (London: Longman, 1874), 1:262 63; cf. Ayling, *Edmund Burke,* 184–85; Thomas W. Copeland, *Our Eminent Friend Edmund Burke: Six Essays* (New Haven: Yale University Press, 1949), 66–67.

4. St Claire, *The Godwins and the Shelleys,* 50.

5. Ibid.

6. There is another possible context for the allegation. In 1759, Burke became the secretary of William Gerard Hamilton (1729–96), a minor politician. Two years later, Hamilton was appointed chief secretary to the lord lieutenant of Ireland and, in 1763, secured an annual pension for Burke of £300 on the Irish Establishment. Burke terminated his connection with Hamilton in 1765, when they had a falling out; consequently, Burke resigned his pension, which had been his main source of income. Thomas W. Copeland, editor of volume 1 of *Correspondence,* notes that the

> agreement Burke made regarding his pension was not to having it cancelled, but to having its income reassigned to another person chosen by Hamilton. Burke remained the nominal holder. The person chosen by Hamilton was Robert Jephson (1763–1803), a wit and playwrite later well known in the literary society of London and Dublin. (*Correspondence,* 1:186–87)

The earlier pension hence might have also served as a basis for the subsequent allegation.

7. Information provided by William St. Claire in a letter (23 January 1990). As early as the 1770s, Price had contested Burke in print.

8. In his *Memories of the Whig Party During My Time* (2 vols. [London, 1852]), Lord Holland does not mention Moore, but he is probably either Peter Moore (1753–1828), who, in 1803, was elected as a radical M.P. for Coventry or, more likely, his brother, Edward, who, according to the *Dictionary of National Biography* (13:823), influenced Lord Holland and the Whig party.

9. In a letter to his friend, Earl Fitzwilliam (5 June 1791), Burke complained that Charles James Fox had condoned

a base charge that I could have no other motive for the part, which during near two years I had taken against the propagation of French principles in this Kingdom, than a secret Bribe which I had received from the Ministers, an impudent calumny, which he well knew his friends . . . had been active in publicly propagating. (*Correspondence*, 6:274)

Other erroneous chestnuts still flourish: "Soon after the appearance of his *Reflections*, Burke was awarded an annual pension by the court of George III" (Jack Fruchtman Jr., *Thomas Paine: Apostle of Freedom* [New York: Four Walls Eight Windows, 1994], 221); "Burke's pension of £ 1500 p.a. began to be paid in 1794" (Gregory Claeys, ed., *Political Writings of the 1790s*, 8 vols. [London: Pickering & Chatto, 1995], 1:17 n. 1; cf. 2:227 n. 2).

10. Burke's Civil List Act (22 Geo. III, C. 82) appears in a variety of sources dealing with English parliamentary history. See, for instance, *The Statutes at Large*, ed. Owen Ruffhead et al. For a learned discussion of Burke's Civil List Act, see the works by E. A. Reitan in "Works Cited." Professor Reitan has kindly advised and guided me through the intricacies of the Civil List.

11. Secret pensions were principally granted, at his "Majesty's pleasure," for reasons of state or to save the recipients the embarrassment of having "it known that their Distresses are so relieved," even though "it is honourable and just Cause, to be thought worthy of Reward" (see article 19, in the Civil List Act of 1782).

12. Among the missing circumstances that Paine fails to mention are the name of the pension (Paine only alludes to but does not mention the Irish Establishment), the specific date when Burke tried to sell or mortgage it, the name (or names) of the person(s) who discovered Burke's concealed name, and whether Burke was still drawing a pension in the 1790s or had stopped because it had been revealed in 1782. If it is the former, Paine does not explain why Burke would have continued drawing a "discovered" pension that exposed him to the very charges Paine makes. If it is the latter, he does not explain how a pension surrendered in 1782 could account for Burke's mercenary opposition to the Revolution in 1790.

13. Aldridge, *Man of Reason*, 319; Fruchtman, *Thomas Paine*, 145.

14. David Freeman Hawke, *Paine* (New York: Harper & Row, 1974), 123. Paine's secret pension lasted from 10 February 1782 to 18 April 1783. In *The American Crisis XIII* (April 1783), Paine noted that his patriotic endeavors had

been directed to conciliate the affections, unite the interests, and draw and keep the mind of the country together; and the better to assist in this foundation work of the revolution, I have avoided all places of profit or office, either in the state I live in, or in the United States; kept myself at a distance from all parties and party connections, and even disregarded all private and inferior concerns. (*CW*, 1:234–35)

15. Hawke, *Paine*, 220; cf. Fruchtman, *Thomas Paine*, 114, 120.

16. Carl B. Cone, *The English Jacobins, Reformers in Late Eighteenth-Century England* (New York: Scribner, 1968), 107; Thomas Cooper, *A Reply to Mr. Burke's invective against Mr. Cooper and Mr. Watt* (Manchester, 1792), 79; Gregory Claeys, *Thomas Paine: Social and Political Thought* (London: Unwin Hyman, 1989), 164.

17. Copeland, *Our Eminent Friend*, 67–68.

18. Dixon Wecter, *Edmund Burke and His Kinsmen: A Study of the Statesman's Financial Integrity and Private Relationships* (Boulder: University of Colorado Studies, 1939), 45 n. 22.

19. In this century, critics of Burke continue to suggest that Burke's public pensions retroactively substantiate, in principle, the unsubstantiated allegations of his eighteenth-century enemies.

5. Paine's Revolutionary Comedy: The Bastille and October Days in the *Rights of Man*

1. Tom Furniss, *Edmund Burke's Aesthetic Ideology: Language, Gender, and Political Economy in Revolution* (Cambridge: Cambridge University Press, 1993), 133.

2. *The Papers of Thomas Jefferson*, ed. Julien P. Boyd (Princeton: Princeton University Press, 1958), 15:267, 273.

3. In 1789, Paine was corresponding with Jefferson about events in France. As the American minister in France, Jefferson provided Paine with some firsthand accounts of the events. On 17 January 1790, Paine sent Burke an enthusiastic report on the Revolution's progress, quoting from a letter Jefferson had written him on 11 July 1789. In *Rights of Man*, Paine makes the January letter and Jefferson's (anonymous) comments an issue. See "Appendix."

4. Jerome D. Wilson and William F. Ricketson, *Thomas Paine* (Boston: Twayne Publishers, 1989), 61–62.

5. See George Rudé, *The Crowd in the French Revolution* (Oxford: Clarendon Press, 1959), 74–75.

6. William Doyle, *The Oxford History of the French Revolution* (Oxford: Clarendon Press, 1989), 122; J. M. Thompson, *The French Revolution* (1943; rprt., New York: Oxford University Press, 1966), 104; Rudé, ibid., 76.

7. See Doyle, *The Oxford History,* 122; Thompson, ibid., 106; Paul H. Beik, "October Days," in *Historical Dictionary of the French Revolution*, ed. Samuel F. Scott and Barry Rothaus, 2 vols. (Westport, Conn.: Greenwood Press, 1989), 2:731–33.

8. Rudé, *The Crowd in the French Revolution*, 61–62.

9. Thompson, *The French Revolution*, 107; Doyle, *The Oxford History*, 122.

10. Frans De Bruyn, "Theater and Countertheater in Burke's *Reflections on the Revolution in France*," in *Burke and the French Revolution*, ed. Steven Blakemore (Athens: University of Georgia Press, 1992), 31.

11. *Révolutions de Paris* 1, no. 13 (3–10 October 1789): 6–10.

12. Ibid., 10.

13. Ibid., 15, 17–18.

14. Ibid., 16–17.

15. Ibid., 19.

16. Darline Gay Levy and Harriet B. Applewhite, "Women and Militant Citizenship in Revolutionary Paris," in *Rebel Daughters: Women and the French Revolution*, ed. Sara E. Melzer and Leslie W. Rabine (New York: Oxford University Press, 1992), 82.

17. *Révolutions de Paris* 1, no. 13 (3–10 October 1789), 20–22.

6. Revolution and the Canon: Paine's Critique of the Old Linguistic Order and the Creation of the Revolutionary Writer

1. In 1782 and 1807, Paine insisted that the Declaratory Act was a principal cause of the American Revolution (Alfred Owen Aldridge, *Thomas Paine's American Ideology* [Newark: University of Delaware Press, 1984], 120). Curiously, Paine did not subsequently note that the Declaratory Act was promulgated by the Rockingham ministry, probably because Burke and the Rockingham Whigs opposed the American war and agreed to the Act (pushed by Pitt) as a compromise by which the Stamp Act could be repealed. See Conor Cruise O'Brien, *The Great Melody: A Thematic Biography of Edmund Burke* (Chicago: The University of Chicago Press, 1992), 111–17. In *Observations on the Nature of Civil Liberty* (1776), Richard Price had attacked the Declaratory Act's language of "slavery" (*Political Writings*, ed. D. O. Thomas [Cambridge: Cambridge University Press, 1991], 37–38).

2. Gerald Bruns, "Canon and Power in the Hebrew Scriptures," *Critical Inquiry* 10 (1984): 464.

3. Aldridge, *Thomas Paine's American Ideology*, 262.

4. Cf. John Locke, who had helped to draft a liberal Constitution for the new colony of Carolina, *The Fundamental Constitutions of Carolina* (1669): the Constitution for Carolina is "to remain the sacred and unalterable form and rule of government of Carolina forever." Cited in Claeys, *Political Writings*, 2:80 n. 2.

5. David A. Wilson, *Paine and Cobbett: The Transatlantic Connection* (Kingston & Montreal: McGill-Queen's University Press, 1988), 45–47. Wilson discusses similarities of style and content in Paine's and Hall's pamphlets. In chapter 1, he discusses the influence of radical Whig discourse on Paine's intellectual formation. Whether or not Paine was reinscribing Hall—and many scholars remain unconvinced—the relevant context is Paine's insistence throughout his writings that he is producing an original, radical critique.

6. See, for instance, *Reflections*, 94–96, 99–100, 157, 166; Hawkins, *Letters on the Female Mind*, 2:69; Nigel Smith, *Literature and Revolution in England, 1640–1660* (New Haven: Yale University Press, 1994), 2; Peter J. Kitson, "'Sages and patriots that being dead do yet speak to us': Readings of the English Revolution in the Late Eighteenth Century," *Prose Studies* 14.3 (December 1991): 205–30. Radical British writers used the regicidal paradigm of the 1640s as a warning to British reactionaries. In France, the Girondins evoked Cromwell and the Long Parliament to stigmatize the Jacobins. Louis XVI spent his last days in the Temple reading Hume on Charles I, contemplating the obvious regicidal parallels. During the king's trial, the revolutionaries used the 1640s paradigm as a legitimate precedent. For an examination of the perceived parallels in revolutionary (1790–99) and Romantic literature, see Joseph Nicholes, "Revolutions Compared: The English Civil War as Political Touchstone in Romantic Literature," in *Revolution and English Romanticism*, ed. Keith Hanley and Raman Selden (New York: St. Martin Press, 1990), 261–76. For parallels in drama, see Kenneth R. Johnston and Joseph Nicholes, "Transitory Actions, Men Betrayed: The French Revolution in the English Revolution in Romantic Drama," *The Wordsworth Circle* 22 (Spring 1992): 76–96.

7. Both the rival readings and the rejections of the French Constitutions (there were two others in 1795 and 1799) were battles over control of the Revolution's meaning. In the trial of Louis XVI, for instance, the condemned Constitution of 1791 was also on trial. A variety of speakers in the National Convention ridiculed and attacked its "weaknesses"

(and those who had, in the prior National Assembly, supported it), especially since the Constitution had sanctioned and protected the king, making the chopping off of his head problematic. See the speeches collected by Michael Walzer, *Regicide and Revolution: Speeches at the Trial of Louis XVI*, trans. Marion Rothstein (Cambridge: Cambridge University Press, 1974).

8. See Bernard Bailyn, *Faces of Revolution: Personalities and Themes in the Struggle for American Independence* (New York: Knopf, 1990), 67–84; Eric Foner, *Tom Paine and Revolutionary America* (New York: Oxford University Press, 1976), 71–106; James T. Boulton, *The Language of Politics in the Age of Wilkes and Burke* (London: Routledge and Kegan Paul, 1963), 134–50; Olivia Smith, *The Politics of Language, 1791–1819* (Oxford: Clarendon Press, 1984), 35–67.

9. *Locke's Two Treatises of Government*, ed. Peter Laslett (Cambridge: Cambridge University Press, 1988), 137–38, 155–57, 163, 168–69, 191–92, 198, 201–2, 220–22, 242. During the American Revolution, Paine had been accused of deriving his style and content from both radical Puritan discourse in the 1640s and subsequent republican discourse in the 1680s and 1690s. Alfred Owen Aldridge argues that Paine was not directly influenced by either radical Puritan or Enlightenment discourse and that any similarities "may be explained by a process of transmission through intermediaries"—republican ideas "kept alive" by eighteenth-century Whig theorists (*Thomas Paine's American Ideology*, 101). His counteremphasis on differences rather than similarities reformulates Paine's own representation of himself as an original, revolutionary writer who really did not read anyone seriously except himself. Paine was, however, a great reader (whether directly or indirectly) of dissident writers, whose thought he revivified in ways that often seemed radically new. While considering some of Paine's original contributions, I stress that his style and many of his ideas were part and parcel of British radical tradition and that, within the context of the macrocosmic French Revolution, Paine's representation of himself waging original revolution is historically central to his critique.

10. E. P. Thompson calls *Rights of Man* a "foundation-text" of English radical discourse (*The Making of the English Working Class* [New York: Pantheon, 1964], 90). Jon P. Klancher argues that Paine "found[s]" radical discourse upon a radical critique of (Burkean) authorizations of conservative textual tradition (*The Making of English Reading Audiences, 1790–1832* [Madison: University of Wisconsin Press, 1987], 108). Paine, however, authorizes his own texts by arguing that the publication of *Common Sense* in 1776 created the "origins" of the American Revolution, out of which flowed the French Revolution and the other revolutionary movements made possible by his causal books (see *CW*, 1:497; 2:1163, 1490, 1495, 1498). He is continually preoccupied with precedent textual origins.

11. Albert Goodwin, *The Friends of Liberty: The English Democratic Movement in the Age of the French Revolution* (Cambridge: Harvard University Press, 1979), 260 n. 234; David V. Erdman, *Commerce Des Lumières: John Oswald and the British in Paris* (Columbia: University of Missouri Press, 1986), 120; cf. 244, 257.

12. See chap. 3, sec. 1, art. 2 of the 1791 Constitution in *A Documentary Survey of the French Revolution*, ed. John Hall Stewart (Toronto: The Macmillan Company, 1951), 246–47. Paine's friend, Thomas Christie, in 1791 had referred to and quoted the law of 22 May 1790 in *Letters on the Revolution of France* (181, 211; appendix, 112–14).

13. Simon Schama, *Citizens: A Chronicle of the French Revolution* (New York: Knopf, 1989), 246. For Paine's comments on Calonne, see *CW*, 1:301–3.

14. This was a standard dissident contention. See Algernon Sidney, *Discourses Concerning Government*, ed. Thomas G. West (1698: Indianapolis: LibertyClassics, 1990),

486, 508. Cf. Daniel Defoe, "The True-Born Englishman" (1700), 11.140–69. In *Constitutional Reform* (1805), Paine quoted Defoe's lines in his critique of the House of Lords' "disgraceful origin" (*CW*, 2:1000).

15. For a discussion of these issues, see Blakemore, *Burke and the Fall of Language*, 81–86; for similar linguistic preoccupations in America and Paine's influence on Noah Webster, see Michael P. Kramer, *Imagining Language in America: From the Revolution to the Civil War* (Princeton: Princeton University Press, 1992), 44–49; for linguistic wars in America, see David Simpson, *The Politics of American English, 1776–1856* (New York: Oxford University Press, 1986); for the linguistic implications of transparency, sincerity, and a "natural" language, see Jay Fleigelman, *Declaring Independence: Jefferson, Natural Language, & the Culture of Performance* (Stanford: Stanford University Press, 1993). In *Representative Words*, Thomas Gustafson provides a luminous account of the Western preoccupation with corrupt language and the respondent endeavor to establish a representative language corresponding to political reform and revolution. Focusing on Paine's American writings, Gustafson sees Paine overturning the traditional British "terms" that had enslaved the American mind and seeking to replace "them with words representative of the natural constitution of things" (*Representative Words: Politics, Literature, and the American Language, 1776–1865* [Cambridge: Cambridge University Press, 1992], 243; see 241–52). Gustafson's comments also apply appropriately to *Rights of Man* and reaffirm what has been the dominant critical consensus of Paine and his language.

16. Cf. Sidney, *Discourses Concerning Government*, 514.

17. The radical Levellers in the 1640s had attacked the English legal system and "the fact that legal proceedings were still conducted in Latin and Norman French," as did the republican Algernon Sidney in *Discourses Concerning Government* (Houston, *Algernon Sidney*, 171). This critique was also a codified commonplace of Whig ideology. In *Commentaries on the Laws of England* (1765–69), William Blackstone referred to the foreign intrusion of the Norman "dialect" with its "obscure glosses, and jarring interpretations" into English civil law. Norman French is a "barbarous dialect" and a "badge of slavery" (*Commentaries on the Laws of England*, 4 vols. [Chicago: The University of Chicago Press, 1979], 4:411, 3:317, 4:409). Paine and other Whigs, however, exaggerated the Norman influence on English legal language: "'Law French' lingered in writings about law until its use was finally forbidden [by Cromwell] in 1650. A statute of 1363 had declared that oral proceedings in the courts of England must be in English rather than French, a language 'which was much unknown in the realm'" (Goldwin Smith, *A Constitutional and Legal History of England* [New York: Dorset Press, 1990], 248). Briefly revived after the Restoration (1660), Law French, as a legal language, was definitively abolished in 1731.

18. J. G. A. Pocock, *The Ancient Constitution and the Feudal Law* (Cambridge: Cambridge University Press, 1957), 232.

19. Ibid.; cf. Paine, *Rights of Man* (*CW*, 1:294–95). By the 1790s, dissident criticism of the House of Commons was commonplace. In *Political Disquisitions* (1774–75), James Burgh had earlier criticized the House of Commons's abusive power and inadequate representation (cf. *CW*, 1:309).

20. Isaac Kramnick makes a case for Paine's radicalness in terms of his critique of paternalistic government and aristocratic distinctions and his antithetical promotion of science and egalitarian merit—a bourgeois ideology he shares with Dissenters and other "radical liberals" (*Republicanism and Bourgeois Radicalism: Political Ideology in Late Eighteenth-Century England and America* [Ithaca: Cornell University Press, 1990], 133–

60). Referring to Paine's "significance for the ideology of revolution in the late eighteenth-century," Kramnick observes that "Paine was self-made Paine; he had created himself, generated himself, given birth to himself. [Painean] men were authors of themselves, in contrast to men bred to privilege, in contrast to those to the man[or] born" (135). Although Kramnick does not pursue the observation, it is, I think, closer to Paine's original and enduring significance: the myth of the self-creating author of world revolution. In another book, I explore this theme in context of Paine's complete oeuvre.

21. Karl Marx, *The Eighteenth Brumaire of Louis Bonaparte*, in *Surveys from Exile*, ed. David Fernbach (1973; New York: Vintage Books, 1974), 147.

22. See Philipe Roger, "The French Revolution as logomachy," in *Language and Rhetoric of the Revolution*, ed. John Renwick (Edinburgh: Edinburgh University Press, 1990), 4–24.

7. Mackintosh, Burke, and the French Revolution

1. Helen Maria Williams, *Letters from France*, ed. Janet Todd, 2 vols. (1790–96; Delmar, N.Y.: Scholars' Facsimiles & Reprints, 1975), 1:4.218–19.

2. Boulton, *The Language of Politics*, 152; see 151–76.

3. *Memoirs of the Life of Sir James Mackintosh*, ed. Robert J. Mackintosh, 2 vols. (Boston: Little, Brown and Company, 1853). The *Memoirs* are usually referred to as James Mackintosh's autobiography, since they include copious quotations from his journals and works along with autobiographical material he had intended to publish. The materials are, however, organized by his son, Robert, who tells the story of his father's life in his own words as well. Although the *Memoirs* is, I think, technically a biography (the word can refer to either a biography or an autobiography, and Robert Mackintosh seems to use it in the latter sense), I follow standard usage in the Works Cited, where it appears under James Mackintosh's name.

4. Patrick O'Leary, *Sir James Mackintosh, the Whig Cicero* (Aberdeen: Aberdeen University Press, 1989); Seamus Deane, *The French Revolution and Enlightenment in England, 1789–1832* (Cambridge: Harvard University Press, 1988), 43–57.

5. Erdman, *Commerce Des Lumières*, 118.

6. O'Leary, *Sir James Mackintosh*, 30.

7. Erdman, *Commerce Des Lumières*, 227.

8. Ibid., 234.

9. See, for instance, ibid., 232 n. 23.

10. O'Leary, *Sir James Mackintosh*, 36.

11. Mackintosh, *Memoirs*, 1:87.

12. Peter Stanlis, *Edmund Burke: The Enlightenment and Revolution* (New Brunswick, N.J.: Transaction Publishers, 1991), 50.

13. Mackintosh, *Memoirs*, 1:91, 94.

14. Ibid., 1:110; see 111–16.

15. William Godwin, *Uncollected Writings* (1785–1822), ed. Jack W. Marken and Burton R. Pollin (Gainesville, Fl.: Scholars' Facsimiles & Reprints, 1968), 302–4.

16. St Claire, *The Godwins and the Shelleys*, 206.

17. O'Leary, *Sir James Mackintosh*, 51; William Hazlitt, *Lectures on the English Poets and the Spirit of the Age* (1825; New York: E. P. Dutton & Co., 1910), 264.

18. Mackintosh, *Memoirs*, 1:125.

19. James T. Boulton, "James Mackintosh: *Vindiciae Gallicae*," *Renaissance and Modern Studies* 21 (1977), 117. Boulton is undoubtedly correct. For instance, part 3 of the *Malleus Maleficarum* (1486), the influential treatise on demonology, includes this prefatory abjuration for those suspected of heresy: "I abjure, renounce, and revoke that heresy" (Russell Hope Robbins, *The Encyclopedia of Witchcraft and Demonology* [New York: Crown Publishers, 1959], 337–38). Mackintosh's language likely comes from even earlier forms for the recantation of heretics and may have been adapted by the Anglican Church. His language, as I will later discuss, was incorporated into various oaths of abjuration by which the British subject abjured allegiance to Rome and the Stuart pretenders.

20. Charles Lamb, *The Complete Works and Letters of Charles Lamb* (New York: The Modern Library, 1935), 701.

21. Mackintosh, *Memoirs*, 2:133.

22. Ibid., 2:131–36.

23. Deane, *The French Revolution*, 56.

24. Cf. *Reflections*, 281, 3rd line from bottom; 296, 4th par., 1.3.

25. Mackintosh, *Memoirs*, 1:312; cf. *Reflections*, 281, last sentence.

26. For instance, Burke, in *Reflections*, complains that "it has been the misfortune . . . of this age, that everything is to be discussed" (188); likewise, Mackintosh complains that "even the fundamental rules of morality themselves have, for the first time, unfortunately for mankind, become the subject of doubt and discussion" (*Works*, 34).

27. Deane, *The French Revolution*, 54.

28. Ibid.

29. See William Christian, "James Mackintosh, Burke, and the Cause of Reform," *Eighteenth-Century Studies* 7 (1973–74): 193–206.

30. Deane, The French Revolution, 44.

8. Mackintosh, Burke, and the Glorious Revolution

1. In England, William III was "the Great Deliverer." In *A Discourse on the Love of Our Country* (1789), Richard Price refers to the English people's "deliverance" from Jacobite popery and slavery (*Political Writings*, 178, 189). In *Reflections*, Burke, responding to people who were equating the Glorious and French Revolutions, refers ironically to criminals and murderers liberated from imprisonment by "their heroic deliverer, the metaphysical Knight of the Sorrowful Countenance" (90), i.e., deranged progressives who, like Don Quixote, are maddened by revolutionary romances, such as Price's *Discourse*. In the *Vindiciae*, Mackintosh castigates Burke for refusing to welcome "the splendid and glorious delivery" of the French people—the adjective *glorious* doubling the resemblance of both Revolutions (*Works*, 404).

2. Paul Kléber Monod, *Jacobitism and the English People, 1688–1788* (Cambridge: Cambridge University Press, 1989), 49–54.

3. The identification of English Dissenters with the promotion of the Revolution was commonplace. Mackintosh, in the *Vindiciae*, denies that the majority of English "advocates" of the Revolution were Dissenters (*Works*, 460–61).

4. J. G. A. Pocock, "Edmund Burke and the Redefinition of Enthusiasm: the Context as Counter-Revolution," in *The French Revolution and the Creation of Modern Political Culture*, ed. François Furet and Mona Ozouf (Oxford: Pergamon Press, 1989), 3:21.

5. J. C. D. Clark, *English Society 1688–1832* (Cambridge: Cambridge University Press, 1985), 46.

6. On 11 December 1688, James II had fled London, but not before he had canceled writs he had issued (under duress) for electing a new Parliament and had personally burned those writs that had not been dispatched. In addition, he canceled the nomination of new sheriffs, needed for carrying out the elections, and dropped the Great Seal into the Thames as his boat sailed silently out of London. Because of the many events that Mackintosh discusses, it is difficult always to keep the technical distinction between the Convention (22 January 1689–22 February 1689) and the Convention Parliament (23 February 1689–winter of 1689–90), when the latter was disbanded by William III and a new Parliament was convoked. Since both were essentially the same body, I use Convention and Convention Parliament interchangeably, unless the distinction is crucial. Mackintosh always refers to the Convention, probably to underscore its illegal status.

7. John Phillip Reid, *The Concept of Representation in the Age of the American Revolution* (Chicago: Chicago University Press, 1989), 2.

8. Burke's usage of *deviation* is in the allusive context of Aristotle's discussion in *The Politics* of "natural" constitutions (monarchy, aristocracy, polity) and their respective deviations into "unnatural" ones (tyranny, oligarchy, democracy). Burke uses the standard English translation *deviation* for the Greek *parekbasis* (see Aristotle, *The Politics*, trans. T. A. Sinclair [London: Penguin Books, 1981], 156–57, 189–90, 206, 211, 215, 222, 229, 239, 242, 259, 320, 334). Burke's point is that the attempt of James II to subvert the "mixed" English constitution (a combination of monarchy, aristocracy, and *democracy*, in its nonpejorative sense) by changing the constitutional monarchy into an absolute monarchy (a tyranny) created a constitutional crisis and imbalance that was resolved by the *temporary* deviation instituted by the Convention Parliament (the Lords and Commons, the "aristocratic" and "democratic" parts of the constitution)—a deviation that restored the constitution's natural balance.

9. Richard Price, *Discourse on the Love of our Country*, in *Political Writings*, 190.

10. After the Glorious Revolution, "Revolution principles" became a popular term contested by Tories and Whigs: Tories associated the Revolution's "principles" with rationalizations of rebellion and treason; for Whigs, they were the liberating foundation principles established by the Revolution (see Kenyon, *Revolution Principles: The Politics of Party, 1689–1720* [Cambridge: Cambridge University Press, 1977], 102–7. In the 1790s, Burke and other conservatives contended that English supporters of the French Revolution were misrepresenting the Glorious Revolution's principles by providing them a radical significance they did not have. In *Reflections,* Burke recalls "erring fancies to the *acts* of the Revolution which we revere, for the discovery of its true *principles*. If the *principles* of the Revolution of 1688 are any where to be found, it is in the Statute called the *Declaration of Right*" (100). Cf. *Vindiciae* in *Works*: "The true admirers of Revolution principles" (454, 456) and Laetitia Matilda Hawkins's hope that Helen Maria Williams's direct experience of the French Revolution will cause "a revolution in your revolution principles" (*Letters on the Female Mind*, 2:180).

11. Lois G. Schwoerer, *The Declaration of Rights, 1689* (Baltimore: The Johns Hopkins University Press, 1981), 274, 280.

12. A phrase with conservative pedigree, used, for instance, with reference to the Duke of Monmouth (Charles II's illegitimate son) and his military rebellion against James II. In his *Letter on Toleration*, John Locke noted that the dissenting churches "were accused of being 'nurseries of factions and seditions'" (Richard Ashcraft, *Revolutionary Politics and Locke's Two Treatises of Government* [Princeton: Princeton University Press, 1986], 358, 505).

13. "William of Normandy in 1066, Henry of Bolingbroke in 1399, and Henry of Richmond in 1485 had invaded [England] . . . claiming rights of their own and offering to redress the grievances of others," just as William of Orange subsequently did in 1688 (J. G. A. Pocock, "The Fourth English Civil War: dissolution, desertion, and alternative histories in the Glorious Revolution," in *The Revolution of 1688–1689, Changing Perspectives*, ed. Lois G. Schwoerer [Cambridge: Cambridge University Press, 1992], 55. William of Orange, however, had tried to avoid all appearance of conquest and had "rejected the advice 'of the greatest lawyers and those that came with him' to declare himself king, by right of conquest, after the example of the victorious Henry VII, and issue writs for Parliament in his name" (Robert Beddard, *A Kingdom without a King: The Journal of the Provisional Government in the Revolution of 1688* [Oxford: Phaidon Press, 1988], 63). In the Glorious Revolution, conquest theory was generally rejected by both Whigs and Tories (Kenyon, *Revolution Principles*, 29–32).

14. Cf. Burke (107), supporters of the French Revolution "take the deviation from the principle [of succession] for the principle."

15. Schwoerer, *The Declaration of Rights*, 217.

16. See, for instance, Locke's discussion of the *"original Compact"* in *The Second Treatise of Government* (pars. 97 and 171).

17. Kenyon, *Revolution Principles*, 39.

18. Gary Wills, *Inventing America: Jefferson's Declaration of Independence* (New York: Vintage Books, 1979), 38.

19. In *Reflections*, Burke quoted Price's notorious "king led in triumph," savagely mocking it throughout (see 159, 162, 165–66, 168–69, 176–78, 180–81). In the *Vindiciae*, Mackintosh alludes to Burke's "triumph," rhetorically triumphing over Burke (*Works*, 404–6, 409, 431, 435, 447, 452, 454, 460).

20. Ashcraft, *Revolutionary Politics*, 568.

21. Ibid., 592–94, 597.

22. Ironically echoing Burke, "A state without the means of change is without the means of its conservation" (*Reflections*, 106).

23. Schwoerer, *The Declaration of Rights*, 283–84.

24. See Lois G. Schwoerer's review of these readings: "Introduction," in *The Revolution of 1688–1689*, 7–8.

25. Mackintosh, *Memoirs*, 1:125.

26. In Schwoerer, *The Declaration of Rights*, 297–98.

27. Originally titled *History of the Revolution in England in 1688*, it was changed by Mackintosh's son, Robert, because he thought it too inclusive: the book deals with the causes leading up to the Revolution, but Mackintosh was unable to complete the entire history.

9. Revolution in Property

1. Goldwin Smith, *A Constitutional and Legal History*, 267–68, 281.

2. Keith Thomas, *Religion and the Decline of Magic* (New York: Charles Scribner's Sons, 1971), 96–98, 100.

3. See *Reflections*, 144, 204, 219, 259, 350. Cf. Mackintosh's revision in *Review of the Causes of the Revolution of 1688*: "The painful consciousness which haunts the possessers of recently confiscated property" (*Works*, 317). For a pertinent discussion of the role of property in Burke's thought, see Francis Canavan, *The Political Economy of Edmund Burke: The Role of Property in His Thought* (New York: Fordham University Press, 1995).

4. Goldwin Smith, *A Constitutional and Legal History*, 341; cf. *Reflections*, 260. The confiscations of (Catholic) property were especially severe in Ireland, although they had actually begun under the reigns of Elizabeth and James I. For rhetorical reasons, neither Burke nor Mackintosh mentions these confiscations. Later, in *Review of the Causes of the Revolution of 1688*, Mackintosh considers the Irish confiscations in detail (*Works*, 314–15).

5. Richard L. Greaves, *The Radical Underground in Britain, 1660–1663* (New York: Oxford University Press, 1986), 135–36.

6. Ashcraft, *Revolutionary Politics*, 202.

7. Pocock, *Virtue, Commerce, and History*, 70.

8. Blackstone, *Commentaries*, 2:385.

9. Ibid., 2:16–19.

10. See P. G. M. Dickson, *The Financial Revolution in England: A Study in the Development of Public Credit, 1688–1756* (London: Macmillan, 1967).

11. Pocock, "Edmund Burke and the Redefinition of Enthusiasm," 28. Michael McKeon notes that the antagonistic relationship between "land and trade" was converted, after the Restoration, into "the newly conceptualized antithesis between the 'landed interest' and the 'monied interest'" and that the former was understood to be distinguished from the latter "not by the status criteria of land ownership or the possession of a county seat but by the quite specialized requirement that they live entirely on income from rents"—from income derived from the land (*The Origins of the English Novel, 1600–1740* [Baltimore: The Johns Hopkins University Press, 1987], 165–66).

12. W. A. Speck, *Reluctant Revolutionaries: Englishmen and the Revolution of 1688* (Oxford: Oxford University Press, 1988), 250.

13. Brian Tierney, *The Crisis of Church and State, 1050–1300* (Toronto: University of Toronto Press, 1989), 25.

14. Will and Ariel Durant, *The Age of Voltaire* (New York: Simon and Schuster, 1965), 13, 283.

15. In Stewart, *A Documentary Survey*, 115.

16. Schama, *Citizens*, 483.

17. Ibid. The source of many of Mackintosh's arguments is the debates in the National Assembly, which Mackintosh presents as if they were his own, apparently to hide their radical origin from the English audience he addresses. He also appropriates, I believe, three arguments made by the Abbé Sieyès in *What Is the Third Estate?* (1789): the distinction between useful producers and useless consumers, the argument against

"corporate interests" and an "esprit de corps," and the contention that the legitimate clergy are paid functionaries of the state (Joseph Emmanuel Sieyès, *What is the Third Estate?*, trans. M. Blondel [New York: Praeger, 1964], 54, 56–57, 94–95, 138, 142, 145, 158, 160, 164–65, 175–76, 185–86). Since these arguments were also used by members of the National Assembly, it is difficult to identify specific French sources that had become the collective ideological property of "the nation."

18. Louis Bergeron, "National Properties," in *A Critical Dictionary of the French Revolution*, ed. François Furet and Mona Ozouf, trans. Arthur Goldhammer (Cambridge: Belknap Press of Harvard University, 1989), 511.

19. Ibid., 512. William of Ockham (1285–1349) had rejected "the papal view that religious communities and churches could own property with the blunt contention that the legal concept of corporation designated a fictive entity and not a real thing, given that only individuals were real substances" (Arthur P. Monahan, *From Personal Duties Towards Personal Rights: Late Medieval and Early Modern Political Thought, 1300–1600* [Kingston & Montreal: McGill-Queen's University Press, 1994], 30). The long ideological roots of the French Revolution have yet to be uncovered.

20. Adam Smith had attacked "corporate spirit" in *The Wealth of Nations* (1776) as propogating feudal institutions and laws that restrained talent and industry and disrupted "natural" market values (*An Inquiry into the Nature of and Causes of the Wealth of Nations*, 2 vols. ed. R. H. Campbell and A. S. Skinner [Indianapolis: LibertyClassics, 1981], 1:136, 142–44). Mackintosh, however, translates into the *Vindiciae* the dominant French discourse of the 1790s aimed specifically at French corporations, which, he subversively suggests, resemble English corporations that must be similarly destroyed. His critique of "corporation spirit" is translated from the French discourse he appropriates: Sieyès and members of the National Assembly criticized esprit de corps as had both French royalists and radicals in the late 1780s, when it became fashionable to attack the "esprit de corps"—those corporations or assemblies advancing an agenda of private, particular interests rather than public, national interests. Cf. Mackintosh's subsequent revision in *Review of the Causes of the Revolution of 1688*: fortunately, "the corporate property of [Oxford and Cambridge] was undisturbed" during the English Civil War; the "corporate spirit . . . is one of the most steady and inflexible principles of human action"; in contrast, under James II, the "invasion of the legal possessions of the Universities . . . was made on principles which tended directly to subject the whole property of the Church to the pleasure of the Crown"; as soon as "the sacredness of legal possession is intentionally violated, the security of all property is endangered" (*Works*, 321, 325).

21. Ashcraft, *Revolutionary Politics*, 560–67, 566.

22. In *Commentaries on the Laws of England* (1765), Blackstone had extolled the 1689 Convention Parliament for avoiding "the visionary theories of some zealous republicans," like Locke, who argued for a "total dissolution of government" (1:206). Mackintosh recognized that Burke, in his account of the Glorious Revolution, rearticulates Blackstone. Hence his linkage and attack on both (*Works*, 450). In *Reflections*, Burke was also conscious of the radical usage of dissolve and dissolution: revolutionaries "always speak" as if there is a singular species of compact between them and their magistrates, which binds the magistrate [cf. Sidney, *Discourses Concerning Government*, 309–16, 412–13, 431, 434], but which has nothing reciprocal in it, but that the majesty of the people has a right to dissolve it without any reason, but its will. (184)

During the Restoration and Glorious Revolution, however, the nation's "ancient edifice" was not "dissolve[d]" (*Reflections*, 106; cf. 105, 160, 171, 194–95, 314, 326–27).

23. [Jacques Anne-Robert Turgot], "Fondation," in *Encyclopédie ou dictionnaire raisonné des sciences des artes et des métiers* (1751–80; Stuttgart, Germany: Friedrich Frommann Verlag, 1966), 7:72–75.

24. In 1790, the Abbé Sieyès had made this point again in a pamphlet dealing with the clergy. Sieyès stressed that the great corporations had to be destroyed, and he "proposed that ecclesiastics, like other public functionaries, become salaried employees of the nation" (William H. Sewell Jr., *A Rhetoric of Bourgeois Revolution: The Abbé Sieyès and What is the Third Estate?* [Durham: Duke University Press, 1994], 132).

25. In Schama, *Citizens*, 483.

26. John Spurr, *The Restoration Church of England, 1646–1689* (New Haven: Yale University Press, 1991), 104.

27. Doyle, *The Oxford History*, 137.

28. Cf. Joseph Priestly, *Letters to the Right Honourable Edmund Burke* (1792): "And if a revisal of this [France's ecclesiastical establishment] would have been proper, why not that of ours also?" (Claeys, *Political Writings*, 2:367).

29. Mackintosh's example unwittingly connects France's new revolutionary order with old, "Gothic" Europe. He bases his historical generalization on Feudal Vassalage, a simplistic, unhistorical generalization with reference to church lands in Europe. Monastic lands in the Middle Ages and before were often granted by powerful families for reasons of piety and/or politics before there was a concept of a state or nation. In *The Wealth of Nations* (1776), Adam Smith had discussed the Catholic Church's original control of land and benefices in France, noting that the Pragmatic Sanction (1438) and the Concordat of Bologna (1511) allowed French kings the power to distribute the major benefices and hence made the Gallic church independent of the papacy (2:798–805). Since Mackintosh employs a fiction of origins by which the king, the state, or the nation always had original possession of the land, he ignores historical examples that would contradict his fiction of origins: he cannot use the doctrine of prescription (employed by Burke), which legitimizes "new" possession over "old" possession, since prescription makes the argument from origins irrelevant. It should be noted, however, that Mackintosh's argument that the real proprietor of church property is the nation or people and that the clergy are only salaried functionaries resembles the argument of Philippe du Plessis Mornay in *Vindiciae, Contra Tyrannos* (1579; ed. and trans. George Garnett [Cambridge: Cambridge University Press, 1994])—the radical Huguenot text that employed feudal analogies to contend that the people were the "true proprietor" of the commonwealth and the king their salaried administrator (18, 89–90, 113, 119, 124, 127, 156). Later, I suggest that Mackintosh allusively evokes this text in his intertextual war with Burke. While the author of *Vindiciae, Contra Tyrannos* has not been definitively established, most scholars believe it to be Mornay.

30. In the first edition of *Vindiciae*, Mackintosh asserts that with "the abolition of nobility" no one was "degraded" (cf. *Reflections*, 206, 210, 246, 266) because "no man can be *degraded* when the rank he possessed no longer exists" (*Vindiciae*, 259).

31. In Stewart, *A Documentary Survey*, 115.

32. Bergeron, "National Properties," 512.

33. For Burke's relationship with Adam Smith, see James Conniff, *The Useful Cobbler: Edmund Burke and the Politics of Progress* (Albany: State University of New York Press, 1994), 113–23.

34. Adam Smith, *The Wealth of Nations*, 1:99, 279, 332–34, 337–38; 2:573, 665–66.

35. Ibid., 1:330–49.

36. Charles Louis de Secondat Montesquieu, *The Spirit of the Laws*, ed. and trans. Anna M. Cohler, Basia Carolyn Miller, and Harold Samuel Stone (Cambridge: Cambridge University Press, 1989), 456.

37. Schama, *Citizens*, 484.

38. Ashcraft, *Revolutionary Politics*, 234–35, 264–70.

39. Pocock notes that "the vocabulary of eighteenth-century England distinguished sharply between commerce and speculation in the public debt" (*Virtue, Commerce, and History*, 200). The public debt was associated with stockjobbing and the monied interest. For the Scottish School's solution to the Country critique, see Pocock, *Virtue, Commerce, and History*, 198–200.

40. A secondary meaning of *Vindiciae* came to mean the liberation of people from oppressive rule. Thus, the standard English translation of *Vindiciae, Contra Tyrannos* is "A Defense of Liberty against Tyrants." Likewise, a secondary meaning of *Vindiciae Gallicae* is "A Defense of Gaul's Liberty." The primary meaning, however, pertains to the dispute over property ownership. I owe these clarifications to Joshua Dorchak, Classics Department, Harvard University. Cf. George Garnett's glossary in Mornay, *Vindiciae, Contra Tyrannos*, lxxxiii.

41. Cf. *Vindiciae*: Burke's book divided public opinion, producing a controversy "which may be regarded as the trial of the French Revolution before the enlightened and independent tribunal of the English public. What its decision has been I shall not presume to decide; for it does not become an advocate to announce the decision of the judge" (*Works*, 460).

10. Revolution in Representation: Electoral and Economic Paradigms in *Vindiciae Gallicae*

1. Peter Jupp, *British and Irish Elections, 1784–1831* (New York: Barnes and Noble, 1973), 78.

2. Ashcraft, *Revolutionary Politics*, 151–64. Ashcraft convincingly argues that the Leveller agenda included "manhood suffrage," the right of any Englishman, twenty-one years or older, to vote, excluding household servants (149–66).

3. Derick Hirst, *The Representative of the People? Voters and Voting under the Early Stuarts* (Cambridge: Cambridge University Press, 1975), 29, 157.

4. Ashcraft, *Revolutionary Politics*, 166.

5. Peter G. J. Pulzer, *Political Representation and Elections: Parties and Voting in Great Britain* (New York: Frederick A. Praeger, 1967), 23.

6. Price, *Political Writings*, 191–92.

7. Ibid., 192; Kramnick, *Republicanism*, 173–74, 177, 240; cf. Adam Smith, *The Wealth of Nations*, 2:933.

8. J. P. Kenyon, *The Civil Wars of England* (New York: Alfred A. Knopf, 1988), 172–73; Ashcraft, *Revolutionary Politics*, 565, 569, 581; A. S. P. Woodhouse, ed. *Puritans and Liberty: Being the Army Debates (1647–49) from the Clarke Manuscripts with Supplementary Documents* (London: Everyman's Library, 1992), 61, 80.

9. In 1689, an anonymous author had published a tract against the radical ideologies of the time, including manhood suffrage. The tract was titled *Reflections upon Our Late and Present Proceedings in England* (Ashcraft, *Revolutionary Politics*, 565, 569). It seems more than coincidental that the full title of Burke's book is *Reflections on the Revolution in France and On the Proceedings in Certain Societies in London Relative To That Event*. Just as Price and other supporters of the French Revolution were evoking a radical language and tradition, Burke also evokes a correspondent conservative tradition and language.

10. Price, *Discourse*, in *Political Writings*, 192, 196.

11. The footnote appears on page 42 of the third and fourth editions but is missing from D. O. Thomas's edition of Price's *Political Writings* (192). James K. Chandler notes that Burke, in *Reflections*, emphasizes Richard Price's criticism of the House of Commons as "a semblance," "a form," "a theory," "a shadow," "a mockery" to underscore Price's Platonic vocabulary: Burke

> wants to suggest a relationship between the Revolutionary critique of the adequacy of *status quo* political representation, on the one hand, and Platonic theory of representation in terms of forms and shadows. . . . In the *Reflections* Burke begins to suggest the epistemological basis of his objections to Platonizing politics. ("Political Liberties: Burke's France and the 'Adequate Representation' of the English," in *The French Revolution and the Creation of Modern Political Culture*, ed. François Furet and Mona Ozouf [Oxford: Pergamon Press, 1989] 3:49–50)

12. Since the seventeenth century, Old Sarum had been the locus classicus of a rotten borough. In the post-1815 reform debates, critics invariably referred, in contrast, to unrepresented industrial towns like Manchester, although "their residents almost always voted in the elections for the county in which the town was situated, and did so on the relatively wide forty-shilling freehold franchise which applied in all counties—a franchise much wider than that applying in many boroughs returning their own MPs" (Clark, *English Society*, 367). In *The Wealth of Nations* (1776), Adam Smith observed that "a great part of the yeomanry have [forty-shilling] freeholds" and could vote; consequently, their "order becomes respectable to their landlords on account of the political consideration which this gives them" (1:392). During the American Revolution, the example of England's county elections was used to contrast the lack of representation in America, as Richard Price did in *Two Tracts on Civil Liberty* (1778): in England "all freeholders and burgesses in boroughs, are [through the county elections] represented." In America, "not one freeholder, or any other person, is represented" (John Phillip Reid, *The Concept of Representation*, 54).

13. Hanna Fenichel Pitkin, *The Concept of Representation* (Berkeley: University of California Press, 1967), 168–89. Pitkin's view of Burke's concept of representation has been widely criticized for, among other things, oversimplification (see Conniff, *The Useful Cobbler*, 137–60, for a critique). Burke did indeed have a more complex understanding of representation, although virtual representation of "interest" was a historical paradigm he also employed. I mention this paradigm in the context of Burke because this is the English model that Mackintosh attacks in the *Vindiciae*, the one that he allusively associates with Burke's position on English representation.

14. John Phillip Reid, *The Concept of Representation*, 2.

15. The following four paragraphs are from my article "Revolution in Representation: Burke's *Reflections on the Revolution in France*," *Eighteenth-Century Life* 15 (November 1991): 12–13.

16. Mackintosh frequently refers to representation as the people's "voice" (cf. *Reflections*, 295–96). In England, until the adoption of the secret ballot in 1872, "voters voted in public. When they went to the polls, they declared their choices before all to see and hear" (David Cresap Moore, *The Politics of Deference: A Study of the mid-nineteenth century English political system* [New York: Barnes & Noble, 1976], 1). The emphasis on public transparency versus private concealment was a logocentric premise of radicals in the 1790s.

17. John Phillip Reid, *The Concept of Representation*, 32; cf. 120.

18. See Stewart, *A Documentary Survey*, 131, art. 27.

19. On 15 January 1790, the National Assembly decreed that the tax equivalent of three days' labor was sixty sous. In *Rights of Man*, Paine declares that "the Constitution of France says, that every man who pays a tax of sixty sous per annum . . . is an elector" (*CW*, 1:280), implying that every active citizen is an elector of the representative to the National Assembly—keeping out of sight the intermediate election in the departments as well as the other two restrictive money qualifications. In the *Vindiciae*, Mackintosh deals with a period in which there were two kinds of elections in France—elections of representatives to the National Assembly and local elections of administrative functionaries in the municipalities, departments, and districts—all of which he discusses. The elections of representatives to the National Assembly entailed a series of intermediate elections. Because there are a confusing number of representatives, I refer to those involved in the intermediate elections as *deputies* (the word Mackintosh uses) and to those who were elected to the National Assembly as *representatives*.

20. In *The Federalist* 9, Alexander Hamilton extols the division of powers and electoral representation as "wholly new discoveries," either "not known . . . or imperfectly known to the ancients."

21. See J. G. A. Pocock, *The Machiavellian Moment: Florentine Political Thought and the Atlantic Republican Tradition* (Princeton: Princeton University Press, 1975), 72, 77.

22. Pocock, *Virtue, Commerce, and History*, 306–7.

23. Cf. Burke's citation of Price: "The inequality in our representation is a 'defect in our constitution . . . [a constitution] excellent chiefly in *form* and *theory*'" (*Reflections*, 145).

24. Stewart, *A Documentary Survey*, 131.

25. Burke erroneously based his observation that members of the National Assembly must wait two years before they could again run for election on legislation passed by the National Assembly (1 October 1789) that was subsequently rescinded (see Christie, *Letters on the Revolution of France*, 181; Appendix, 45).

26. Stewart, *A Documentary Survey*, 132.

27. John Phillip Reid, *The Concept of Representation*, 98–106.

28. Christie, *Letters on the Revolution of France*, 198.

29. The Abbé Sieyès had made a similar point in a pamphlet published in October 1789. See Sewell, *A Rhetoric of Bourgeois Revolution*, 179.

30. The "intoxication of an election mob" alludes to England, conjuring up the (criticized) English canvass, by which a candidate or MP would spend money, often

lavishly—purchasing large amounts of food and liquor for the voters he was wooing. Such a practice often came across as bribery. In *The Rights of Men*, Wollstonecraft refers to "the thoughtless extravagance of an electioneering frolic," the "effervesence of spirits," and the little, "tyrannical arts of canvassing" corresponding to the "venality" of the people's "votes" (*WMW*, 5:36). William Blackstone noted that it was against the law for any candidate to provide "any money or entertainment to his electors" and that the electors had to take both "the oath of abjuration and that against bribery and corruption," although he thinks it "might not be amiss, if the members elected were bound to take the latter oath ... which in all probability would be much more effectual, than administering it only to the electors" (*Commentaries*, 1:174).

31. Sieyès, *What is the Third Estate?* 106–18.

32. Jean-Jacques Rousseau, *The Social Contract*, trans. Maurice Cranston (Harmondsworth: Penguin Books, 1968), 69–74.

33. Lionel A. McKenzie, "The French Revolution and English Parliamentary Reform: James Mackintosh and the *Vindiciae Gallicae*," *Eighteenth-Century Studies* 14 (1981): 264–82.

34. Discussing the variety of available discourses in the late eighteenth century used by bourgeois radicals and the semantic evolution of key words such as *virtue* and *corruption*, Isaac Kramnick emphasizes that it was common to mix or conflate different discourses and "languages" (e.g., classic republican or civic humanism with work-ethic Protestant discourse): what today would be considered a contradiction would not be considered such in the late eighteenth century (Kramnick, *Republicanism*, 260–88). This does not, however, mean that the contradiction does not exist. Kramnick's useful point is helpful in the context of the bourgeois radicals he considers, but it cannot (and this he does not do) reductively explain all "radical" or, for that matter, "conservative" contradictions. Mackintosh, for instance, has a radical bourgeois perspective, but he is contextually compelled to respond to specific contradictions noted by Burke by resorting to a series of discordant discourses. Burke forces him either to ignore the contradictions or to choose contradictory arguments. Deconstructing the French fiction of one, unified representation, Burke realizes the fiction cannot be defended consistently.

35. Dickson, *The Financial Revolution*, passim.

36. Gary Henzi, "'An Itch of Gaming': The South Sea Bubble and the Novels of Daniel Defoe," *Eighteenth-Century Life* (February 1993): 33.

37. Pocock, *Virtue, Commerce, and History*, 66.

38. Ibid., 200.

39. Durant, *The Age of Voltaire*, 56.

40. Michael Foucault, *The Order of Things: An Archeology of the Human Sciences*, trans. A. M. Sheridan Smith (New York: Vintage Books, 1973), passim.

41. In England, the financial revolution of the late 1690s and the catastrophe of the South Sea Bubble (1720) created a crisis in representation. Sandra Sherman notes that "the idea that credit was a regime outside representation, that it was a mirage of signifiers lacking signifieds, precipitated a radical critique." A variety of pamphlets opposed "the fact that credit operates in a regime of simulacra where signs refer only to themselves, rather than to some actual fund of value represented to buyer and seller" ("Credit, Simulation, and the Ideology of the Contract in the Early Eighteenth Century," *Eighteenth-Century Life* 19 (November 1995): 86, 92.

42. S. B. Harris, *The Assignats* (Cambridge: Harvard University Press, 1930), 8, 17, 19, 68. It is possible that Burke, who followed the debates in the National Assembly closely, incorporated these criticisms into *Reflections*.

43. Ibid., 17, 19.

44. Ibid., 69.

45. Christie, *Letters on the Revolution of France*, appendix, 104, 106.

46. The following five paragraphs are from Blakemore, "Revolution in Representation," 13–14.

47. See James Chandler for an astute analysis of Burke's belief that, in England, gold and silver specie acknowledge themselves "creatures" of property, "owning their debt to what they stand for" and hence admitting "the limits of their capacity to stand for it," an admission by which "they become representative of humanity's lasting conventional credit," whereas "paper currency . . . [in France] disowns its relation to gold and silver and thus also to the relation in which they stand to the principle of property." Property, for Burke, "is a matter not only of owning but also of owning up" (Chandler, "Political Liberties," in *The French Revolution and the Creation of Modern Political Culture*, 48).

48. Williams, *Letters from France*, 1:2.64–65.

49. Paine, additionally, follows Adam Smith, who, in *The Wealth of Nations*, noted that the issue of paper money tends to divert gold and silver abroad: "The substitution of paper in the room of gold and silver money, replaces a very expedient instrument of commerce with one much less costly, and sometimes equally convenient" (1:292). Although Smith considers both the advantages and disadvantages of paper money, Paine rewrites Smith's positive point (see 1:294) pejoratively: England's funding system "operates to multiply paper and *to substitute it in the room of money* . . . the more opportunities are afforded to export specie; and it admits of a possibility . . . in increasing paper till there is no money left" (*CW*, 1:323, my emphasis). Cf. *The Wealth of Nations*: "The judicious operations of banking, by substituting paper in the room of a great part of . . . gold and silver, enables the country to convert a great part of this dead stock into active and productive stock; into stock which produces something to the country" (1:321). For Paine's familiarity with *The Wealth of Nations*, see Jack Fruchtman Jr., *Thomas Paine and the Religion of Nature* (Baltimore: The Johns Hopkins University Press, 1993), 101–4, 112–14, 192 n. 5. The dangers of paper money were a common concern of both Left and Right. Richard Price, for instance, had criticized England's "sinking fund" in 1772, in a pamphlet titled *An Appeal to the Public on the Subject of the National Debt*. In *Observations on the Nature of Civil Liberty* (1776), he distinguished between "real" specie and fictitious paper: "Specie represents some real value in goods or commodities. . . . [P]aper represents . . . nothing but specie. . . . Paper, therefore, represents coin, and coin represents real value. . . . [O]ne is a sign of wealth," the "other is the sign of that sign." By issuing a proliferating paper currency, public banks substitute "fictitious [wealth] for real wealth" (Price, *Political Writings*, 58, 60; cf. 148–49). Tom Furniss argues that, in *Reflections*, Burke projects his anxieties about British speculation and paper onto revolutionary France (*Edmund Burke's Aesthetic Ideology*, 231–35). One wonders, however, why Burke would project onto France something that was already there in a more instructive, exorbitant form.

50. Michel Bruguière, "Assignats," in *A Critical Dictionary of the French Revolution*, 431.

51. A better historical example is the confiscation of church lands by Henry VIII, who sold or granted the lands to the "propertied classes who shared in the plunder from the

church" and who, consequently, became bound to the House of Tudor (Goldwin Smith, *A Constitutional and Legal History*, 267–68). Mackintosh avoids this pejorative comparison, since it remakes Burke's antirevolutionary point in *Reflections* (217–19); he prefers the 1690s resemblance rather than that of the 1530s.

52. Bruguière, "Assignats," 429; Harris, *Assignats*, 14.

53. Bruguière, ibid., 428; J. F. Bosher, *The French Revolution* (New York: W. W. Norton, 1988), 145

54. Harris, *Assignats*, 65.

Conclusion

1. See Nicholas Rogers, "The Urban Opposition to Whig Oligarchy, 1720–60," in *The Origins of Anglo-American Radicalism*, ed. Margaret C. Jacob and James A. Jacob (Atlantic Highlands, N.J.: Humanities Press International, 1991), 152–68. Cf. Charles Pigott, *Strictures On The New Political Tenets Of The Rt. Hon. Edmund Burke* (1791):

The Tories, in Queen Anne's, and in succeeding reigns, were often the popular party, the strenuous advocates for liberty, while the Whig ministry . . . occasionally preached the stupid doctrines of non-resistance; and . . . repelled every effort to stem the torrent of corruption, and the power of the crown. (Claeys, *Political Writings*, 2:139)

2. Jeffrey T. Nealon, "The Discipline of Deconstruction," *PMLA* (October 1992): 1274. Nealon's emphasis.

3. Ibid., 1270.

4. Leo Damrosch, *Fictions of Reality in the Age of Hume and Johnson* (Madison: The University of Wisconsin Press, 1989).

Works Cited

Aldridge, Alfred Owen. *Man of Reason: The Life of Thomas Paine*. Philadelphia: J. B. Lippincott, 1959.

————. *Thomas Paine's American Ideology*. Newark: University of Delaware Press, 1984.

Alexander, Meena. *Women and Romanticism: Mary Wollstonecraft, Dorothy Wordsworth, and Mary Shelley*. Totowa, N.J.: Barnes and Noble Books, 1989.

Arendt, Hannah. *On Revolution*. Harmondsworth: Penguin, 1963.

Aristotle. *The Politics*. Translated by T. A. Sinclair. London: Penguin Books, 1981.

Ashcraft, Richard. *Revolutionary Politics and Locke's Two Treatises of Government*. Princeton: Princeton University Press, 1986.

Ayling, Stanley. *Edmund Burke: His Life and Opinions*. New York: St. Martin's Press, 1988.

Bailyn, Bernard. *Faces of Revolution: Personalities and Themes in the Struggle for American Independence*. New York: Knopf, 1990.

Barker-Benfield, G. J. *The Culture of Sensibility: Sex and Society in Eighteenth-Century Britain*. Chicago: The University of Chicago Press, 1992.

Beddard, Robert. *A Kingdom without a King: The Journal of the Provisional Government in the Revolution of 1688*. Oxford: Phaidon Press, 1988.

Beik, Paul H. "October Days." In *Historical Dictionary of the French Revolution, 1789–1799*, edited by Samuel F. Scott and Barry Rothaus, 2:731–33. 2 vols. Westport, Conn.: Greenwood Press, 1985.

Bergeron, Louis. "National Properties." In *A Critical Dictionary of the French Revolution*, edited by François Furet and Mona Ozouf, 511–18. Translated by Arthur Goldhammer. Cambridge: Belknap Press of Harvard University, 1989.

Blackstone, William. *Commentaries on the Laws of England*. 4 vols. Chicago: The University of Chicago Press, 1979.

Blakemore, Steven. *Burke and the Fall of Language: The French Revolution as Linguistic Event*. Hanover, N.H.: University Press of New England, 1988.

————, ed. *Burke and the French Revolution: Bicentennial Essays*. Athens: University of Georgia Press, 1992.

————. "Misrepresenting the Text: Price, Burke, and the October Days of 1789." *The Friend: Comment on Romanticism* 1 (October 1992): 1–9.

————. "Repression and Resemblance: Burke's Critique of the Revolution." *Consortium on Revolutionary Europe* 1 (1989): 33–42.

————. "Revolution in Representation: Burke's *Reflections on the Revolution in France*." *Eighteenth-Century Life* 15 (November 1991): 1–18.

Bosher, J. F. *The French Revolution*. New York: W. W. Norton, 1988.

Boulton, James T. "James Mackintosh: *Vindiciae Gallicae*." *Renaissance and Modern Studies* 21 (1977): 106–18.

————. *The Language of Politics in the Age of Wilkes and Burke*. London: Routledge and Kegan Paul, 1963.

Bruguière, Michel. "Assignats." In *A Critical Dictionary of the French Revolution*, edited by François Furet and Mona Ozouf, translated by Arthur Goldhammer, 426–36. Cambridge: The Belknap Press of Harvard University Press, 1989.

Bruns, Gerald. "Canon and Power in the Hebrew Scriptures." *Critical Inquiry* 10 (1984): 462–80.

Burke, Edmund. *The Correspondence of Edmund Burke*. Edited by Thomas W. Copeland et al. 10 vols. Chicago: The University of Chicago Press, 1958–78.

————. *A Philosophical Enquiry into the Origin of our Ideas of the Sublime and Beautiful*. 1757. Edited by J. T. Boulton. New York: Columbia University Press, 1958.

————. *Reflections on the Revolution in France*. 1790. Edited by Conor Cruise O'Brien. Harmondsworth: Penguin Classics, 1986.

————. *The Speeches of the Right Honourable Edmund Burke*. 4 vols. London: Longman and Hurst Rees, 1816.

Canavan, Francis. *The Political Economy of Edmund Burke: The Role of Property in His Thought*. New York: Fordham University Press, 1995.

Chandler, James K. "Poetical Liberties: Burke's France and the 'Adequate Representation' of the English." In *The French Revolution and the Creation of Modern Political Culture*, edited by François Furet and Mona Ozouf, 45–58. Vol. 3. Oxford: Pergamon Press, 1989.

Chapman, Gerald W. *Edmund Burke: The Practical Imagination*. Cambridge: Harvard University Press, 1967.

Cheyne, George. *The English Malady*. 1733. Reprint. Delmar, N.Y.: Scholars' Facsimiles & Reprints, 1976.

Christian, William. "James Mackintosh, Burke, and the Cause of Reform." *Eighteenth-Century Studies* 7 (1973–74): 193–206.

Christie, Thomas. *Letters on the Revolution of France*. London: J. Johnson, 1791.

Claeys, Gregory, ed. *Political Writings of the 1790s*. 8 vols. London: Pickering & Chatto, 1995.

————. *Thomas Paine: Social and Political Thought*. London: Unwin Hyman, 1989.

Clark, J. C. D. *English Society 1688–1832*. Cambridge: Cambridge University Press, 1985.

Cone, Carl B. *Burke and the Nature of Politics*. 2 vols. Lexington: University of Kentucky Press, 1957, 1964.

————. *The English Jacobins, Reformers in Late Eighteenth-Century England*. New York: Scribner, 1968.

Conger, Syndy McMillen. *Mary Wollstonecraft and the Language of Sensibility*. Rutherford, N.J.: Fairleigh Dickinson University Press, 1994.

Conniff, James. *The Useful Cobbler: Edmund Burke and the Politics of Progress*. Albany: State University of New York Press, 1994.

Cooper, Thomas. *A Reply to Mr. Burke's invective against Mr. Cooper and Mr. Watt*. Manchester, 1792.

Copeland, Thomas W. *Our Eminent Friend Edmund Burke: Six Essays*. New Haven: Yale University Press, 1949.

Damrosch, Leo. *Fictions of Reality in the Age of Hume and Johnson*. Madison: The University of Wisconsin Press, 1989.

Deane, Seamus. *The French Revolution and Enlightenment in England, 1789–1832*. Cambridge: Harvard University Press, 1988.

De Bruyn, Frans. "Theater and Countertheater in Burke's *Reflections on the Revolution in France*." In *Burke and the French Revolution: Bicentennial Essays*, edited by Steven Blakemore, 28–68. Athens: University of Georgia Press, 1992.

De Quincey, Thomas. *The Collected Writings of Thomas De Quincey*. Edited by David Masson. 14 vols. Edinburgh: Adam and Charles Black, 1890.

Dickson, P. G. M. *The Financial Revolution in England: A Study in the Development of Public Credit, 1688–1756*. London: Macmillan, 1967.

Doyle, William. *The Oxford History of the French Revolution*. Oxford: Clarendon, 1989.

Durant, Will and Ariel. *The Age of Voltaire*. New York: Simon and Schuster, 1965.

Elliot, Sir Gilbert. *Life and Letters of Sir Gilbert Elliot*. Edited by the Countess of Minto. 3 vols. London: Longman, 1874.

Erdman, David V. *Commerce Des Lumières: John Oswald and the British in Paris*. Columbia: University of Missouri Press, 1986.

Ferguson, Frances. "The Sublime of Edmund Burke, or the Bathos of Experience." *Glyph* 8 (1981): 62–78.

———. "Wollstonecraft Our Contemporary." In *Gender and Theory: Dialogues on Feminist Criticism*, edited by Linda Kauffman, 51–62. Oxford: Basil Blackwell, 1989.

Ferguson, Moira, and Janet Todd. *Mary Wollstonecraft*. Boston: Twayne Publishers, 1984.

Fleigelman, Jay. *Declaring Independence: Jefferson, Natural Language, & the Culture of Performance*. Stanford: Stanford University Press, 1993.

Flexner, Eleanor. *Mary Wollstonecraft: A Biography*. New York: Coward, McCann & Geoghegan, Inc., 1972.

Foner, Eric. *Tom Paine and Revolutionary America*. New York: Oxford University Press, 1976.

Foucault, Michel. *Madness and Civilization: A History of Insanity in the Age of Reason*. Translated by Richard Howard. New York: Vintage Books, 1988.

———. *The Order of Things: An Archeology of the Human Sciences*. Translated by A. M. Sheridan Smith. New York: Vintage Books, 1973.

Fruchtman, Jack, Jr. *Thomas Paine: Apostle of Freedom*. New York: Four Walls Eight Windows, 1994.

———. *Thomas Paine and the Religion of Nature*. Baltimore: The Johns Hopkins University Press, 1993.

Furet, François, and Mona Ozouf, eds. *A Critical Dictionary of the French Revolution.* Translated by Arthur Goldhammer. Cambridge: Harvard University Press, 1989.

Furniss, Tom. *Edmund Burke's Aesthetic Ideology: Language, Gender, and Political Economy in Revolution.* Cambridge: Cambridge University Press, 1993.

Godwin, William. *Memoirs of Mary Wollstonecraft.* 1798. Reprint. New York: Haskel House Publishers, 1927.

———. *Uncollected Writings (1785–1822).* Edited by Jack W. Marken and Burton R. Pollin. Gainesville, Fl.: Scholars' Facsimiles & Reprints, 1968.

Goodwin, Albert. *The Friends of Liberty: The English Democratic Movement in the Age of the French Revolution.* Cambridge: Harvard University Press, 1979.

Greaves, Richard L. *The Radical Underground in Britain, 1660–1663.* New York: Oxford University Press, 1986.

Gustafson, Thomas. *Representative Words: Politics, Literature, and the American Language, 1776–1865.* Cambridge: Cambridge University Press, 1992.

Gutwirth, Madelyn. *The Twilight of the Goddesses: Women and Representation in the French Revolutionary Era.* New Brunswick, N.J.: Rutgers University Press, 1992.

Harris, S. B. *The Assignats.* Cambridge: Harvard University Press, 1930.

Hawke, David Freeman. *Paine.* New York: Harper & Row, 1974.

Hawkins, Laetitia Matilda. *Letters on the Female Mind, Its Powers and Pursuits. Addressed to Miss H. M. Williams, With particular reference to Her Letters From France.* 2 vols. London: Hookham & Carpenter, 1793.

Hazlitt, William. *Lectures on the English Poets and the Spirit of the Age.* 1825. New York: E. P. Dutton & Co., 1910.

Henzi, Gary. "'An Itch of Gaming': The South Sea Bubble and the Novels of Daniel Defoe." *Eighteenth-Century Life* (February 1993): 32–45.

Hirst, Derick. *The Representative of the People? Voters and Voting under the Early Stuarts.* Cambridge: Cambridge University Press, 1975.

Holland, Lord. *Memories of the Whig Party During My Time.* 2 vols. London, 1852.

Houston, Alan Craig. *Algernon Sidney and the Republican Heritage in England and America.* Princeton: Princeton University Press, 1991.

Isnard, Marcel. "*Vindiciae Gallicae* Revisited." *The Yearbook of English Studies* 19 (1989): 219–30.

Jacobus, Mary. "The Difference of View." In *Women Writing and Writing About Women,* edited by Mary Jacobus, 10–21. New York: Barnes and Noble, 1979.

Jefferson, Thomas. *The Papers of Thomas Jefferson.* Edited by Julian P. Boyd. Vol. 15. Princeton: Princeton University Press, 1958.

Johnston, Kenneth R. and Joseph Nicholes. "Transitory Actions, Men Betrayed: The French Revolution in the English Revolution in Romantic Drama." *The Wordsworth Circle* 22 (Spring 1992): 76–96.

Jupp, Peter. *British and Irish Elections, 1784–1831.* New York: Barnes and Noble, 1973.

Kaplan, Cora. *Sea Changes: Essays on Culture and Feminism.* London: Verso, 1986.

Kelly, Gary. *Revolutionary Feminism: The Mind and Career of Mary Wollstonecraft.* New York: St. Martin's Press, 1992

Kenyon, J. P. *The Civil Wars of England.* New York: Alfred A. Knopf, 1988.

———. *Revolution Principles: The Politics of Party, 1689–1720*. Cambridge: Cambridge University Press, 1977.

Kitson, Peter J. "'Sages and patriots that being dead do yet speak to us': Readings of the English Revolution in the Late Eighteenth Century." *Prose Studies* 14.3 (December 1991): 205–30.

Klancher, Jon P. *The Making of English Reading Audiences, 1790–1832*. Madison: University of Wisconsin Press, 1987.

Kramer, Michael P. *Imagining Language in America: From the Revolution to the Civil War*. Princeton: Princeton University Press, 1992.

Kramnick, Isaac. *The Rage of Edmund Burke: Portrait of an Ambivalent Conservative*. New York: Basic Books, 1977.

———. *Republicanism and Bourgeois Radicalism: Political Ideology in Late Eighteenth-Century England and America*. Ithaca: Cornell University Press, 1990.

Lamb, Charles. *The Complete Works and Letters of Charles Lamb*. New York: The Modern Library, 1935.

Levy, Darline Gay and Harriet B. Applewhite. "Women and Militant Citizenship in Revolutionary Paris." In *Rebel Daughters: Women and the French Revolution*, edited by Sara E. Melzer and Leslie W. Rabine, 79–101. New York: Oxford University Press, 1992.

Lloyd, Genevieve. *The Man of Reason: "Male" and "Female" in Western Philosophy*. Minneapolis: University of Minnesota Press, 1984.

Locke, John. *An Essay Concerning Human Understanding*. Edited by Alexander Campbell Fraser. 2 vols. 1690. Reprint. New York: Dover Publications, Inc., 1959.

———. *Locke's Two Treatises of Government*. Edited by Peter Laslett. Cambridge: Cambridge University Press, 1988.

MacKintosh, James. *Vindiciae Gallicae*. 1791. Reprint. Spelsbury, Oxford: Woodstock Books, 1989.

———. *Memoirs of the Life of Sir James Mackintosh*. Edited by Robert J. Mackintosh. 2 vols. Boston: Little, Brown and Company, 1853.

———. *The Miscellaneous Works of the Right Honourable Sir James Mackintosh*. Edited by Robert J. Mackintosh. 3 vols. in one. New York: D. Appleton, 1870.

Marx, Karl. *The Eighteenth Brumaire of Louis Bonaparte*. In *Surveys from Exile*, edited by David Fernbach. Pelican Marx Library, 1973. Reprint. New York: Vintage Books, 1974.

McKenzie, Lionel A. "The French Revolution and English Parliamentary Reform: James Mackintosh and the *Vindiciae Gallicae*." *Eighteenth-Century Studies* 14 (1981): 264–82.

McKeon, Michael. *The Origins of the English Novel, 1600–1740*. Baltimore: The Johns Hopkins University Press, 1987.

Monahan, Arthur P. *From Personal Duties Towards Personal Rights: Late Medieval and Early Modern Political Thought, 1300–1600*. Kingston and Montreal: McGill-Queen's University Press, 1994.

Monod, Paul Kléber. *Jacobitism and the English People, 1688–1788*. Cambridge: Cambridge University Press, 1989.

Montesquieu, Charles Louis de Secondat. *The Spirit of the Laws*. Edited and translated by Anna M. Cohler, Basia Carolyn Miller, Harold Samuel Stone. Cambridge: Cambridge University Press, 1989.

Moore, David Cresa *The Politics of Deference: A Study of the mid-nineteenth century English political system*. New York: Barnes & Noble, 1976.

More, Hannah. *Essays on Various Subjects Principally Designed for Young Ladies*. In *The Works of Hannah More*, 11 vols. New York: Harper, 1847.

[Mornay, Phillipe du Plessis]. *Vindiciae, Contra Tryannos*. Edited and translated by George Garnett. Cambridge: Cambridge University Press, 1994.

Nealon, Jeffrey T. "The Discipline of Deconstruction." *PMLA* (October 1992): 1266–79.

Nicholes, Joseph. "Revolutions Compared: The English Civil War as Political Touchstone in Romantic Literature." In *Revolution and English Romanticism*, edited by Keith Hanley and Raman Selden, 261–76. New York: St. Martin's Press, 1990.

O'Brien, Conor Cruise. *The Great Melody: A Thematic Biography of Edmund Burke*. Chicago: The University of Chicago Press, 1992.

O'Leary, Patrick. *Sir James Mackintosh, the Whig Cicero*. Aberdeen: Aberdeen University Press, 1989.

Paine, Thomas. *The Complete Writings of Thomas Paine*. Edited by Philip S. Foner. 2 vols. New York: The Citadel Press, 1945.

Paulson, Ronald. *Representations of Revolution, 1784–1820*. New Haven: Yale University Press, 1983.

Pigott, Charles. *Strictures on The New Political Tenets Of The Rt. Hon. Edmund Burke*. 1791. In *Political Writings of the 1790s*, edited by Gregory Claeys, 2:118–53. London: Pickering & Chatto, 1995.

Pitkin, Hanna Fenichel. *The Concept of Representation*. Berkeley: University of California Press, 1967.

Pocock, J. G. A. *The Ancient Constitution and the Feudal Law*. Cambridge: Cambridge University Press, 1957.

———. "Edmund Burke and the Redefinition of Enthusiasm: the Context as Counter-Revolution." In *The French Revolution and the Creation of Modern Political Culture*, edited by François Furet and Mona Ozouf, 3:19–43. Oxford: Pergamon Press, 1989.

———. "The Fourth English Civil War: dissolution, desertion, and alternative histories in the Glorious Revolution." In *The Revolution of 1688–1689, Changing Perspectives*, edited by Lois G. Schwoerer, 52–64. Cambridge: Cambridge University Press, 1992.

———. *The Machiavellian Moment: Florentine Political Thought and the Atlantic Republican Tradition*. Princeton: Princeton University Press, 1975.

———. *Virtue, Commerce, and History: Essays on Political Thought and History, Chiefly in the Eighteenth Century*. Cambridge: Cambridge University Press, 1985.

Poovey, Mary. *The Proper Lady and the Woman Writer: Ideology as Style in the Works of Mary Wollstonecraft, Mary Shelley, and Jane Austin*. Chicago: The University of Chicago Press, 1984.

Porter, Roy. *Mind-Forg'd Manacles: A History of Madness in England from the Restoration to the Regency*. Cambridge: Harvard University Press, 1987.

Potkay, Adam. *The Fate of Eloquence in the Age of Hume*. Ithaca: Cornell University Press, 1994.

Price, Richard *A Discourse on the Love of our Country*. 4th ed. London: T. Cadell, 1790.

———. *Political Writings*. Edited by D. O. Thomas. Cambridge: Cambridge University Press, 1991.

Priestly, Joseph. *Letters to the Right Honourable Edmund Burke*. 1792. In *Political Writings of the 1790s*, edited by Gregory Claes, 2:316–85. London: Pickering & Chatto, 1995.

Pulzer, Peter G. J. *Political Representation and Elections: Parties and Voting in Great Britain*. New York: Frederick A. Praeger, 1967.

Reid, Christopher. "Burke, the Regency Crisis, and the 'Antagonist World of Madness.'" *Eighteenth-Century Life* 16 (May 1992): 59–75.

———. "Burke's Tragic Muse: Sarah Siddons and the 'Feminization' of the *Reflections*." In *Burke and the French Revolution: Bicentennial Essays*, edited by Steven Blakemore, 1–27. Athens: University Press of Georgia, 1992.

Reid, John Philli *The Concept of Representation in the Age of the American Revolution*. Chicago: The University of Chicago Press, 1989.

Reitan, E. A. "Edmund Burke and the Civil List, 1769–1782." *The Burke Newsletter* 8 (Fall 1966): 604–18.

———. "Edmund Burke and Economic Reform, 1779–83." *Studies in Eighteenth-Century Culture* 14 (1985): 129–58.

Révolutions de Paris. Vol. 1, no. 13, 3–10 October 1789: 1–48.

Richardson, Samuel. *Clarissa: or, The History of a Young Lady*. 1748. 4 vols. London: John Dent, 1932.

Robbins, Russell Hope. *The Encyclopedia of Witchcraft and Demonology*. New York: Crown Publishers, 1959.

Roger, Philipe. "The French Revolution as logomachy." In *Language and Rhetoric of the Revolution*, edited by John Renwick, 4–24. Edinburgh: Edinburgh University Press, 1990.

Rogers, Katherine. *Feminism in Eighteenth-Century England*. Urbana: University of Illinois Press, 1982.

Rogers, Nicholas. "The Urban Opposition to Whig Oligarchy, 1720–60." In *The Origins of Anglo-American Radicalism*, edited by Margaret C. Jacob and James A. Jacob, 152–68. Atlantic Highlands, N.J.: Humanities Press International, Inc., 1991.

Rousseau, George S. "Nerves, Spirits, and Fibers: Towards Defining the Organs of Sensibility with a Postscript 1976." *The Blue Guitar* 2 (1976): 125–53.

Rousseau, Jean-Jacques. *The Social Contract*. Translated by Maurice Cranston. Harmondsworth: Penguin Books, 1968.

Rudé, George. *The Crowd in the French Revolution*. Oxford: Clarendon Press, 1959.

Sapiro, Virginia. *A Vindication of Political Virtue: The Political Theory of Mary Wollstonecraft*. Chicago: The University of Chicago Press, 1992.

Schama, Simon. *Citizens: A Chronicle of the French Revolution*. New York: Knopf, 1989.

Schwoerer, Lois G. *The Declaration of Rights, 1689*. Baltimore: The Johns Hopkins University Press, 1981.

———. "Introduction." In *The Revolution of 1688–1689: Changing Perspectives*, edited by Lois G. Schwoerer, 1–20. Cambridge: Cambridge University Press, 1992.

Sewell, William H. Jr. *A Rhetoric of Bourgeois Revolution: The Abbé Sieyes and What is the Third Estate?* Durham: Duke University Press, 1994.

Sherman, Sandra. "Credit, Simulation, and the Ideology of the Contract in the Early Eighteenth Century." *Eighteenth-Century Life* 19 (November 1995): 86–102.

Showalter, Elaine. *The Female Malady: Women, Madness, and English Culture, 1830–1980*. New York: Pantheon, 1985.

Sidney, Algernon. *Discourses Concerning Government*. Edited by Thomas G. West. 1698. Reprint. Indianapolis: LibertyClassics, 1990.

Sieyès, Joseph Emmanuel. *What is the Third Estate?* Translated by M. Blondel. New York: Praeger, 1964.

Simpson, David. *The Politics of American English, 1776–1856*. New York: Oxford University Press, 1986.

Slavney, Phillip R. *Perspectives on "Hysteria."* Baltimore: The Johns Hopkins University Press, 1990.

Smith, Adam. *An Inquiry into the Nature of and Causes of the Wealth of Nations*. Edited by R. H. Campbell and A. S. Skinner. 1776. 2 vols. Reprint. Indianapolis: LibertyClassics, 1981.

Smith, Goldwin. *A Constitutional and Legal History of England*. New York: Dorset Press, 1990.

Smith, Nigel. *Literature and Revolution in England, 1640–1660*. New Haven: Yale University Press, 1994.

Smith, Olivia. *The Politics of Language, 1791–1819*. Oxford: Clarendon Press, 1984.

Speck, W. A. *Reluctant Revolutionaries: Englishmen and the Revolution of 1688*. Oxford: Oxford University Press, 1988.

Spurr, John. *The Restoration Church of England, 1646–1689*. New Haven: Yale University Press, 1991.

St Claire, William. *The Godwins and the Shelleys: A Biography of a Family*. New York: W. W. Norton, 1989.

Stanlis, Peter. *Edmund Burke: The Enlightenment and Revolution*. New Brunswick, N.J.: Transaction Publishers, 1991.

Stewart, John Hall, ed., *A Documentary Survey of the French Revolution*. Toronto: The Macmillan Company, 1951.

Thomas, Keith. *Religion and the Decline of Magic*. New York: Charles Scribner's Sons, 1971.

Thompson, E. P. *The Making of the English Working Class*. New York: Pantheon, 1964.

Thompson, J. M. *The French Revolution*. Oxford: Basil Blackwell, 1943. Reprint. New York: Oxford University Press, 1966.

Tierney, Brian. *The Crisis of Church and State, 1050–1300*. Toronto: University of Toronto Press, 1989.

Tims, Margaret. *Mary Wollstonecraft: A Social Pioneer*. London: Millington Books Ltd., 1976.

[Turgot, Anne-Robert Jacques]. "Fondation." In *Encyclopédie ou dictionnaire raisonné des sciences des artes et des métiers*, 7:72–76. Nouvelle impression en facsimilé de la première édition de 1751–1780. Stuttgart, Germany: Friedrich Frommann Verlag, 1966.

Walzer, Michael, ed. *Regicide and Revolution: Speeches at the Trial of Louis XVI*. Translated by Marion Rothstein. Cambridge: Cambridge University Press, 1974.

Wardle, Ralph M., ed. *Collected Letters of Mary Wollstonecraft*. Ithaca: Cornell University Press, 1979.

———. *Mary Wollstonecraft: A Critical Biography*. Lawrence: University of Kansas Press, 1951.

Wecter, Dixon. *Edmund Burke and His Kinsmen: A Study of the Statesman's Financial Integrity and Private Relationships*. Boulder: University of Colorado Studies, 1939.

White, Hayden. *Tropics of Discourse: Essays in Cultural Criticism*. Baltimore: The Johns Hopkins University Press, 1978.

Williams, Helen Maria. *Letters from France*. 1790–96. Edited by Janet Todd. 2 vols. Delmar, N.Y.: Scholars' Facsimiles & Reprints, 1975.

Wills, Gary. *Inventing America: Jefferson's Declaration of Independence*. New York: Vintage Books, 1979.

Wilson, David A. *Paine and Cobbett: The Transatlantic Connection*. Kingston and Montreal: McGill-Queen's University Press, 1988.

Wilson, Jerome D., and William F. Ricketson. *Thomas Paine*. Boston: Twayne Publishers, 1989.

Wollstonecraft, Mary. *The Works of Mary Wollstonecraft*. Edited by Janet Todd and Marilyn Butler. 7 vols. New York: New York University Press, 1989.

Woodhouse, A. S. P., ed. *Puritans and Liberty: Being the Army Debates (1647–49) from the Clarke Manuscripts with Supplementary Documents*. London: Everyman's Library, 1992.

Index